CHRISTIE'S GUIDE TO COLLECTING

CHRISTIE'S
GUIDE
TO COLLECTING

Edited by
Robert Cumming

PRENTICE-HALL, INC.
Englewood Cliffs, New Jersey 07632

Frontispiece: Gainsborough: *Portrait of James Christie*
(Malibu, The J. Paul Getty Museum).

Library of Congress Cataloging in Publication Data

Cumming, Robert
  Christie's guide to collecting.

  Includes bibliography and index.
  1.   Art – collectors and collecting.
  I.   Title
ISBN 0-13-133620-7

Printed and bound in Great Britain by Butler & Tanner Limited,
Frome, Somerset

CONTENTS

FOREWORD

The main aims of *Christie's Guide to Collecting* are to encourage the spirit and traditions of private collecting and to offer down-to-earth advice on questions which are frequently asked. Two of collecting's major pleasures are discussion and investigation, and so I hope the book will encourage a spirit of inquiry as well as offer good sound advice. Indeed, it makes no claim to raise all the issues or offer all the answers; but collectors who want to build up knowledge, experience and self-confidence need to know the scope and basic principles of their chosen subject and activity, and this is a principal motive of the book. It is much easier to seek and make sense of advice from others if you understand the context in which the advice is given. All of the contributors have been chosen because they have up-to-date and active experience in the fields on which they write, and for all of them their involvement in the world of art and collecting is as much a way of life as a job.

Much of what is said will seem straightforward to people in the know, but that is the point, for the book is written for people who want to know, and good advice is never over-complicated. Experts often forget that there was a time when they too did not have the answers to basic questions at their fingertips, and further did not know what questions to ask or snags to look out for. Ultimately the greatest satisfaction is finding out the answers to each detailed or individual question, and collecting is an activity where individual pieces, taste, and detail are the life blood. Equally, however, it is important to realize at the outset that there are no books, however comprehensive, that can give all the details in advance. A good teacher shows his student how to see and understand the general principles so that he or she can have the confidence to work out or discover the precise and detailed answer for the particular case in hand, and all our contributors have been asked to follow this premise. Thus I hope the book will have a wide appeal to new collectors of all sorts of works of art and objects, virtually anywhere. Although there are many detailed examples in the text it should not require too much imagination to work from them to others, and to parallel examples which may be closer to the collector's particular interest. Experienced collectors should find it useful to have such a diversity of opinion and information gathered together in one volume, and perhaps they will be encouraged to look at things they have previously neglected, or think afresh about familiar ideas.

Since so much of collecting is concerned with looking, I have tried to select illustrations which supplement the text by making a visual point, or which provide an important, amusing or memorable image. Some have been taken from *Punch*, for in its heyday its gifted artists provided particularly acute observations on the aspirations and anxieties of its readers, and not surprisingly the enjoyment of art along with collecting and its attendant concerns featured regularly. Many of them have been taken from Christie's own archives, although the principles and cases they illustrate usually apply to collecting and the art market as a whole. Christie's are naturally proud of their history and traditions, skills and achievements, but they are, of course, well aware that there are many other auction houses, dealers and institutions who are equally proud of theirs. Half of the chapters in the book are written by people outside Christie's, since we have tried to give the collector advice and information which is broadly based and free-thinking.

A book such as this obviously owes a great deal to a vast number of people who over a long period of time have given help, encouragement and advice to the contributors, to enable them to pass on their expertise and enthusiasm to others. For specific help and advice on different chapters the contributors collectively would like to thank the following: Richard Falkiner, Ken Grouet, D. Taylor, James Scott-Webb, Jonathan Ashley-Smith, Gillian Lewis, Peter van Geersdael, Elisabeth Hamilton-Eddy, the Council for Museums in Scotland, Timothy Clifford and Penny Jenkins.

I would like to express personal thanks to many colleagues in Christie's throughout the world who have been most generous in supplying help and information, in particular to Susan Whitaker who typed many revisions of the manuscript. I must also thank past and present students at Christie's Fine Arts Course who, by design or accident, have raised many of the topics which this book discusses. At Phaidon Press I would like to thank Jean-Claude Peissel and Bernard Dod who came into the project at a late stage: the latter made many useful suggestions and his meticulous and professional supervision overcame many problems. Andrew Decker read the text and made many useful suggestions regarding practice in the United States. Above all, however, I would like to thank my wife, Carolyn, for her help and constant and loving support.

Robert Cumming
May 1984

Part I

BECOMING A COLLECTOR

1
COLLECTING

Maecenas in pursuit of the Fine Arts – scene Pall Mall, a frosty morning. *The Marquis of Stafford (1758–1833), who later became First Duke of Stafford, was one of the great collectors and patrons of his day. His most spectacular purchase was a joint venture to acquire the cream of the collection of the Duc d'Orléans after the French Revolution. He was one of the first owners of pictures in London to allow visits from the public. This cartoon by Gillray likens him to Maecenas, one of the greatest patrons of the Roman Augustan age, and shows him on his way to a sale at Christie's.*

Collecting is a curious activity. It evades any precise definition as to who does it, why, or of what a collection consists. Kings, presidents, and millionaires with vast fortunes collect. But so do children and magpies who have no money. Abstract entities such as governments, corporations and companies collect. Some people are quite rational and organized about it; others, totally frantic. It is not necessary to human existence in the physical sense, but it is so widespread that it must satisfy some part of the human psyche. Most people go about it in a quiet and friendly way; a few are ruthless, and fraud, theft and even murder have been committed in the name of collecting. Some fortunes have been made by it, but an equal number of bankruptcies have been caused by it. One thing, however, is constant. Very few people regret it. One of the greatest, richest and most unscrupulous collectors ever, on the night before he died, walked round his collection and is reputed to have said with anguish, 'I must leave all this! What trouble I had to acquire these things! I shall never see them again where I am going.' He was Cardinal Mazarin, Louis XIV's right hand man, and the time was March 1661. Few collectors can have hoped to emulate Cardinal Mazarin, but many will have felt as he did when faced with the prospect of parting from a much loved and cared for collection.

Motives and senses

Comparisons are often made between the urge to collect and the urge to love, and there is a great deal of truth in them. Admittedly, there is no single motive for collecting, any more than for loving, but how dull it would be if there were. At one end of the spectrum are those whose approach is entirely detached and intellectual, at the other, those whose approach is purely sensual. Some collectors are most strongly moved by the spirit of inquiry and the desire to know, and like a work of art because it presents a problem to be solved; others want only the inexplicable quickening of the pulse that is caused by the contemplation of something appealing to them. Most collectors probably share something of both emotions. The true connection between collecting and loving is almost certainly the desire to possess. The desire is not always fulfilled – maybe it is the nature of the human condition that it most frequently is not – but the excitement and the hope drive the collector on.

There is a story – perhaps apocryphal, but more likely true – of a group of well-to-do and impeccably behaved ladies who arranged a private visit to see a selection of the exquisite drawings held by one of the great public collections in London. They were taken to a small room in the heart of the building, and the curator and his assistant showed them a choice selection which caused great satisfaction. Suddenly one of the ladies lurched at the table, seized a Cézanne drawing, and ran for the door. She did not get very far. Some time later when she and everyone else had been calmed down with cups of sweet tea she was asked what had caused her alarming act of madness. She had no real explanation, other than to say she had been so overwhelmed by the beauty of the drawing that she had to possess it. Any true collector will know exactly what she meant, though such examples of total loss of control are fortunately rare.

We have five physical senses: sight, touch, hearing, taste and smell. For the collector the first two are the most important, and Leonardo da Vinci argued, with prejudice, that sight was the sovereign of them all. Tastes and smells are too elusive to collect, except in special circumstances; the one exception is the wine connoisseur, whose bottles contain the liquid that will send him, through his nose and palate, into ecstasies of pleasure. Sounds can be collected by means of modern technology, and there is a thriving market in old recordings. But the common link between collectors from the earliest times to our own is the wish to look and to handle: books are often collected because they look beautiful and feel satisfying rather than for their written content. Though interlinked, sight and touch are entirely different, especially in one crucial feature. The eye is often fooled: the sense of touch but rarely. We often mistake what we see – a *trompe-l'oeil* painting which convinces that it is the real thing, for example. But any substance – marble, wood, silk, silver, porcelain – has a unique feel of texture, temperature and weight, and it is unusual for the eye and hand to be fooled simultaneously. This is one of the reasons why experts who are in any doubt about authenticity insist on handling the object in question.

Like love, collecting can be the most fulfilling, stimulating and rewarding of human activities, and demands to be shared with others. Occasionally it is so obsessive that it becomes destructive, and instead of opening new horizons leads to a dead end. By all means make sacrifices for collecting, but do not be tempted to die for it, or to follow the example of the rich collector who became obsessed with pots after making his first purchase from a stall in the Portobello Road street market in London. Thereafter his house became filled with pots of all periods, styles, shapes and sizes. When fellow enthusiasts discovered that there was nothing to eat in the house because even the kitchen cupboards, larder and refrigerator contained nothing but pots, even they admitted that the collector's enthusiasm had gone too far!

Private collecting   All civilized societies have collected for one reason or another, and the role of private collecting is one of the most intriguing aspects of collecting history. It comes and goes, and the leadership shifts between different groups and classes,

Brueghel: Allegory of Sight (*Madrid, Prado*). *The variety of objects (from paintings to scientific instruments) and the mixed and crowded display capture the spirit of the 17th-century cabinet of curiosities. The Habsburg Emperor Rudolf II was one of the principal collectors of the age, his collection being seized in the aftermath of war by Queen Christina of Sweden, and subsequently dispersed. Brueghel's painting is one of a series of allegories of the five senses.*

and passes from one nation to another. The significance and leadership can be plotted – just as it can be for public collecting – but unique to private collecting are those courageous individuals who swim against the tide and collect what nearly everyone else disregards. Golden ages of private collecting are of two types. There are those epochs when collecting is a necessary part of the life-style of rich men, and large and varied collections are built up, often with great personal flair and discrimination. The Renaissance princes of the sixteenth century are an oustanding example, and they were educated in the belief that patronage of the arts and collecting were as essential as military prowess. The other notable periods are those in which outstanding collections are made, not by men and women of great wealth, but by those who notice and take an interest in what others fail to see. In the early nineteenth century superb collections of Italian maiolica and early Italian Renaissance paintings were made for modest expenditure because most collectors dismissed them as primitive and unworthy of consideration. Later in the century the same was true of African tribal art; and the early collectors of modern European paintings and sculpture were also few and far between and had, in retrospect, unbelievable opportunities for collecting.

The Greek and Roman civilizations fostered private collecting, but the tradition died out for all practical purposes in the medieval world. It came as a new discovery to early Renaissance collectors to find that in antiquity, which they much admired, leading figures, and even Caesar himself, had considered collecting to be important. Our modern tradition, like most of our artistic traditions, is really a child of the Renaissance. It is the free-thinking individual

Cardinal Mazarin in the Gallery of his Town House (*engraving by Nanteuil after van Schuppen*). *When Cardinal Mazarin died most of his collection was acquired by Louis XIV, and it is now in the Louvre, Paris. The illustration also shows that sculpture was then displayed more prominently than paintings.*

Tapestry, Dame à la Licorne (*Paris, Musée Cluny*). *This tapestry dates from late 15th or early 16th century, and was probably made in Brussels. There are 6 in the series, 5 of them thought to represent the 5 senses, and the 6th, shown here, to be dedicated to the recipient. Unicorn horns were believed to be effective against poison, and as late as 1789 instruments of 'unicorn horn' were used in French Court ceremonial to test food for poison. Late in the 17th century the Royal Society in London tested a cup, claimed to be of unicorn horn, to disprove the superstition. The animal's ferocity was supposed to have been subdued by the sight of a virgin, hence the symbolic connection with the Virgin Mary. The horns which owners thought to be from a unicorn probably came from the narwhal, an Arctic whale.*

who stands at the heart of Renaissance art and civilization, and private collecting was a means of asserting and extending this individuality. Although the outward forms of art and our conception of the universe have changed, this idea remains one of the main purposes in collecting at its best, and one of the keys to a person's character is still to see what objects he or she chooses to live with, and what books are on the open shelf.

There is a famous inventory of the Medici collection, made after the death of Lorenzo the Magnificent in 1492, which is worth pausing over, if only as a reminder that collecting priorities are not timeless or universal. Listed among the contents were the three famous paintings by Uccello of the Battle of San Romano; a painting by van Eyck; the horn of a unicorn; numerous antique cameos; and Chinese porcelain. The National Gallery in London, the Louvre in Paris and the Uffizi in Florence are now the proud possessors of the paintings by Uccello, with a market value that is virtually incalculable; and we no longer believe in unicorns. The 1492 valuation put the van Eyck at 30 florins; the three paintings by Uccello together at less than 300 florins; the antique cameos at an average 500 florins each. The horn of the unicorn was valued at 6,000 florins.

Seventeenth-century Holland, the first prosperous middle-class trading nation, attached great importance to collecting, and the foundations of modern auctioneering and dealing were laid in Amsterdam. John Evelyn, the celebrated English diarist, noted their collecting activities with interest. He called the well-known Dutch landscapes and interior scenes 'Landskips, and Drolleries, as they call those clownship representations', and then went on: 'The reason of this store of pictures and their cheapnesse proceede from their want of land, to employ their stocke; so 'tis an ordinary thing to find, a common Farmour lay out two, or 3,000 pounds in this commodity, their hands are full of them, and they vend them at their Kermas'es [fairs] to very great gaines.' His note of surprise is worth considering since it indicates that other nations did not yet share the Dutch financial approach to collecting. Speculative collecting in Holland reached a peak in 1636 with tulip mania, when unbelievable sums were paid for single tulip bulbs which would produce rare and previously unseen blooms. The bubble eventually burst, and many speculative collectors were badly hurt.

Away from Holland autocratic monarchs concentrated their attention on their treasure chambers and 'Wunderkammern', and any self-respecting collector had his own cabinet of curiosities. Inside was a hotch-potch of everything collectable: jewels, works of art, scientific instruments, antiques, natural history, Mexican headdresses, porcelain and shoes from China; anything. The things were collected not necessarily for their aesthetic merit, but also because they were interesting, curious, and provided information. And they were, incidentally, an indication that man's knowledge of the world was no longer centred on the Mediterranean and Roman civilization but now embraced the Americas, the Indies, and the Far East, for voyages of discovery from Columbus onward had given glimpses of unknown continents, full of rare and exotic peoples and objects.

Collecting took on a different complexion in the eighteenth century. It became much more orderly, and against a general intellectual background of scientific and philosophical discussion and investigation things were collected because of their beauty, or their archaeological or scientific significance, rather than for their curiosity. This was the great age of the British as collectors. They streamed to the Continent in their thousands, prosperous and confident, following the Grand Tour which took them to their ultimate goal: Italy. When they returned after three to four years they brought with them quantities of works of art and souvenirs with which to adorn their newly built country houses. Lord Burlington, one of the great arbiters of taste, is said to have arrived at Dover in 1719 with no fewer than 848 pieces of luggage, the majority of which contained works of art and souvenirs. This massive influx of fine art, and many other objects, from the highest quality to the out-and-out fake, made Britain into the great treasure house of Europe. So she has remained, for in spite of economic decline, taxation and inflation there has been no war or revolution to cause the forcible break-up of the private collections which continued to be formed on an increasing scale during the nineteenth century. One only has to think of the treasures that came into the hands of British private collectors as a consequence of the French Revolution to realize how different it might have been. During this long golden age of collecting London developed an expertise and a tradition in auctioneering and dealing which have been maintained more or less unbroken to the present, and this is one reason for her continuing place at the centre of the modern commercial art world.

The nineteenth century had an unprecedented obsession with material objects, an obsession recorded in meticulous detail in many paintings of the period. Contemporary photographs, too, show houses crammed with objects, and on the strength of the new industrial prosperity vast new collections were accumulated all over Europe. Many collections continued to be dispersed on the death of a collector, much as they had been in the eighteenth century, thereby benefiting the following generation and contributing to the reputation of these centuries as the most fortunate for the private collector. New fashions in collecting flourished in the nineteenth century as early decorative arts, early Italian painting, and many neglected subjects came to prominence.

By the turn of the twentieth century, however, the pattern was changing radically. Museums were beginning to become important rivals to private collectors, a notable example being the Kaiser-Friedrich-Museum in Berlin. The blossoming of modern art movements and the interest in Eastern and African civilizations produced new types of collectors with new ideas and priorities. The rapidly growing prosperity of the United States led to a different breed of new collectors with deep and full pockets and a competitive desire to strengthen their European background by the acquisition of European art. The famous millionaires such as Henry C. Frick, Andrew Mellon and J. P. Morgan had large appetites for collecting, and there was a continual flow of objects from Europe westwards across the Atlantic. However, unlike their European counterparts of earlier generations they were also buying immortality, and on their death their private collections were bequeathed to institutions bearing their names which continue to flourish in what is now the domain of public collecting.

Public collecting

The ideal Renaissance prince was brought up to be an active patron and collector of the arts for public as well as private purposes. As a private collector he generally had more resources and more scope than his inferiors, and there are many spectacular examples of enlightened interest and courageous patronage and collecting. François I of France persuaded Leonardo da Vinci to live his last years at Cloux, and built a collection of Italian paintings of which the most famous was the *Mona Lisa*; Charles I of England acquired the spectacular collection of the Dukes of Mantua from under the noses of the Italians themselves and in circumstances worthy of a modern thriller. But collecting was also used by monarchs as an instrument of state. Magnificent outward display was a manifestation of absolute public authority. The Royal collection needed to outshine that of anyone else. This became for a time an almost obligatory characteristic of European monarchy, and reached its peak at the court of Louis XIV in the seventeenth century. Versailles with all its treasure was the embodiment of the French State, and a complete art industry, the 'Manufacture Royale des Meubles de la Couronne', was set up to support it. Similarly the Papacy used patronage and collecting of the arts to strengthen its spiritual and temporal authority. Works of art were also used to buy diplomatic and political favours, just as international credit, subsidized grain and armaments are regularly used today.

Royal collections were not public in the sense of being accessible – except to the most select. The idea that collections should be open to all was in fact first raised by the Roman writer Pliny, although it never emerged as a practical reality until the eighteenth century. Early examples of the public collection in its present meaning are the Ashmolean Museum at Oxford, opened in 1683, and the British Museum, opened in 1759. Before the Revolution of 1789 there were unfulfilled plans to make the French Royal Collections publicly available in the Louvre, and these were brought to fruition by the new regime. However, it is Napoleon who takes credit for establishing the modern institution of a national gallery

Dismantled chariots found in the tomb of Tutenkhamun. *Reverence for death and the desire to see that the dead were well provided for was one of the first motives for forming a collection, which was then buried with the dead body. The treasures in the tomb of Tutenkhamun were intended to accompany him into the next world. The principal beneficiaries were usually the thieves who looted the tombs, or, in this case, modern archaeology.*

representing the finest art. As his armies moved through Europe they sent back to Paris all the most celebrated works from all the best collections to form one immense display in the Louvre. Many artists (but not the conquered nations) welcomed the convenience of such a central storehouse, and as partial justification Napoleon claimed that all men of artistic genius, of any period, were honorary Frenchmen. After his defeat most of the captured treasures were returned, but his example had taken hold, and by the mid-nineteenth century nearly every European capital had its own national gallery open to the public.

The public collections founded in the nineteenth century had two main aims: in some cases a declaration of national pride; and in others a specific desire to instruct and thereby raise aesthetic and moral awareness. In the twentieth century the formation and expansion of public collections and, in the United Kingdom, the opening of private collections to public view have developed at an increasing rate, mostly to good effect, but likely to raise important questions for the future. For example, should the Elgin Marbles, removed from the Parthenon and brought to London in 1803, be returned to Athens from where they came? Should important tribal art be returned to the African nations which now govern the tribes that produced them? Even if the arguments in favour of returning nationally significant cultural property to the nations from which it was taken are mistaken, they still need to be answered. Many of the older and larger public institutions have built up vast collections by purchase and bequest, and yet their works are sometimes effectively inaccessible because they have insufficient room to display them, or do so in such lamentable conditions that they discourage all but the most determined. Just as a conscientious private collector will dispose of minor items to build a better and more manageable collection, should not museums have the same power, to encourage them to improve their collections and presentation? Do public bodies give sufficient encouragement to the private collector – remembering that many of their greatest treasures are in their care thanks to the courage, taste and foresight of private individuals? Can they be effective patrons when they can only display, not use, objects? Can they be inspired collectors of contemporary art if they have to take a decision by majority vote in a committee rather than through the personal belief of the single individual?

Private collecting today

The historical pattern of collecting is inevitably illustrated by the spectacular names and events which rise like mountain peaks above the foothills. Lavish-spending collectors still exist and are inevitably given the most publicity. However, no one should forget that the lower slopes of mountain ranges are in many ways just as interesting as the peaks, and because they are more accessible are thereby much more inviting. Nor should collectors be discouraged by the apparent power and appetite of public bodies and well-endowed private institutions, or by the seemingly endless rise in prices that tends to put even modest objects out of reach. The balance between public and private collecting swings backwards and forwards. Fashions change. It may no longer be possible to buy an old master drawing of quality for the price of a good suit – it was until quite recently – but there are always objects of great interest and beauty to be purchased by those who are not tied to whatever is in fashion at the moment.

Future generations may shake their heads in disbelief at our present collecting mania, and we seem to have re-adopted the seventeenth-century notion of collecting objects as much for their curiosity as for their aesthetic qualities. How else can we explain high prices for indifferent paintings, utility furniture, old gramophones, second-hand shoes, or stuffed animals? We have also, as then, confused collecting and speculation and paid ridiculous prices for our own

equivalent of the black tulip. Nostalgia has been a strong sentiment too, so that biscuit tins or toy trains seem desirable because they are reminders of another and preferable age. However, it should be remembered that in the long run collections are impermanent, and that we recall past civilizations and previous generations by the objects and works of art that they created. It is unhealthy when private collectors become so obsessed by the past that they overlook the artists and craftsmen of their own time. Supporting young artists and craftsmen by collecting their work can be one of the most rewarding occupations. It does not require a great deal of money, and there is, of course, an active personal engagement in the activity of creation which no other form of collecting can offer.

Private collectors need courage, patience, energy, individuality and perhaps a touch of madness. An endless supply of money is fortunately not necessary. Many of the most exciting collections have been built on a modest income. Many of the dullest have been built with a limitless cheque book. Collections full of expensive objects which reveal only expensive advice are invariably depressing. If objects and works of art are bought only because someone said they are the thing to have, or the right name to follow, or are arranged by an interior decorator who considers that this is the tasteful way to show them off, in other words if the collector has no personal interest and commitment, the result is always apparent, and always painful. Collecting is not like that. What matters is the collector with, say, just a few pieces, who has a passion for each one; or the collection that includes among its priceless objects things that are ridiculous, wrong and in bad taste, the despair of uncomprehending friends and advisers, but there because the collector wants them, and because, like the treasures, they have personal meaning; or the collection which has no great amount of objects or financial value, but which is the extension and revelation of an individual's character. The great thing about collecting is that virtually anything is worth trying, and nothing is too insignificant or too grand for consideration.

(*Left*) **The Athenian Acropolis from the west, seen from the Hill of Philopappos.** *The Greeks had public collections of works of art, but not in the modern sense. The Elgin Marbles, for example, were part of the architectural decoration of the Parthenon. The Greek word 'mouseion' meant a sanctuary dedicated to the muses – more akin to a modern academy of advanced learning. Fine paintings were grouped in 'pinakothekai', although what exactly was displayed, and how, is uncertain. The north-west wing of the Acropolis – the Propylaea – shown in the photograph on the far left, contained a pinakotheka.*

(*Right*) **Christie's Inaugural Exhibition, August 1982.** *Christie's have recently revived the tradition of using their salerooms to exhibit the work of practising artists. The Exhibition is now held annually in the Great Rooms, St. James's, in August, and shows a selection of works from students at London art schools. All works on show are for sale.*

2

ACQUIRING AN EYE AND EXPERTISE

Boy: 'Well, all I can say is, Mother, if that's what they do at Umbrian schools I'm jolly glad I belong to an English one.' Punch, 30 June 1909.

Anyone new to collecting will soon find that he or she is advised to 'follow your eye', 'form your own judgement', 'have a good look and then decide'. Indeed it is the advice given by many of the contributors to this book. To the newcomer such advice may seem unhelpful and possibly annoying. How can you 'follow your eye' if you have not even taken the first steps? There is no simple answer to this. However, anyone learning a sport – tennis or golf for example – is expected to try to hit the ball during the first lesson. That, after all, is the main object of the game. With practice and instruction the hitting gets better and more varied, and occasionally a top-class player emerges. It is the same with collecting. Anyone who has expressed sufficient interest to start collecting has almost certainly responded visually at some time to a work of art or object. It is out of that initial response that a trained eye can be built. As in all endeavours some people have more flair and natural ability than others. World-class sportsmen are rare and unusual people, but there is no reason why anyone with the initial interest and with application, patience and enthusiasm should not become a capable club player. The development of a good eye is no different.

Connoisseurship

A connoisseur is literally 'one who knows', and the term is used for anyone with scholarly and aesthetic expertise in the arts. A true connoisseur can illuminate an object with a wide range of knowledge and critical judgements – about its authorship, date, the society which produced it, its use (especially if it is an object from the decorative arts), its meaning (especially if it is a painting), the history of its ownership, the location of related works, and an assessment of its quality and condition. He may even know its market price. Thus a good eye is one that is backed up by knowledge, supported by a good visual memory, and independent enough to make individual judgements and fresh observations. An eye which has no scholarship to control its waywardness often makes careless errors of an elementary nature; and an eye which has its independent sensitivity smothered by too much undigested knowledge often fails to notice the unexpected or to see things that have been overlooked. There is a splendid example of two types of connoisseurship of the best sort from recent saleroom history which deserves to become a legend. When the contents of the Rothschild mansion at Mentmore were auctioned in 1977 by Sotheby's, there was a picture in the collection of moderate size, of an indeterminate mythological subject obscured by several layers of dirt and dark varnish. Its identification was a problem, but the cataloguer rightly identified it as French eighteenth-century, and then ascribed it to the artist Carle van Loo, once highly regarded, but now scarcely a name to conjure with or to bring the highest prices. On the evening before the auction, Peter Wilson, Chairman of Sotheby's, was shown round and stopped in front of the painting, not having seen it before. On being told it was ascribed to van Loo he is reputed to have said, 'How interesting. It might almost be a Fragonard,' and walked on. The sale was attended by experts from all over the world, including scholars and museum curators. The painting in question was sold for a modest figure to David Carritt, a former Director of Christie's and then the Director in London of Artemis, the international art dealing company. A few weeks later David Carritt revealed that the now cleaned painting was in fact an exceptionally rare early work by Fragonard of *Psyche Showing her Sisters her Gifts from Cupid*, and produced the scholarly and historical evidence to put his opinion beyond dispute. Shortly afterwards it was sold to the National Gallery in London for an undisclosed but substantial sum.

Peter Wilson was not primarily an expert in French paintings, but the instinct

Fragonard: Psyche Showing her Sisters her Gifts from Cupid. *The painting, now in the National Gallery, London, was miscatalogued as by Carle van Loo. It is an early work by Fragonard.*

of his eye and expertise had been quite correct. David Carritt was an expert in French paintings and a considerable scholar. He knew that such a painting had once existed, and his eye and his knowledge enabled him to pick out this unpromising and miscatalogued object and not only to see it for what it was, but to prove it. Such stories are rare, but there is no better example of what an 'eye' and 'expertise' are all about.

Developing an eye

There are no short cuts to developing an eye, and contrary to the belief of many young students of the arts, it cannot be done simply by sitting in a library reading books and looking at photographs. Two qualities are needed: a willingness to get out and about and look at things at first hand, which is time- and energy-consuming; and the courage to form an incorrect opinion and then discover why it is wrong. This requires self-discipline. For example, when you go to a museum do not, like the great majority, look at the label first and then the work in question. Look at the object first, form an opinion, and then check, remembering that the label, like the Mentmore catalogue entry, *may* be wrong. Start with simple questions. In a room of furniture, you might begin, for example, by attempting to date pieces to the nearest century; then attempt to give each piece a nationality. As your expertise develops you can then increase the difficulty of the questions. What was its use? What is the style? What is the wood? What is the correct terminology for this or that decorative feature? What is the date to the nearest decade? Are there signs of restoration or alteration? Does it have the characteristics of a particular maker or designer? Is it a good example or one of

Tahitian wood stool (*sold by Christie's 7 July 1982*). *The stool is extremely rare and one of only four known to exist. It comes from Tahiti, and was made in the late 18th or early 19th century. It was sold for £25,950 ($45,100). Before that it is said to have been sold by a country antique dealer for a modest price in the belief that it was an example of Art Nouveau furniture. Careful examination would have shown that the piece was carved from a single block of wood and that an Art Nouveau identification was unlikely.*

indifferent design and quality? Keep a notebook in your pocket and record anything that you do not know the answer to so that you can check later in a reference book or by asking an expert.

If you are a genuine beginner start your eye on the best pieces. Not only are the great artists more exciting visually; they are the ones who establish the key prototypes from which the others learned; they give you a feel of real quality – and they give you the chronological framework into which the others fit. Also, many lesser pieces which are affordable by the ordinary collector gain in interest when you can see what or whose shining light they reflect.

An auction room is one of the best places to develop an eye, and certainly an ideal place to refine it. There is a continual changing display of objects. Above all, they can be handled: drawers can be opened, porcelain and sculpture felt, silver handled for weight, the backs of pictures examined. Furthermore, the arrangement is usefully unpredictable. In a museum handling is obviously forbidden, and displays tend to be chronological or logically grouped by school or factory or style. For anyone trying to develop an eye, as opposed to building detailed knowledge, this is not ideal, since it becomes possible to predict what will be coming next, and the eye gets lazy. A good tennis coach varies the sequence of shots that his trainee has to play: in that way a player becomes used to the unexpected and can perform confidently under match conditions against skilled opposition. The sheer variety of the salcroom provides the same test, as well as the fact that there will be pieces of good and bad quality lumped together, and those that are damaged, altered or mistakenly catalogued. Buy a catalogue, keep it firmly closed until you have formed a factual and critical opinion on a piece at whatever level of knowledge you choose, then see what the catalogue has to say, and, when you begin to develop some genuine expertise, decide whether the cataloguer is right or not.

The sort of exercise suggested above – which incidentally is not only fun but continually played by art experts on their own and with or against their colleagues – presupposes access to museums, antique shops or the saleroom. If these are not available try it with postcards. Every time you visit a museum buy a lot of cards, and preferably of things you do not recognize rather than your favourite works of art. Take a random selection and shuffle them – the disadvantage of book illustrations is that their order and juxtaposition become increasingly familiar and predictable – and then try and arrange them by subjects, styles, nationalities, artists, techniques, or whatever.

Another variation is to use buildings and architecture. Do not pass a building of any interest without trying to date it, and give yourself a real test in a street where historical styles and building types follow in rapid and haphazard succession. Above all, do not forget to look up to examine the top floor, and roofline. Looking

Boucher: Le Déjeuner (*Paris, Louvre*). *Paintings, prints and drawings, together with diaries, memoirs and novels provide a rich source of background information about the fine and decorative arts, their use, and their display. Boucher provides an intimate view of the Rococo style and mid-18th-century life. The painting is dated 1739.*

at buildings has two advantages. Firstly, few buildings remain unaltered over the years. New additions, new windows and doors are added, bricks are covered in stucco, and so on. A sharp eye is needed to spot these sorts of details. Secondly, they are a good way of learning to put works of art in context. No object or work of art was made to exist in isolation. Always try to visualize the interiors, buildings, fashions that are contemporary; in other words, try to furnish and decorate the building in your mind's eye, and imagine its social use and the daily routine of its inhabitants. Many of the words used to describe architectural features are also a routine part of the vocabulary of the fine and decorative arts.

Whenever possible take the opportunity to visit private collections. Clubs and societies (see Chapter 4) often organize private visits to well-known collections in circumstances where owners and curators are willing to allow greater freedom than usual, or to open cabinets and cupboards, and bring out objects which are normally out of sight because they are too fragile for public display or considered insufficiently interesting to the general public. Clubs may also be able to visit collections which are not open to the public. Similarly, do not neglect the countless small museums which exist all over the world. When you travel or go abroad, always take a good guide or directory which lists these places, because they can contain unexpected gems, and the pleasure of finding something relatively unknown and overlooked is always sweet. In Britain the enormous number of country houses open to the public in the spring and summer months is a particular bonus. No other country in the world has such a vast resource to delight the collector, since nowhere else do they exist in such number or with such rich contents. The majority contain fascinating ranges of objects which were collected over the generations by a single family, and many display them as still part of a daily life in which the habit of collecting is taken for granted. As in the saleroom, there is the attraction of an unpredictable mixture of styles, objects and quality, and the possibility of seeing something that is totally new.

In fact there are so many opportunities for seeing objects, and often so little time to linger in a museum or private collection, that it becomes essential to develop a good visual memory. After an outing make a concerted effort to recall buildings and rooms, and in particular to remember the arrangement and placing of objects and pictures in a room. If you have seen a key picture or piece of furniture, memorize it as well as you can. Making a sketch – however clumsy – of its form and significant details will help enormously, since sketching makes you look and investigate. If you have a camera by all means use it, but use it wisely. Although a photograph can be studied afterwards, it is no substitute for careful looking at the object itself. That is the priority. When that is done take a photograph to act as an aide memoire. A camera used undiscriminatingly in the end prevents you from looking at anything properly.

There are a number of well-known dangers to avoid. If you are a beginner try to avoid looking at too many objects or works of art at one time. It needs iron discipline to restrict yourself, but in the end it will bring its own reward. For example, six paintings properly looked at and remembered in a couple of hours represent a better use of the time than sixty which are glanced at, only to be forgotten, or even worse, subsequently muddled in the memory.

It is very easy, after a short while, to have a rush of blood to the head and think that one suddenly knows the answer to everything. A true expert realizes that the more he or she knows the greater grows the awareness of his or her ignorance. The benefit in this somewhat alarming prospect is that no one in the art world need fear boredom or satiety. And in any case, after using the eye and looking assiduously, in the next stage should come the reading, study and research.

Another danger is that as your eye becomes attuned to observing and recognizing more detail, so it can become obsessed and be led terribly astray. When looking at anything for the first time, stand well back from it and take it in as a whole: subject-matter, size, proportion, balance, colouring. Once these are grasped, then, and only then, look at the details. It is all too easy to mistake the trees for the wood, and often an isolated detail is convincing, but actually misleading, whereas what is important is that *all* parts should relate together correctly.

Techniques and materials
It is very important to gain a thorough understanding of techniques of production and the basic materials which are used by artists and craftsmen. There are two reasons for this. Knowing what techniques were available at a particular time or place is of the greatest possible help in identifying objects correctly, and, of course, detecting fakes and forgeries, many of which contain techniques or materials incompatible with the supposed identity of the piece. A sound knowledge of techniques also enables you to 'see' basic but important distinctions. A good example is printmaking. Many people initially find it difficult to distinguish between etchings, engravings and aquatints, for instance, and are even more confused when shown a high-quality photographic reproduction of one of them. However, a sound knowledge in detail of the technical processes involved enables you to see the type of sharp-edged line that cannot be made by the etching process, which involves biting into a plate with acid, but can be made by engraving, which involves cutting into a copper plate with a sharp-edged tool. It is not necessary to become an expert in the techniques in question, but you should consider some practical instruction in your chosen field, either through classes or demonstrations, so that you have a crystal clear idea of all the stages of production. A realization of the difficulties is also salutory, and makes one considerably more respectful of the achievements – and failures – of artists and craftsmen.

The second reason for understanding techniques is aesthetic. Much aesthetic pleasure can be gained by understanding how well an artist or craftsman manipulates his material within its natural limitations and the limits of his craft, and how well he marries design and idea with the available materials. For example, silver as a metal has a number of inherent qualities. It is soft and pliable. This means it can be manipulated into curved shapes; it also means that its surface can be decorated by cutting and removing the metal (engraving), by pushing the metal from one place to another (chasing) or by beating it from behind to make embossed patterns or shapes (repoussé). It also has a very pleasing colour and can be polished to reflect the light. The best silver pieces have a combination of shape, decoration, colour and surface texture interacting together to produce a result which is marvellous to look at and which the hands long to feel and hold. Many people would say that the silversmiths of the mid-eighteenth century produced the finest masterpieces, since they created an ideal marriage between the inherent qualities of their material and the fanciful swirling forms and details of rococo decoration. Other metals have their own inherent qualities. Steel, for example, is a hard and unyielding metal, but with much greater strength than silver. Like silver, it has colour and takes a high polish, although the colour is colder. It marries well with designs that are crisp, hard-edged and somewhat austere. When craftsmen fail to find a union between their designs and their material, the result is inevitably disappointing, and regrettably one can point to too many examples of work by modern silversmiths in which they seem to have done their best to make silver look and act like stainless steel.

These considerations inevitably lead on to the interesting but difficult question of quality. What is it and how does one recognize it? To some degree it is a subjective judgement, although collectors, connoisseurs and experts in a particular field will show a fair consensus of opinion. It is a multiple assessment based on knowing what an artist or craftsman is or was attempting to do and in what circumstances; evaluating the idea or meaning in a work; assessing the formal qualities of design; appreciating the choice and handling of materials. Experts will inevitably disagree on an absolute standard of quality because they give different weight to the many individual factors involved. Contemporary painting and sculpture are particularly difficult to assess in terms of quality, since the relative merit of contemporary ideas is always difficult to judge compared with those that have stood the test of time, and recently it has been fashionable for many artists and craftsmen to place a low priority on individual craftsmanship, and in many cases to delegate it entirely to someone else or to an industrial process. On the other hand, this very uncertainty makes contemporary art that much more exciting for many collectors.

A collector with a good eye is often able to recognize quality even though he cannot immediately identify or date and place the object or work of art in question. Be suspicious of the experts who will only make a judgement on quality when they have discovered who the artist or craftsman is. Finally, do not fall into the trap of thinking that the be all and end all of expertise is the ability to provide the correct name and date. It is very satisfying to be able to do so, but a true expert will reach such a conclusion only with caution, and only after assimilating, assessing and enjoying all the other qualities which the object presents.

An interest in studying the arts in a historical context is no new phenomenon. Pliny's *Natural History*, dating from the first century AD, contained chapters on painting and sculpture. The outstanding treatise of the Renaissance, which still

Art history

Coffee pot by Paul de Lamerie, dated 1738.
A superb example of the marriage between craftsmanship, design and material. Paul de Lamerie (1688–1751) was of Huguenot descent and practised in London. He was one of the first craftsmen to introduce the Rococo style in England, and the greatest silversmith of his age.

remains an important source of information, is Giorgio Vasari's *Lives of the Most Excellent Painters Sculptors and Architects*, first published in 1550. However, art history as a serious academic discipline in its own right is of comparatively recent date, originating in Germany in the late nineteenth century. Universities throughout the world now have departments of art history. Indeed in the last twenty years, art history has become an increasingly fashionable area of study.

Modern art history has developed a number of important disciplines. Initially scholars concentrated on formal analysis, showing how the arts could be seen to develop historically as a continual evolution of different styles, each with their own identifiable characteristics. This approach is still central to art-historical studies, and the terms High Renaissance, Mannerist, Baroque or Rococo, as descriptive of general styles applicable to all the arts, are part of the everyday vocabulary of art history (and of collecting). The founder and originator of this approach was the German art historian Heinrich Wölfflin (1864–1945), and his writings should still be studied.

Another important area of study is iconography, meaning the description and

Mantegna: **Studies of Saint Andrew and Two Saints with Books** (*sold by Christie's 24 June 1980 for £165,000 ($286,100)). This fine drawing was bought at Christie's in 1959 by Baron Hatvany, who exemplified many of the best aims and ideals of the private collector. Noel Annesley wrote* (Christie's Review, *1980): 'Paul Hatvany and his wife were on a cruise when news came that Hitler had invaded Austria. Being Jewish he could not return there, and he elected to come to England. . . . His interest in art, largely dormant since student days, was rekindled when he found himself a man of leisure, and it soon became a passion. He began to attend lectures at the Courtauld Institute, and increasingly visited the salerooms and the dealers, not restricting himself, as have many collectors, to one particular field, but studying and buying across the whole spectrum of art . . . He developed remarkable connoisseurship, always more sensual than intellectual. He made mistakes, but often gained from them, and throughout he was reading and looking voraciously and retaining most of what he read and saw. Initially suspicious of 'experts' and often adventurous and stubborn enough not to heed their advice, he enjoyed friendships with many leading art historians and dealers once he had evidence of their knowledge and integrity. Yet he preferred, having listened to what they had to say, to form his own judgement, and to chance his arm at auction, not baulking at a high price, and many of his most notable acquisitions, for example the Mantegna . . . were made in this way.'*

investigation of meaning in artistic images. This embraces the interpretation of symbolism, and the explanation of imagery in terms of the culture for which it was created. Present-day interpretations and readings of images are often very different from those of the age with which they were contemporary, and meanings are often lost entirely until rediscovered by the scholar who can show how and why they were significant.

Iconographical studies can also show how the use of images develops out of a particular tradition: for example, the depiction of landscape depends on a long tradition of developing images, and to interpret a landscape painting fully it is important to know where it fits in this overall development. Aby Warburg (1866–1929) and Erwin Panofsky (1892–1968) were perhaps the greatest scholars in this tradition, and their works should also be studied.

Recent new research has often turned to the history of collecting and patronage, Professor Haskell at Oxford being one of the foremost scholars in this field. Scholars are also increasingly preoccupied with seeing and understanding art in its social context.

Most art historical studies in the universities concentrate on the fine arts – painting, sculpture and architecture. The decorative arts – furniture, and ceramics, for example – have received relatively little attention from the university scholars. Arts and humanities faculties tend to fight shy of subjects which raise questions of craft and technology, and it is worth noting that European artists since the Renaissance have consciously sought to make an intellectual distinction between the fine arts and the decorative arts. Leonardo da Vinci was one of the foremost advocates, arguing that an artist should be considered better than an artisan or craftsman, since his work is to be primarily judged for the power of the intellect and imagination, not for manual dexterity. The intended consequence of the argument was to elevate artists to the social and intellectual company of princes and courtiers, and to leave craftsmen several rungs below on the social ladder. Most present-day research on the decorative arts has been carried out by museum curators, dealers, auctioneers and collectors, although the position is changing and some universities do now laudably include the decorative arts as part of their art history curriculum. Needless to say, the art-historical principles and the intellectual disciplines involved in the study of the decorative arts are precisely the same and just as rigorous as they are for the fine arts.

A basic knowledge of art history is essential for the well-informed collector – and of course many collectors are considerable scholars in their own right. Most serious writing about the visual arts is now undertaken by people with an academic art history qualification. This has meant a steady improvement in the quality and reliability of information available, but it does of course mean that the reader must be familiar with art-historical concepts and the vocabulary of art history. Initially this must mean concentrated study, just as learning another language with any degree of proficiency means application and hard work. If you can join one of the many full or part time courses that are available the work will be both easier and more pleasurable (see Chapter 4).

As well as using the best works of art history, do not neglect to read around your subject to fill in the general social and cultural background. None of the arts exists in a vacuum. For example, Dutch painting evolved to fulfil a social need, which explains both the imagery, small physical size and large numbers of Dutch paintings. Teapots, kettles, and cups also evolved to fulfil a social need, and their shapes, forms and sizes reflect fashion, economics, and social ceremony. Novels, diaries and memoirs provide a wealth of background information as well as the necessary relaxation and entertainment that should be a feature of all serious study.

Read all books with a critical eye. Unfortunately, there is a great deal of bad art history and art criticism, and you need to be aware of this. It would be invidious to pick out examples, but there are certain guidelines that can be stated. Good writers are always scrupulous about the accuracy of their information, and the way in which they marshal their evidence. They also display a willingness to use their eyes and examine specific works of art in detail and discover new facts. They are also notable for their ability to avoid jargon, complicated arguments, obscure language, and meaningless generalizations and abstractions. Inferior art history is the opposite, and in particular tends merely to repeat what others have seen and said, rather than see afresh and make an original contribution.

Remember, however, that the most important sources of information for the scholar and collector are primary sources: namely the works of art and objects themselves, and the documents and writings with which they are contemporary. Subsequent writings are secondary sources, and they can only report or comment on the primary sources. They are important in so far as they explain and illuminate the primary sources: that is their function. If you find they do not fulfil this basic purpose, then you should put them on one side and ignore them.

Research and handling information

Anyone who sets out to look at new objects, check facts and look up references is undertaking art-historical research. It may sound pretentious to describe it thus, but it is worth emphasizing that the ordinary collector and the most specialized

An important George III harewood and marquetry commode (*sold by Christie's at Godmersham Park, June 1983*). '*The semi-elliptical top with ormolu gadrooned border inlaid with a half fan medallion banded with satinwood and rosewood heart-shaped foliate chains, the frieze with a drawer inlaid with fluted lunettes and husk swags divided by urns, the centre with three drawers and ring handles framed by two cupboard doors inlaid with classical urns hung with ribbon-tied berried laurel swags divided by uprights inlaid with flowering branches, on tapering ormolu feet cast with upspringing acanthus, the rear feet replaced. 43in wide, $22\frac{1}{2}$in high.*' Verbal descriptions of furniture can have an almost gastronomical richness. A thorough knowledge of the vocabulary of the arts is essential, since the ability to describe correctly is an integral part of perception and memory.*

scholar are engaged in exactly the same activity. There is no particular mystery about research and scholarship. First of all you need motivation – a genuine enthusiasm for your chosen subject and a strong desire to learn more about it. On top of this you must be prepared to work hard, since there is a lot to learn in any field, and knowledge and sure judgement will be yours only if you are prepared to work to acquire them. A successful researcher must always be critical and unwilling to accept anything without good evidence and good reason; patient and persistent in searching for information and unravelling problems; attentive to detail and scrupulous in checking facts; dispassionate in argument and honest in admitting mistakes or accepting unwelcome conclusions. Not everybody is gifted with outstanding memory and intellectual powers, but good habits of eye and mind can be cultivated, and with enthusiasm, persistence and integrity any ordinary collector can acquire genuine and valuable expertise.

No one can expect to memorize vast quantities of information, and an important part of research consists not in learning facts but in knowing where to look for them when they are needed. This is partly a matter of experience; as you acquire expertise you learn which reference books you can trust, which experts you can turn to, and which avenues of investigation are most likely to be fruitful (see also Chapters 3 and 4). It is also a matter of being well organized in your own research. Detailed advice on how to organize research and record information would not be possible in a general book such as this, and individual needs and purposes are anyhow infinitely varied. However, there are some basic principles which it is all too easy to overlook. Before embarking on research of any kind – cataloguing a collection, taking notes from books, seeking out advice – it pays to

Hogarth: A Midnight Moddern Conversation. *Ralph Bernal built a marvellous collection of works which were unfashionable, such as ceramics and medieval works of art. His sale at Christie's in 1855 lasted 32 days with 4,294 lots. He was not a rich man but he had a truly discriminating eye, which gave rise to many stories. He bought this example of Hogarth's engraving from the print dealer Dominic Colnaghi for a small sum. It is an extremely rare early state in which the word 'modern' is misspelled 'moddern'. Colnaghi had failed to spot this.*

work out in some detail how to organize information so that it is useful to you and can be readily recalled when you need it. This sounds obvious, but in practice it can require a lot of thought, and things such as card indexes and classification systems can be a pleasure to use or a nightmare according to how well or ill they have been devised. Whatever methods you adopt, it is always necessary to be thorough and systematic. If you copy a document, double check that the transcription is accurate; if you take notes, make sure that they are full enough for you to understand them when you return to them later. Above all, always remember to make a proper record of the source of any information you acquire, for unless the source can be verified, the information is useless. Always record the author, title and publication details (date, publisher, volume number and correct title of journals) of any book or article you consult.

To become a real expert is not easy, and the greatest experts have an undoubted advantage in being born with great natural gifts. This should not discourage us, however, for doing research and acquiring knowledge is basically a matter of enthusiasm, hard work and common sense – homely qualities that we can all aspire to.

Financial expertise

Provided that an object is correctly identified and assessed in terms of quality, and provided there is a regular market for that type of object, there is little problem in arriving at a fairly accurate estimate of its price. There is less magic in this type of estimation than is sometimes thought. There are plenty of price guides published, and visits to an antique market or saleroom will soon give the collector a feel for price. Difficulties arise only when an object is so rare or of such outstanding quality that there is no existing yardstick by which it can be judged. What is the value of the last remaining manuscript by Leonardo da Vinci left in private hands, or a Rubens drawing of exceptional quality? Such questions are not likely to worry the average collector, although he will probably watch the answers with interest. It is largely a matter of having a broadly intelligent guess and then waiting to see where the bidding stops. It is much the same when a major company becomes the subject of a takeover bid. The final price can be disappointing, or exceed all reasonable expectations.

Some collectors seem blessed with good fortune, returning from a flea market or out of the way place with some treasure bought at a ridiculously low price. A few people are blessed with good luck, and do seem to have an instinct for unearthing what other eyes overlook. But behind such 'finds' there are usually many hours and days of unreported foot slogging and disappointments which are rewarded by these discoveries. As in most things, people tend to tell of their triumphs not their failures, and most brilliant achievement is the fruit of the old adage 'ten per cent inspiration, ninety per cent perspiration'.

Conclusion

It takes a long time to build expertise, but it is a refreshing feature of the collecting world that other enthusiasts are willing to share theirs quite freely. Learning, like collecting, should not be done in isolation. One of the first steps, therefore, is to discover what resources are available in the form of books, journals, professional advice, clubs, societies, courses, and then to use them. Ask questions, be persistent, and when you begin to acquire some expertise, please remember to put as much back into the system as you have taken out.

3
SEEKING ADVICE
AND FINDING INFORMATION

Daumier: Les Artistes (*lithograph*). *'Tell me, do you suppose I will find it difficult to sell this study for a good price?' 'No . . . only you will have to find someone who is mad about poplars.' Honoré Daumier (1808–79) poked fun at all aspects of French society. Landscape painting was not well regarded in 1865, and two decades later Monet's famous paintings of poplars provoked ridicule in many quarters.*

The collector is surrounded by innumerable sources of information, but with no clear idea of how to gain access to them and how to assess their accuracy or usefulness, he or she will never make effective use of them. The actual process of gaining information should be one of the greatest pleasures, and collectors are in the unusual position of being able to develop a high level of expertise without a conventional academic background. Some of the greatest collectors have been largely self-taught, having made the best use of the vast amount of information and advice that is available.

An additional bonus is that most of this information and advice is either free, or can be acquired at minimal cost. Collecting objects will be as expensive as the means or the fanaticism of each individual collector will allow, but learning about them need not cost anything. Indeed, many collectors ultimately realize that assimilating information and knowledge can be as enjoyable and as rewarding as collecting the objects themselves. Information is cheap to acquire, and provided a workable system of recording it has been devised (see Chapter 2), it can be easily stored without special equipment. It does not take up much space, and there is little risk of it being lost or stolen. It can even bring its own rewards, in the form of articles, books, or lectures. Many collectors find that expertise is itself a marketable commodity, and a means of subsidizing the collecting habit.

Information is of many kinds, and it is necessary to have a clear idea about what you are going to be seeking, and where. The most basic information is provided

City Museum and Art Gallery, Stoke-on-Trent, Staffordshire. *The museum is situated in the heart of the English Potteries and contains one of the largest collections of international ceramics in the world. The museum is also notable for its didactic displays which explain the techniques of making and decorating ceramics.*

by the objects themselves, whether they be paintings, pots, cigarette cards or old kitchen utensils. It is important for collectors to see and handle as much as they can within their chosen field, for a rich store of first-hand knowledge is the basis of all expertise. Secondly, there are all the facts that need to be assimilated *about* the objects you are interested in, and here you are as likely to be turning to books and articles as to the objects themselves. Every field has its own body of information to be mastered; usually there is a lot to be learnt, and a good memory helps, although very often it is not so much a matter of learning facts as learning where to find them when you need them. Thirdly, there is the general, social and art-historical knowledge that comes from wide reading. Finally, there is the information in primary source material such as contemporary letters, inventories and other documents; here one is engaged in specialized research in archives and libraries.

Sources of information and advice for collectors can be divided in seven main groups: museums, galleries and other public collections; private collections; auction houses; dealers and others professionally involved in the collecting business; books; magazines; and miscellaneous sources such as libraries and archives, classes and lectures, societies, and radio and television. Most of these are freely available, or accessible at a small cost. There are also ways of buying information, but these can be expensive, involving the services of professionals such as art consultants, valuers, investment counsellors and so on, who normally operate on a well-defined fee system.

The most valuable source of free information, much of which may be inaccurate, but which is often amusing and entertaining none the less, is conversation. In the end, the best and most enjoyable way to learn is to talk to other collectors, to dealers, in short to anyone who shares the enthusiasm for collecting.

All museums and galleries that are regularly open to the public can be regarded as depositories of information. Much of this information is contained in the objects and collections on view, and in the related labels or museum publications, such as exhibition catalogues. The ease with which information can be extracted from any display will vary greatly from one museum to another. By and large in the United Kingdom, the best and most informative collections are to be found in the major national museums, although many smaller museums are also important, and can be particularly useful if they have specialized collections. These may either reflect local industries or regional features, or they may underline the activities or interests of local collectors or benefactors. A regional museum can often be more useful in its own special field than a national museum, and may in any case have a better and more accessible collection. Small local museums with general collections can be fascinating but they are unlikely to be of much use to the serious collector. The basic rule is always to go to the best museum or the best collection available in any particular field, and call in advance to learn whether a special exhibition has temporarily replaced the permanent collection.

Museums, galleries and public collections

There are literally hundreds of museums and galleries, many of which have clearly defined areas of specialization. There are museums devoted to agriculture, medicine, photography, chairs, dolls' houses, fire-engines, shoes, glass, stamps, magic, theatre and a host of other subjects. Some of the more specialized ones are either privately owned or operated by trusts or charities or foundations. They may have restricted visiting times, and will certainly have a small staff, some of whom may be part-time or volunteers, and who may have neither the time nor the

Getty Museum, Malibu, California. *The building is a replica of the Villa dei Papiri, excavated at Herculaneum, and was never seen by the museum's founder, the oil millionaire J. Paul Getty, who lived in England. His endowment makes it the richest museum in the world, with an estimated income of US $1.5 million per week.*

expertise to handle detailed inquiries. Surprisingly, visiting hours are also restricted at some large and wealthy museums in the United States, where nearly all museums are governed and supported by charities and foundations. There are many excellent publications giving details of museums and galleries open to the public, and a list will be found in Appendix C.

Most museums can only display a small part of their collections at any one time, and so there are often large reserve collections. While these are rarely accessible to the general public, they can be visited by serious students or collectors, but only by appointment.

If you have a query ask the museum staff. In the United Kingdom many museums are well staffed and funded directly by the government, and although curators are generally hidden from view, and sometimes encourage an aura of inaccessibility, they are employed to serve the public. In the United States, most museums receive federal subsidies that pay for only a fraction of their operations and acquisitions, and though curators may be happy to provide information, the very large museums in major cities do not have staff that are generally available to answer general questions or give advice about collecting. Many curators are involved in research of their own and may be understandably possessive about detailed information, but they should be willing and able to give information about objects in their care. Inquiries can be made by post, by telephone, or in person. Of these, the last is generally the most useful, but appointments should always be made well in advance, and with the relevant department or expert.

Most museums are prepared to give opinions on objects brought in by visitors. Because it is very time-consuming, they may have set times for this service, and so it is vital to check before making a visit. Take the object, or a good photograph of it, with full details of size, material, any maker's marks, and condition. If a visit is

Wadsworth Athenaeum, Hertford, Connecticut. *The Wadsworth Athenaeum is the oldest museum in continuous operation in the United States. It was opened in 1844 on land owned by Daniel Wadsworth, an amateur architect who financed part of the project and gave paintings by Trumbull and Cole. The Avery Court shown here was the first museum building in the International style in the United States, and was opened in 1934. The central sculpture is by the Flemish sculptor Pietro Fran Carille (1548–1618).*

impossible, then an inquiry can be made by post. In this case a good photograph accompanied by all the relevant information should be sent, and never the object itself. It may take some time for postal inquiries to be answered. Opinions given by museum staff are precisely that. They are informal, not legally binding in any way, and they may not be used to help the owner sell or advertise the object. Valuations are never given by museum staff.

Many large musems have education departments which organize lecture programmes. Held generally at lunchtime or in the early evening, and given by expert museum staff, they are either free or have a small charge. Programmes are normally published by the museum well in advance, and they may additionally be advertised in some daily, weekly or local newspapers, or on local radio. The public affairs, membership, and press offices of museums keep track of lecture programmes and provide information about the programmes to telephone callers.

National and specialist museums are likely to have a reference library. Established originally for their own staff, many are now available for public use, although some form of reader's ticket or library card is usually required. Books and other material may not be borrowed, but can be used for reference or research within the confines of the library. Such libraries often hold books, journals and documents not readily available elsewhere.

In the United Kingdom a large number of former private houses are open to the public. Many of them contain remarkable collections, in some cases unmatched by any public museum, often with the advantage of being displayed in their original context. They are either privately owned or in the care of bodies such as the National Trust or the Department of the Environment. Visiting times may be restricted and access is likely to be limited, so serious students might find it useful

Private collections

to try to arrange a private visit, perhaps with a group of fellow enthusiasts. Many houses, particularly those still in private ownership, are operated on a tight budget, and are unlikely to have staff able to handle serious inquiries. Only a few of the largest will have expert curatorial or library staff.

In the United States very few private houses are open to the public in the same way, partly because of the different taxation regulations in the two countries. The National Trust for Historic Preservation tends houses of architectural interest, and though nearly all the houses maintained by the Trust have 'period rooms', the houses are open because of their architecture rather than their collections.

Visiting private collections has a long tradition in the United Kingdom, but virtually none in the United States, where collections that are not sold are usually donated to museums, universities or other institutions committed to the preservation of art and the continued study and enjoyment of it. Although today's mass visits were physically and socially inconceivable in the eighteenth century (for example, Blenheim Palace, seat of the Duke of Marlborough, now has over 35,000 visitors a year to the house alone, and many more visit the park and grounds), the following entry from a diary of 1787 is revealing. It refers to Blenheim Palace, and it is worth remembering that the house was completed only in 1722. 'Mr C went with me to the house, following a great crowd, which we hoped would soon pass away; and in the interior, I got a sight of the china room, well fill'd I believe, and with several elegant services; after we enter'd the hall, we fell in with a corps of 30 observers – what a plague and fatigue! However we travelled through the rooms, and were shown the great works of Rubens which are, in my eyes, disgusting and indecent.'

There are a number of publications which give details of private collections open to the public, and these are listed in Appendix 4.

Auction houses

In the course of many decades the old-established auction houses have inevitably acquired an extraordinary wide range of information. Much of this concerns prices and the patterns and movement of art and collector markets, and so they are the primary source of information about price and values, both actual and historical. As far as any prices can be regarded as definitive in the very changeable world of collecting, these are the ones established by auction houses, and they are the basis for many newspaper and magazine articles and for the various collectors' price guides that are published each year. Auction houses are useful sources of information in a number of other ways. First, the sales themselves provide a unique opportunity for collectors to study the continually changing galaxy of objects during the pre-sale view days or exhibitions. Second, major sales are now supported by detailed catalogues, and these are often well-researched and lavishly illustrated (see also Chapter 13). These are useful as sources of original information and cost less than conventional books; they also remain as permanent records long after the actual sale has been forgotten. Old catalogues are useful as research documents, and it is worth remembering that many early catalogues are now available in microfilm or microfiche form. Major auction houses also publish price lists after each sale.

Third, the general level of expertise among auction house staff is very high, and a serious collector will find it quite easy to establish a regular contact or even friendship with the relevant experts and thus benefit from their knowledge. British auction house porters can also be useful. They have great experience of seeing and handling objects, and will often give interesting advice. In addition, many of them are trainee experts.

The main centre of visible activity in any large auction house is the front counter, or reception area. Any person may take any object, or a good photograph of an object, at any time during office hours to the front counter for an informal opinion or valuation, though it is best to make an appointment with an expert before a visit. This is a very useful service for the collector. Opinions and valuations are based on the experience gained from earlier sales of similar objects, and arc always verbal. They are generally dispassionate, although the expert will obviously hope that it will be such as to encourage the collector to want to buy or sell at auction. An auction house can also supply a formal written valuation of any object or collection, but for this service there is always a charge.

Directories of auction houses are listed in Appendix 3.

Dealers

Many collectors attribute much of their success, and their pleasure, to the friendships they have been able to establish with dealers. However, art and antique dealers live and operate in a competitive world in which their principal weapons are knowledge and experience. For most dealers, the way in which their skill, often gained at considerable personal expense, is used will mark the difference between success and failure. As a result, dealers are by nature possessivc of their knowledge, and are generally unwilling to pass it on to casual inquirers. But to a familiar and valued client, a dealer will be immensely helpful.

Making friends with a dealer is a bit like conducting a love affair. At the start, the outcome is both uncertain and tantalizing. The first meetings follow the traditional ritual of courtship, making progress by careful stages, accepting a few setbacks but remaining optimistic about the outcome. Bit by bit the dealer lowers his guard; gradually information begins to slip out, encouraged by the enthusiasm of, and business with, the collector. Many great collections, for example the Schreiber collection of ceramics in the Victoria and Albert Museum, are the result of successful relationships between collectors and dealers,

Christie's front counter, 8 King Street, London W1. *Informal opinions and valuations can be obtained free of charge and without an appointment at most auction houses.*

relationships in which the dealer often played the dominant role, guiding and advising at all stages and controlling the nature and style of the collection.

Remember that a dealer is not in business to give free advice (see also Chapter 14). He is in business to buy and sell well, and so his advice may be coloured by commercial considerations. It is, for example, an unusual dealer who will advise a collector he does not know to buy or sell at auction, even if this is clearly the best course of action. Any discussion about values must be seen in the context of the market place. No dealer can afford to be dispassionate about price, for his livelihood depends on his profit margin. It is always a good idea to approach more than one dealer for advice, especially about the value of any object. In the first place, one dealer may well be saying what he thinks the collector wants to hear, a simple process of flattery to encourage business. In the second place, he may simply be wrong – the level of expertise among dealers varies greatly, and even the best can make mistakes. Most importantly, there is nearly always room for genuine differences of opinion about quality, condition, attribution or other factors involved in an object's appraisal.

Aim high. Seek out the best dealer in any particular field. At the top level, the information will generally be more accurate, the approach more intelligent, the stock more interesting and the price better related to the market. Conversation and shared experience have helped dealers to turn many small collectors into great collectors, and in any case, regular visits to leading dealers provide collectors with marvellous opportunities to see, examine, handle and discuss objects that are often of museum quality.

Directories of dealers are listed in Appendix 3.

Books   A good library is an essential part of any collection, but it is vital to be able to judge the value of any book. Some of the most useful books about antiques and collections have been written by dealers, for a good dealer can understand better than anyone the needs and interests of collectors. Regrettably, however, there are plenty of badly written, boring and useless books. The tide of popular enthusiasm that has engulfed the world of antiques during the last fifteen years has inspired a flood of books. Of these, the majority need never have been published; they would have been of greater use to the world had they been left in their original state: as trees. Most of these books simply repeat and reiterate the same information, much of which is in any case inaccurate. To give one example: about forty books about Wedgwood pottery have been published this century, but the serious collector need only bother with about half a dozen of them. Publishers are often remarkably unadventurous, only following where others have already trod. Each year sees the appearance of many books of apparent similarity, all covering the same basic subjects and periods, while huge areas of collector interest are still undocumented. For example, it is still difficult to find informative books about the decorative arts of the nineteenth century.

The most recently published book is not necessarily the best. Some of the best books for collectors were written up to a hundred years ago and have not been improved upon. In most areas of collecting there are books that have become standards, most of which can be easily identified. Original copies can be hard to find, but a large number have now been reprinted by publishers who realize that they are not likely to find anything better. Original copies of classic books fetch high prices, and so the aspiring collector will have to become a regular reader of booksellers' lists and book auction catalogues. There are now many book dealers who specialize in art, architecture and antiques books.

Finding the best books on any particular subject is not difficult (see also Chapter 2). A visit to the art and antiques section of a major public library or a large bookshop is always a good idea, in order to see and examine everything that is available. Such a visit will reveal the repetitive nature of most books. Advice from specialist booksellers can also be useful, for they will know which books are worth having, and which can be safely ignored. Advice should also be sought from other collectors, from dealers and from museum staff. Any book that is of use and interest rapidly acquires a reputation and a status that is recognized by collectors and dealers alike, and so the essential components of any library can readily be identified. Apart from these standard reference books, collectors should also look out for the less obvious material that is connected with their subject, for example old trade catalogues, publicity material, exhibition and sale catalogues and so on.

A recent phenomenon has been the publication of annual price guides. These are now published to cover a wide range of subjects, some remarkably obscure. Nearly all the prices quoted for a specific object, or a price range for a type of object, are taken from recent auction sales, and so in broad terms reflect the state of the market at any particular time. They are useful for basic groundwork, or for checking prices from other sources, but they should not be used as infallible gospels. These books encourage beginners to treat art and antiques like second-hand cars, but the art market is very different. No two objects are ever exactly the same, so prices and values are inevitably far more flexible. They are also affected by a vast range of outside factors (see Chapter 6). In checking on the price of a print, for instance, the reader may find that there are different states or strikes of the same print which command widely differing prices, factors not always mentioned in the guides. When possible, it is helpful to refer to the original

Frontispiece to the 1568 edition of Vasari's 'Lives of the Artists'. *Vasari is one of the key sources of information on Renaissance painters.*

auction catalogue in which the print was described, a rule that applies to other types of property as well. Price guides will probably be most interesting in fifty years' time, when they will give a fascinating picture of the collecting habits and trends of the second half of the twentieth century.

A bibliography of some of the classic books for the collector is given in Appendix A.

Magazines   Since the nineteenth century, art magazines have been of great importance and interest for collectors. The first art magazines appeared in France and Germany in the late eighteenth century, but they did not develop on a large scale until the middle of the nineteenth, prompted by advances in printing technology such as lithography and photo-engraving. It has been calculated that between 500 and 1,000 different art magazines have been published in Europe, Russia and America during the last 150 years. Most of these have been short-lived, highly specialized and of limited interest. However, there are many magazines published since the 1850s that are of lasting value. A typical example is the *Art Journal*. Launched in London in 1839 as the *Art-Union*, relaunched in 1849 as the *Art Journal*, this magazine reported on the fine and the decorative arts in a lively style until its demise in 1911. Particularly interesting now are the special catalogue supplements published to coincide with many of the great nineteenth-century international exhibitions. *The Connoisseur* was launched in 1901 as 'the magazine for collectors', and became, during its heyday, the leading international periodical for the antique trade. In the United States, the *American Art-Union Bulletin* began publication in 1847, the *Art Journal* in 1875. *Art News* started in 1902 and is still publishing. Today, there are in most countries many art magazines which commonly include antiques, fine arts, collecting, interior design and decoration and architecture among their spheres of interest. They often include the word 'collector' or 'collecting' in their title: *Collectors' Guide, Antique Collecting, Antique Collector, Collecting Now*. Popular interest in antiques and collecting means that many newspapers and consumer magazines frequently include art, antiques and collecting features. The fashion magazine *Vogue*, for example, has a regular antique or collecting column.

Apart from specialist academic journals, such as the *Burlington Magazine*, most of today's magazines are consciously ephemeral, with articles that are only of limited interest, and rarely containing information that serious collectors cannot find elsewhere. It is advisable to examine magazines at public libraries or on the display shelves of major stationers before deciding to buy or order on a regular basis. This sort of amateur market research will in fact reveal that many of the better general interest magazines, *Country Life, House and Garden,* the *Illustrated London News* and *Architectural Digest* for example, often contain more useful and more interesting articles than those magazines specifically devoted to antiques and collecting. This is explained by their larger circulations, which allows their editors to commission better, and thus more expensive, writers and photographers. More specialized magazines, however, particularly those published by learned societies and the more prestigious collectors' clubs, can usually attract expert contributions for little or no fee, and for the serious collector these are important publications.

Any serious collector ought to include in his library the major magazines of the past, for many gain in interest with the passage of time. A run of the *Studio*, for example, from its launch in 1893 to its effective demise during the early 1960s, is an invaluable record of design and decorative art, and critical opinion, during that period. It was primarily a magazine about contemporary art and design, but many of the objects featured have with time become collectable. Specialist magazines can also be of great interest. The *Pottery Gazette and Glass Trades Review*, for instance, is a vital source of information for any serious ceramic collector, far more valuable than any book about Victorian ceramics. The *Maine Antiques Digest* covers the various Americana markets regularly, and also runs in-depth and well-informed features on specified objects and areas. Old magazines are hard to find in good condition, although bound sets often occur in country auctions. Complete runs can sometimes be found in major libraries, such as the Victoria and Albert Museum Library and the British Library in the United Kingdom, or the Frick Collection and the New York Public Art Reference Library in the United States, or in the relevant specialist museum.

As well as those in museums and galleries, large public reference and lending libraries can be useful sources of information. Many reference libraries can be freely used but others, such as university libraries, require some form of membership or reader's ticket. Less accessible, but sometimes more valuable, are the libraries owned by societies, clubs, institutions and similar bodies. Many of these are highly specialized and are often only available to members or by appointment. Examples are the libraries at the Royal Academy and at the Society of Antiquaries. United States societies, being relatively new, lack the facilities of the British ones, though members often have impressive personal libraries and are willing to lend books. The libraries and archives owned by industrial companies, professional bodies and families should not be forgotten either. These are usually private, but many are either accessible by appointment, or are on loan to institutions with wider public access. Where they are still in private hands, such

Libraries and archives

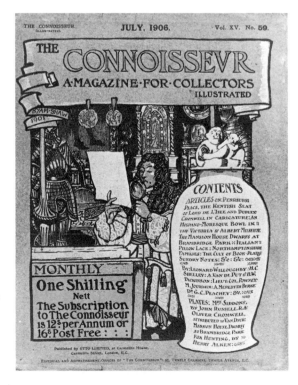

The Connoisseur, July 1906. *An example of a famous magazine at a time when magazines for collectors were produced in great numbers and to a very high standard. Magazines from the period should be included in any serious library on collecting.*

libraries and archives may well range from a properly organized and fully catalogued collection under the care of a professional archivist to a room packed with dusty boxes containing a random and completely unsorted pile of documents. A collector may therefore have to be prepared to work hard, sometimes physically and mentally, get his hands dirty, and allow plenty of time in the pursuit of knowledge.

It is necessary to have a knowledge of research procedures and cataloguing systems in order to reap the full benefit of a library (see Chapter 2). There is always a mass of information to be found, but gaining access to it is a matter of knowing what to do, which questions to ask and how to ask them. A basic rule is not to be intimidated and not to hesitate to ask for advice if you have any difficulty; library staff usually go out of their way to be helpful. One secret of success if to do your homework in advance: make sure you know exactly what you are looking for and check that you have the correct names and titles and dates of the books and journals you wish to consult. By the same token, when you have found what you are looking for, make sure that your notes will be intelligible when you get home, and that you have made a proper record of the source you have taken information from.

Antiques as entertainment

The phenomenal interest in antiques and collecting that has developed in the United Kingdom during the last two decades has been reflected in one particularly obvious way, namely in numerous radio and television programmes. Roadshows, 'phone-ins, discussions and quiz shows are now a feature of the collectors' world, and through them many experts have become household names. Most of these programmes are by their nature fairly general, but for a collector lucky enough to ask the right question at the right time they can be a source of free information. However, serious collectors should always remember that all such programmes are essentially planned as entertainment, reflecting a popular awareness of antiques, collecting and nostalgia, and an even greater public interest in prices and value. In the United States in particular, the major auction houses and many museums and clubs hold 'heirloom discovery days', during which visiting experts give advice on objects brought to a specified location. The advice is usually given in exchange for a modest contribution to the organization sponsoring it.

Assessing advice

This chapter has attempted to show collectors that they are surrounded by many sources of free advice and information, generally accessible after a minimum outlay of effort. Most of these are based on the principle that might best be expressed as 'picking someone else's brains'. The information that results from this process may emerge willingly or grudgingly, and any assessment of its accuracy and value is up to the collector.

Remember that any piece of information can be coloured by prejudice, by omission, by forgetfulness, and by conscious or unconscious inaccuracy. Books are often wrong, and so are experts. The way to cope with this problem is simply to check. Ideally, do not accept any piece of information at face value. So fanatical a distrust may be impractical, and compromise is inevitable. In any case you will soon learn which sources of information are trustworthy. Any opinion expressed by an expert can always be checked against the opinion of another expert, granted that there are probably as many shades of opinion as there are experts. But an area of common agreement will usually emerge, although in the end you have to decide which opinion is most soundly based, and make your own judgement. If you are not happy with the information given by a museum official, by an auction house expert or by a dealer, ask another official, expert or dealer. Never display distrust or disbelief, as this will only result in antagonism. Simply go somewhere else and ask again. Don't try to trap people, and avoid the temptation to play one expert against another. By and large, it is not a good start to a relationship with one expert to ask him or her to undermine the reputation or knowledge of another, even if the two are known to dislike each other. You will merely make the expert wonder when it will be his turn for character assassination, and he will simply hold back information which could be used against him, but which might be valuable to you. When trying to sell an object for cash or establish its value, any price offered by any dealer should always be checked against another offer. In many cases the best way to proceed is to establish the market value of the object by taking it to an auction house for an informal opinion and valuation before approaching any dealer. By this means, the collector will at least know roughly how much to expect, and in any case it is advisable to consider the alternative methods of disposal.

The key to success is to be patient, to exploit the best sources available, to ask the right questions, to fear no man (or woman) however grand they may seem, and to be prepared to check the accuracy of any piece of information. A good collector will also be generous with his time and knowledge. He has to give as well as take, remembering at all times the laborious way in which he gained his own knowledge.

BBC Antiques Road Show. *Art and antiques have been increasingly used as a form of popular entertainment in recent years. This photograph shows Arthur Negus and Roger Warner examining a piece of furniture on the BBC programme Antiques Road Show. Members of the public are encouraged to bring objects to the studio for consideration by a group of 12–15 specialists. During the day approximately 3,000 visitors bring 6,000–9,000 objects, and points of interest are videotaped for the programme. Discoveries are rare, an exception being a Ming 'Monk's Cap' ewer which had been bought for 50 pence, was identified on the programme, and later sold for £13,000.*

4
CLUBS, SOCIETIES AND EDUCATIONAL COURSES

Rowlandson: Christie's Saleroom (*detail*) (*London, Christie's*). *Rowlandson's drawing illustrates the clublike atmosphere of the saleroom in the 18th century.*

The eccentric millionaire collector has long been one of the most popular figures of journalistic mythology. He commands unimaginable wealth, is deeply secretive and lives above an extensive, humidity-controlled cellar, somewhere in South America. He is a Silas Marner, hoarding not solid gold sovereigns but superb works of art, and unlike the mass of humanity, he takes his greatest pleasure from the knowledge that he is an audience of one — no one else can share his delight in the ownership and contemplation of the most beautiful products of human genius.

He is made the romantic excuse for many of the most notorious art robberies, when the police and the newspapers cannot come up with a more practical and prosaic explanation. It is a pity that he almost certainly does not exist. If he did he would be the pure collector, the equivalent of a Casanova or a medieval monastic, someone who loves beautiful objects obsessively and for their own sake, without regard for the pleasures of sharing and the esteem which fellow connoisseurs accord to the possessors of the best.

In fact, 'eccentric' and 'millionaire' are perhaps more accurate words to describe this fictional character than 'collector'. To behave in such a way he would have to be very unusual as well as very rich indeed, for few genuine collectors would be entirely happy with a strictly private hoard, however splendid; so much of the pleasure of collecting is derived from the admiration — and sometimes envy — of one's contemporaries. This is why so many collectors are gregarious, and societies dedicated to the most unlikely objects abound and flourish. A collectors' society is partly for study and the exchange of both knowledge and pieces, but it also exists in part for display.

In this sense antique shops or auction rooms have often fulfilled the function of a society, and Christie's Great Rooms in St. James's were, and still are, a meeting place for collectors to drop in and exchange information for social as well as commercial reasons. Antique shops, however, have a longer history, their antecedents being found in the lumber rooms of the money lenders. 'Lumber' is derived from the Lombards, who were the first Christian usurers, and the 'Lombard' room was the strong-room in which they stored the pledges and the pawns of princes.

The United Kingdom has an ancient tradition of societies for collectors and connoisseurs which is unmatched in the United States. Societies that formally brought together a select group of individuals who were interested in history first appear in England in the sixteenth century. The Society of Antiquaries traces its origins back to the later years of the reign of Queen Elizabeth I. The Royal Society was founded in that of Charles II, in 1660, and although neither was specifically intended to encourage collecting they did so incidentally by bringing together potential collectors. The seventeenth century saw the beginning of what could aptly be termed the 'Age of the Antiquary', and it is but a short step from recording the past to collecting it, from scholarship to acquisitive connoisseurship. Samuel Pepys regularly used only one or two bookbinders for his famous library, but he showed the spirit of the true collector when he arranged for a single volume to be bound by another leading craftsman whom he admired, merely to acquire a specimen of his work.

It is perhaps worth pausing on the history of a slightly later society, which has linked many of the greatest collectors of the last 250 years, although once again it was not founded with that in view. This is the Dilettanti Society, which first met in about 1732. It was formed by a group of young men who had made the Grand

Tour to Italy — or who may indeed have been actually on it, since there is some evidence that the first meeting took place in Venice — with the intention of dining together and encouraging the Fine Arts, and in particular the taste for classical sculpture and antiquities. Horace Walpole made a largely unjust gibe that the real qualification for membership was being drunk, and conviviality has certainly always played a great part in the proceedings of the Society, which still dines regularly today. However, the membership was composed not only of young, and sometimes dissipated, aristocrats and the rich, but also of artists, antiquaries and scholars, and it came to play an important part in forming the cultural tastes of eighteenth- and nineteenth-century Britain.

In the 1760s the Dilettanti encouraged the foundation of the Royal Academy in London, and although their own scheme came to nothing, they later funded travelling scholarships for Academy students, and Presidents and other distinguished Academicians have regularly been appointed Portrait Painters to the Society.

While the various societies mentioned so far were not formed for collectors, the Burlington Fine Arts' Club, which began life as the Fine Arts' Club in 1856 and sadly went into liquidation in 1951, was founded specifically 'to bring together Amateurs, Collectors and others interested in Art; to afford ready means for consultation between persons of special knowledge and experience in matters relating to the Fine Arts; and to provide accommodation for showing and comparing rare works in the possession of members and their friends'. It was a typical club for like-minded gentlemen, with its own premises and a membership limited to 500. For many years its exhibitions, both of the collections of members and loaned from elsewhere, were an important part of the cultural life of London.

The United States of America has a long and still continuing tradition not of societies but of widely based cultural groups, which have often set up museums and similar institutions. Works of art in the recognized sense were rare in the early days, and fossils, shells and the like took their places beside them in the cabinets of curiosities formed by collectors, but already by 1779 the Fine Arts had been added to the curriculum at the College of William and Mary at Williamsburg, on the prompting of Thomas Jefferson. The earliest museum in colonial America was the one opened by the Charleston Library Society in 1773, but it was and remains devoted to natural history. The earliest art museum was that established by Charles Willson Peale in Philadelphia, which was opened to the public in 1786. Peale was also the founder of the Pennsylvania Academy of Fine Arts, begun in 1809 and still surviving as 'America's oldest art institution'.

The endowment of museums and institutes by private collectors also began early, but they were not the only patrons of contemporary American artists. The Pennsylvania Academy of Fine Arts, for instance, built a splendid collection, and also held annual exhibitions which often gave aspiring artists and architects their first chance to gain a reputation. While these and many similar bodies obviously did a great deal to stimulate an interest in the arts, and inspired many collectors, they were not collectors' societies as such. However, their archives and publications, for example the many volumes produced by the New York Historical Society, can be of vital importance to the collector today.

Present-day societies

In the United Kingdom the changed economic and social conditions of the second half of the twentieth century have caused the decline and closure of many of the gentlemen's clubs with exclusive membership. At the same time, however, totally new types of clubs and societies have come into being, with membership

Sir Joshua Reynolds: The Society of Dilettanti (*London, Society of Dilettanti*). *The painting shows a group of members in 1777, including Sir William Hamilton, the friend of Nelson, whose remarkable collection of antiquities is now in the British Museum.*

open to all and running into thousands, and relying on the postal service and eye-catching magazines – not dinners or soirées – to keep their members informed and involved. Art enthusiasts and collectors in particular have benefited from this type of organization, and some of the organizations have played a significant part in encouraging the interests and tastes of a very wide range of people.

The tradition of museum-centred collecting groups continues today in the United States. Partly because the nation is so large, there are very few national societies, if any, of interest to collectors of fine and decorative arts. In lieu of such societies, collectors join museums which sponsor lecture series and discussions of areas of collecting. The hosts of these meetings come either from the museums' staff or from those of galleries and auctioneers, and on occasion curators and trade members will co-chair the lectures. Additional sub-groups of members also exist, such as 'Friends of the American Wing at the Metropolitan Museum of Art', which is true of most museum memberships in the United States. Although different in name from British societies, the purpose of such groups remains the gathering and exchange of information about art and antiques.

The most eminent and academic of the British specialist societies, such as the Royal Asiatic Society, will normally require an aspiring member to go through due processes of assessment and election, and their numbers are limited. Election should be regarded as an accolade for the collector who has proved the seriousness of his credentials and the value of his knowledge, rather than an aid for the acquiring of that knowledge. Do not be overawed by the imposing gravity and distinction of such organizations and their members, even if you cannot yet

Johann Zoffany: Charles Towneley and his Friends in the Park Street Gallery, Westminster (*Burnley, Towneley Hall Art Gallery and Museums*). *Many 18th-century connoisseurs and collectors had a passion for sculptures and antiquities. Towneley gave his collection to the British Museum.*

aspire to membership yourself. Many of them have excellent reference libraries and will be happy to help and encourage you with genuine inquiries and researches.

Any reputable dealer specializing in your field should know of at least one relevant body which could provide a starting point. Museums will usually know of local groups, and the experts at salerooms should be able to provide the names and addresses of national and international organizations in their field.

Given the vast increase in interest in all forms of art and antiques over the last few decades, it would be surprising if a collectors' organization of some sort did not exist for almost every imaginable product of the ingenuity and craftsmanship of the past. Manhole covers, share certificates, button-hooks, post, cigarette and playing cards, toy theatres, wine labels, bodkins, treen, fans, lead soldiers, Beleek and banknotes, all things are provided with a (preferably Latin) name, a newsletter, scholarly attention and a society. The eccentricities and foibles of individuals have been institutionalized as those who once pursued their bizarre interests in private have come out of the closet – and there is doubtless by now a closet collectors' club – and have realized that their predilections are even more enjoyable when shared.

Although fine and decorative arts collectors in the United States remain closely tied to museums, societies made up of collectors interested in 'collectibles' have burgeoned. Collectibles, in United States terms, means anything from automobile parts to baseball cards. Over 150 such societies now exist, and many of them are open to anyone. Some are fanatically exclusive and require sponsorship by a member for admission, in which case you will have to find a member and persuade him of your interest in the field before even being considered for membership.

In the unlikely event that there really is no existing society to cater for your interest, then by all means form one yourself. That is if you are convinced that the interest is really worth pursuing. If so, gather together as many apostles as are known to you and as many potential converts. Contact museums, dealers and specialists. Advertise your project in the local papers, and, if your ambition is great enough, in the diary columns of the nationals. Then come to terms with an amenable printer and you are ready to become Secretary, Chairman or President of a collectors' society devoted entirely to your own interest.

Details of the major clubs and societies of interest to the collector, with addresses, will be found below.

Educational courses

The last twenty-five years have seen a remarkable development in adult education, and here too the art addict and collector has been a major beneficiary. There are any number of courses lasting a day, a week, a weekend, or spread out over one evening a week for a year, that aim to instruct and encourage a specific interest. Most of them neither pose the threat of an examination nor offer a certificate. Rather, they are a variation on the traditional concept of a society, with people coming together to exchange views and opinions and having the opportunity to listen to an expert give a lecture or paper on a subject of mutual interest, with the chance to pick his brains. Such courses are run by dealers, auction houses, collectors' organizations, and enterprising individuals. Others are run by the extra-mural bodies of universities, museums and local education authorities. A few inquiries will soon reveal what is available and which have a good reputation.

Recently, the auction houses Christie's and Sotheby's in London have added educational courses to their services. Both see it as a responsibility to provide authoritative instruction in the type of objects passing through the saleroom, and one of Christie's aims is to provide an up-to-date forum in which to encourage a serious and scholarly interest in collecting. Indeed, this has always been part of their activity. Until some twenty years ago, Christie's consisted, as it always had, of one saleroom in St. James's, run by a dozen or so partners. They could be continually on hand in the saleroom to give advice and encouragement to their clients old and new and talk about the objects and works on view. I. O. Chance, a former Chairman, summed up this atmosphere in an article he wrote on his retirement in 1974: 'I joined the firm in February 1930 [with] my old friend and colleague Arthur Grimwade ... what we did not realize then was that we were living in the last days of the Age of Elegance. The Great Rooms were in a sense a club where the dilettanti and the fashionable world foregathered in the morning to view the sales and exchange gossip before going to a lunch party or to their clubs.' Today Christie's have eight salerooms worldwide, and a much busier programme of sales than could then have been dreamed of. The former elegance, with morning coats and top hats, may have gone, and the club-like atmosphere largely disappeared, but the supply of information and encouragement to collectors has not been neglected. By offering a wide variety of courses of general and specialized interest, and by bringing together a broad cross-section of ages, nationalities, backgrounds and interests within the fold of their auction rooms, they have further developed one of their traditional functions.

Clubs and societies in the United Kingdom

These can roughly be divided into the broadly cultural and the specialized. In the broadly cultural category we can include the numerous Friends of this or that worthy body, societies concerned with the overall culture of various periods, educational groups, organizers of lectures and the most eminent members of the heritage lobby, the National Art Collections Fund and the National Trust.

Nowadays almost every museum, academy and institute has its Friends, and there is even a British Association of Friends of Museums – the Friends of the Friends as it were – which operates from 32 Eaton Place, Kemp Town, Brighton, Sussex, BN2 1EG. Basically they are fund-raising groups, and in return for subscriptions and support they accord their members various privileges. Few of them are of direct interest to the collector as such, but almost any of them may organize lectures and visits which can be of benefit to him, and obviously when such groups are comparatively small the individual member can influence the choice of subjects and activities.

The largest such organization in Britain is the Friends of the Royal Academy, whose membership had grown to just under 30,000 by the end of its sixth year of existence. Tours organized in that year, 1982, included visits to Hertfordshire, Essex, Hampshire, Crete, Bruges, Provence and Andalucia, as well as a study tour to France intended for younger connoisseurs. It has, incidentally, one of the most convenient and well-appointed Friends' Rooms in London, and for many collectors, footsore from tramping Bond Street and St. James's, the subscription is worthwhile for this if nothing else.

Other metropolitan groups include the Friends of the Victoria and Albert Museum, of the Tate Gallery and of the Courtauld Institute. The Courtauld, in Portman Square, with its photographic archives, is an essential tool for anyone concerned with paintings, and its Friends are allowed free entry to the weekly lectures during University term time, to private views and to special functions, as well as discounts on photographs ordered for their private research.

The interests of the Georgian Group and the Victorian Society are largely obvious from their titles, although there are inevitable overlaps between them, and the latter is not automatically closed to the twentieth century. The prime concern of both is with architecture, but the Victorian Society in particular interprets this broadly to cover furnishings, crafts, works of art and sometimes even paintings. Their addresses are: The Georgian Group, 2 Chester Street, London SW1X 7BB; The Victorian Society, 1 Priory Gardens, London W4 1TT. To these well-established groups we can now add the 30s Society, whose focus of attention is the art and architecture of the 1930s; its address is 3 Parks Square West, London NW1 4LJ.

The work of the National Trust is well known, that of the National Art Collections Fund less so, and in both cases the point is more what collectors should be doing to help them than the other way around. The NACF was founded in 1903 at a time when paintings and works of art were leaving Britain at an alarming rate, as has happened again in more recent years. It is a private and independent organization, and its importance lies not only in the launching of appeals and the provision of grants to needy museums, but also in its ability to put pressure on passing governments and ever-present bureaucrats. To do this effectively it needs growing membership, and collectors in search of a truly worthwhile cause, and tax relief, should apply to the Membership Department, Granby House, 95 Southwark Street, London SE1 0JA. Naturally, the visits and activities organized by the NACF, like those of the National Trust, 42 Queen Anne's Gate, London SW1 9AS, can also prove to be of practical benefit.

Another useful umbrella organization is the National Association of Decorative and Fine Art Societies, 38 Ebury Street, London SW1W 0LU, which was founded

Staff and students of Christie's Fine Arts Course. *The photograph was taken for a brochure to illustrate the variety of instruction and information now available to collectors, and the benefit of study in small groups when objects can be handled and closely examined.*

in 1968 and links societies throughout England whose interest is to increase enjoyment, knowledge and care of the arts and to stimulate interest in the preservation of the heritage. Many of the member groups also have a Voluntary Conservation Corps, whose members are trained in restoration techniques by experts. The main asset of NADFAS is its jealously guarded list of expert lecturers which is made available to the member societies.

Turning to more specialized societies, we may begin with scholarly organizations such as the Royal and the British Numismatic Societies, the Royal Asiatic Society, the Society of Jewellery Historians, the Antiquarian Horological Society and the Royal Anthropological Institute. These bodies exist primarily to promote scholarship and many of their members will be academics. Nevertheless, they are valuable for collectors also, and their journals are likely to be among the most important publications in their particular fields.

Somewhere in between comes the Old Water-Colour Society's Club. The OWS, or nowadays more formally the Royal Society of Painters in Watercolours, was founded in 1804 by a group of leading practitioners to hold exhibitions of watercolours only, where they would be judged on their own merits. The OWS was lucky in one of its Victorian secretaries, J. J. Jenkins, who was perhaps a better and more assiduous art historian than he was an artist. He compiled a mass of material on the history of watercolour painting and the lives of its practitioners, which provided the bulk of J. L Roget's *History of the Old Water-Colour Society*, first published in 1891 and reissued in 1972. This is a vital tool for anyone interested in the subject. The Society numbers collectors as well as painters among its members, and its invaluable annual volumes are themselves collectors' items. The Society, and its Club, are now to be found at the Bankside Gallery, 48 Hopton Street, Blackfriars, London SE1 9JH.

'**Hans across the sea**?' (Punch, *12 May 1909*). *Holbein's celebrated portrait of Christina of Denmark, Duchess of Milan, had been sold to Colnaghi's by the Duke of Norfolk, and their proposed sale for £72,000 to an American caused a storm of protest. The newly founded National Art Collections Fund raised an equivalent sum in six weeks, and bought the painting, which now hangs in the National Gallery, London. It is one of the first of its many purchases of works of art which it was considered should remain in Britain. The NACF followed the examples set by the Société des Amis du Louvre, the Kaiser Friedrich Museums-Verein in Berlin, and the Dutch Rembrandt Society, and acts as a focal point for private effort to assist museums and galleries to acquire works of art and items of historical importance.*

Clubs specifically for collectors nearly all cater for specialized interests. The exception is the Antique Collectors' Club, which was founded in 1966, a modern successor to the old Burlington Fine Arts Club, as is indicated by its motto: 'For Collectors – By Collectors – About Collecting'. Instead of a clubhouse off Piccadilly and a limited membership, it has a monthly magazine, *Antique Collecting*, which links individual collectors and regional groups. In origin the Club is a vehicle for a highly successful publishing organization which specializes in reference books and price guides to antiques. These are characterized by a practical and down-to-earth approach to their subjects, using, for instance, illustrations of the more common pieces to be found in shops and sales, rather than the grand and rare from museums, which would be unlikely to come the way of most collectors.

Antique Collecting is free to members and it deals with practical problems such as prices, investment potential, the individual features of an object which can affect the price for better or worse, fakes, forgeries and sources of supply. It also provides a forum in which members can buy and sell among themselves, taking only a token introductory commission for the service. Furthermore, the Club organizes weekend seminars and other events, while the local groups hold meetings and lectures. There are now perhaps 100 branches throughout the country with a total membership of more than 10,000, and some branches have been set up abroad.

Details of the Club, its publications, local branches and membership can be obtained from its headquarters, 5 Church Street, Woodbridge, Suffolk, 1PIZ 1DS.

Specialized collectors' clubs number thousands in the United Kingdom, covering almost every conceivable object that can be collected. In popular collecting subjects, numerous local clubs have been set up. There are, for example, at least 300 philatelic groups in Britain, many of them linked in a

Linley Sambourne House, 18 Stafford Terrace, London. *The house was owned and lived in by the Victorian artist Linley Sambourne (1844–1910), who drew many cartoons for Punch. It has remained virtually unchanged since his death, and is now open to the public and looked after by the Victorian Society.*

national Federation. At the top there are two prestigious societies. According to one expert, one of them is for the wealthy and one for everyman – although the wealthy are naturally not barred. Local societies are exactly what you would expect, with those in centres like Bournemouth, Liverpool, Manchester and Sheffield having some 200–300 members in the area. In many cases the President and Chairman will be senior philatelists, and members or even officers of one of the National Societies. In this field there are also specialist societies limited to one subject, such as the Great Britain Philatelic Society, which has some 400 members.

In the same way local societies of doll fanciers abound, and many of them are connected to, or at any rate in contact with, the Doll Club of Great Britain. At the top of the pile for collectors of ceramics and porcelain are groups such as the China Society and the Oriental Ceramic Society, the English Ceramic Circle, the Northern Ceramic Society and, for specialists, the Wedgwood Society.

Unfortunately in the nature of things, many groups, particularly local and highly specialized ones, change their addresses and secretaries with frustrating frequency. There is no central register at present, and it is often best to trace them through their publications, in libraries, newsagents, adult education centres, and sometimes through advertisements for meetings and lectures in local newspapers. Large reference libraries will have directories or other listings of publications which can be a useful starting point. Current names and addresses of secretaries will generally be found in the latest issue of any magazine or bulletin.

A newsletter or magazine is almost the hallmark of a self-respecting society, and something, somewhere, is published on almost every subject that is likely to attract collectors. In the field of mechanical music, for instance, both the City of London Phonograph and Gramophone Society and the Musical Box Society of Great Britain produce journals, as do at least three bodies in the United States, two in West Germany and one in France. Equally numerous are the specialist magazines which are not the mouthpieces of any one body, but may well carry information on useful organizations in your area. Here one might cite the bi-monthly newspaper *Collectors' Gazette*, published in Sutton in Ashfield and dealing with transport-related toys and ephemera, or *Modellers' World*, which also covers toys. Such publications also advertise regular dealers' and collectors' 'swap meets' which will put you in touch with other addicts and aficionados.

Clubs and societies in the United States

Clubs and societies do not have the tradition in the United States that they enjoy in Great Britain. Although there is an arm of the Victorian Society in the United States, this is the exception, not the rule. One of the few other national societies is Questers Inc., whose members study antiques and attend meetings for discussions and exchanges of information. Membership of Questers is by invitation only, and they are generally uncooperative with efforts to gain membership as they do not give out names of members who might sponsor a collector.

Still, there are over 150 collectors' *clubs* and groups scattered throughout the United States, many of which are listed in *The Kovels' Collectors' Source Book* (see Appendix 3). As mentioned earlier, museums' members can attend lectures sponsored by the institutions, and dealers, whether they handle stamps, books, American furniture, or dolls, know of the clubs open to collectors. It is impractical for many collectors to attend meetings of nationwide organizations unless the group has a regional group that holds meetings. As in the United Kingdom these clubs have newsletters which range in content from scholarly articles to social notes.

5
ATTRIBUTIONS, FAKES AND FORGERIES

Auctioneer: 'Lot 52. A genuine Turner. Painted during the artist's lifetime. What offers, gentlemen?' Punch, 13 June 1900.

Works of art don't tell lies. They are what they are. It is the labels we put on them that can be misleading, wrong or even downright dishonest. The most famous painting in the world, the *Mona Lisa*, is mislabelled since there is no evidence to support the tradition that she is Madonna Lisa, the wife of Francesco del Giocondo. The painting is by Leonardo da Vinci, but we do not know who is portrayed.

Definitions   'Fake' and 'forgery' are charged and highly emotive words, and before examining specific examples in different fields a list of commonly used terms, and their correct meanings, must be given, since even respected art historians have been known to use them incorrectly.

A *fake* in the technical sense of the word is any work of art deliberately made or altered to pretend to be something older or better than it is. A good example would be a fake sofa table where the turned and splayed supports of a Regency dressing glass had been used to replace the legs of a Victorian sofa table, transforming it into an elegant 'Regency' example.

A *forgery* is 'the making of something in fraudulent imitation of something else'. The key concept here is imitation of something else. A Louis XV style commode fraudulently made so that it will be mistaken for an already existing piece is a forgery. A commode made so that it has the general characteristics of the Louis XV style, but not in imitation of a known piece, is a fake.

A *copy* is 'an imitation of an original'. As long as it remains honest and does not pretend to be the original it is a copy, but if it is then added to or altered so that the distinguishing marks of a copy are removed, it becomes a forgery. Thus an imitation by John Smith of a known work by Picasso, signed 'John Smith', is a copy. If John Smith's signature is removed and a signature 'Picasso' added to make people believe that this is Picasso's actual work, the copy becomes a forgery.

A *reproduction* is a term specifically used for copies of pictures or prints made by photographic or mechanical means. It is also used to describe furniture made in imitation of earlier styles.

A *replica* is the term used to denote a copy of a picture made by the artist himself (for example, portrait painters often used to paint more than one version for different members of the family), but it can also be used to mean a facsimile or copy or reproduction.

A *facsimile* is 'an exact copy'.

Counterfeit is a word usually intended for fake or forged money. *Sham* and *spurious* are words used to describe a fake or forgery.

A *pastiche* or *pasticcio* is a painting or work of art created in the manner of a specific artist. In a pastiche, the pasticheur can incorporate images from several different paintings by the artist being imitated so that the pastiche seems familiar to the viewer, but with the connotation that it is not by that artist. Since it is not a direct copy of an existing painting it is not a forgery, and because it does not pretend to be anything else it is not a fake.

An *attribution* is an opinion ascribing an unidentified work of art to a particular artist or craftsman. Thus 'attributed to Raphael' means there is no indisputable evidence that he did in fact paint the picture, but the circumstantial and stylistic evidence makes it the probable opinion. A *misattribution* is an opinion which is subsequently proved to be incorrect by the production of factual evidence. Thus a document which proved that the painting 'attributed to Raphael' was in fact by another artist would mean that the picture had been misattributed.

The collector needs to gain a sufficient general understanding of his chosen field to know whether he is likely to come across the range of mis-descriptions set out above. Some are more common in one area of collecting than another. But it should be emphasized at the outset that the average collector of modest means should not become neurotic about fakes, forgeries and misattributions. Their existence is an integral part of collecting, and the problems they pose should be enjoyed, not feared. An interesting and acknowledged fake may be much more enjoyable than something genuine but dull. A collector who becomes obsessed by authenticity – like one who becomes obsessed by financial considerations – misunderstands the true nature of collecting, and is paradoxically more likely to fall victim of a fraudulent work or deal.

Unfortunately there is no rule of thumb for detecting fakes, forgeries and the different types of copies. Recognizing them is part and parcel of general expertise, experience and connoisseurship (see also Chapter 2), and there is no one, however eminent, who has not made mistakes which in retrospect look very silly. Under the headings below, some of the major problems and characteristics are described, as well as some of the more spectacular mistakes. Scientific analysis can identify the physical materials of an object and establish negative propositions, for example, that a particular painting contains paint which had not been invented by its supposed date. But a clever forger or faker will go to great lengths to get these facts right. What no forger, faker or copier can reproduce, however, is the state of mind under which the original artist worked. They can only imitate a style or mannerism, they cannot create it. There is of necessity something missing in the quality of the work, and in the end it is detectable, just as a mimic, however clever, cannot reproduce the person imitated, and in the end will fall into error, or raise the suspicion of someone who knows the real person well.

Every work of art has a history, and an examination of this history is known as the *provenance*. In an ideal case (which is rare) there is firm evidence which links all the owners in a continuous chain from the moment the work was created, to the possession of the present owner. The *Mona Lisa* has a virtually cast-iron provenance. A fake, forgery or copy, unless contemporary with the work it copies, can have no comparable history, which is why fraudulent documents or other evidence are manufactured to create an apparently convincing, but spurious, provenance. A work which emerges 'out of the blue' inevitably arouses suspicion, although occasionally perfectly genuine works of art which have been hidden for years do emerge with no long provenance. Objects don't have to have an exciting and varied history. Provenance is an important matter only in the case of the rarest and most expensive works. Minor items are bought, sold, bequeathed and exchanged without anyone bothering to record the fact, and so in evidential terms they have no provenance.

Competent specialist auctioneers, dealers and museum curators have no difficulty in identifying most works of art in their particular field, but misattributions do occur and the collector should keep an eye open for them. Also, there are still a number of fields such as antiquities – Egyptian and Greek artefacts for example – where things turn up and nobody knows for sure what they are. Some collectors buy fakes, forgeries and copies for what they are, in their own right. Fragonard, for example, is known to have copied Rembrandt, and these copies would certainly be a worthwhile acquisition for an admirer, and not cheap.

The specialist is unlikely to be deceived by an old forgery, because he has been trained to look for it, but he can be caught by a new one. The most recent case is

(*Left*) **Vermeer: Young Woman with a Water Jug** (*New York, Metropolitan Museum of Art*). *This painting is indisputably by Vermeer and has a fine provenance dating back to 1838. Nevertheless, it was at various times attributed to Metsu and de Hooch, and was not firmly identified as by Vermeer until the late 19th century when scholarly research began to establish a definite identity for his work.*

(*Right*) **Vermeer: The Girl with a Red Hat** (*Washington, National Gallery of Art, Andrew W. Mellon Collection 1937*). *The attribution to Vermeer is doubted by some scholars, who draw attention to features which they consider uncharacteristic of Vermeer, viz. it is painted on panel, and has a close-up snapshot quality; the handling of space is ambiguous, and the lion head finial on the chair faces the wrong way.*

that of a prisoner in a gaol pottery class faking the work of the contemporary English potter Bernard Leach, and getting away with it for a time. But as soon as an unusually large number of pieces start turning up, the informed dealer or expert will begin to wonder why. He or she will then re-examine pieces, and if they are wrong find out and begin to recognize the individuality of the faker. Eventually the source of the fakes will be exposed.

It should also be added that details such as signatures on paintings, marks on ceramics or porcelain, and labels on the back of frames or on furniture are more easily added, changed, faked or transposed than anything else. By all means pay attention to them, but let the work itself dictate your final opinion.

Paintings and drawings

The vast majority of pictures and drawings on the market are fairly straightforward and most unlikely to be up- or downgraded. That does not mean, however, that attributions are easy. A visit to a saleroom will reveal acres of canvas of modest or indifferent quality whose true authorship will never be known. Interest in attributions and styles is, however, one of the characteristics of picture collecting, especially in the field of old masters. Saleroom records are full of pictures deemed by well-known specialists to be copies, yet bought by others at the price of a masterpiece, because they believe, or hope, that is what they have discovered. By the same token some pictures fail to sell because no buyer believes in the attribution given, or is prepared to take the risk that it might be proved

Han van Meegeren: Christ
and the Disciples at Emmaus
(*Rotterdam, Museum Boymans-
van Beuningen*). *This now notorious
painting was bought in 1937 by
Bredius, a Dutch scholar who
believed it was a genuine work by
Vermeer. The wooden poses and
sentimental faces now appear to be
obviously wrong, but every
generation has its blind spots which
are exploited by the unscrupulous.*

wrong. Since the Renaissance lesser artists have copied the works and styles of more famous predecessors and found a market for their work. Artists themselves have produced a number of versions of the same picture either assisted by their pupils or by delegating the whole exercise to studio assistants. Ultimately the collector must, like everyone else, rely on his own eye and expertise to guide him over those shadowy pictures where opinions are divided and solid evidence unavailable. And even then he should not allow such matters to inhibit the purchase of a picture which appeals strongly through sheer beauty and artistry.

The problem only becomes acute when the collector is spending large sums on a single picture. No one wants to wake up next morning to find the leading scholar on that artist has proclaimed that it is by one of his lesser contemporaries. Recently a picture formerly attributed to Rembrandt and sold as such in all good faith by a reputable dealer was reattributed to Jan Lievens, a close friend of Rembrandt, and resold for about one tenth of the price of a Rembrandt. Some purchases are made more thrilling by being a financial gamble, and the individual collector has to assess the strength of his own pocket and courage. The excitement of buying a painting with a lesser attribution in the hope that the next scholar to become an authority on that artist will upgrade the attribution and make the collector's fortune is not to be underrated.

The condition of a painting or work of art is also very important. A painting can be so heavily and sometimes so cleverly restored that it is virtually a new piece and therefore not much better than a forgery. Broken fragments of two or more works of art can be skilfully joined together with or without modern additions, but the result is a fake. To a student these are essential pieces for study, for it is by seeing a clever forgery or fake that one can start to understand the essential difference between it and the original.

One of the most notorious fakers of the last fifty years was Han van Meegeren, a Dutch painter of no particular inspiration, but with considerable manual skills and knowledge of techniques. His picture of *Christ and the Disciples at Emmaus* was bought by the Director of the Boymans Museum in Rotterdam in 1937 as a previously undiscovered work by Vermeer, which was precisely what van Meegeren intended. Now hung on display by the present Director of the Museum, it is a curious object with a distantly 1930s feel and stylization about it, to which Bredius, the Director who bought it, and a great authority on Vermeer, was oblivious. Van Meegeren went to great lengths to fool Bredius. He bought genuine Dutch canvases of the seventeenth century, scraped the original pictures off but left the old ground paint. He used the same badger brushes and researched the correct paints of the period. He studied the life of Vermeer, which was not well known. Nothing at that time was known about the years when he was under the influence of Caravaggio, but he was supposed to have painted religious pictures, and van Meegeren knew that Bredius had an ambition to find these. Research, hard physical work, patience and skill all played their part, but the rewards were high, and while van Meegeren was lucky to get £200 for one of his own pictures, he was able to get up to £100,000 for the best of his fakes. He eventually revealed his activities when under arrest in 1945, charged with collaboration with the Nazis. It should be said, in all fairness, that not all experts were convinced by van Meegeren's 'Vermeers'. However, like most successful forgers and fakers on a grand scale, he chose his victims carefully, in this case an old man who was already in a state of mind to be convinced by a type of painting he had always hoped might exist.

Every decade since the war has produced its great art scandal, and there is nothing that the newspapers like better. In the 1950s Jean Pierre Schecrown was engaged in doing watercolour fakes of many of the modern artists, in the 1960s it was the turn of David Stein, and in the 1970s Elmyr de Hory's name was on everybody's lips. More recently an English artist called Tom Keating found that he had a talent for producing fake Samuel Palmers. Sometimes the artists said that they wished to get their own back on a society which refused to recognize their genius; sometimes they were exploited by clever, ruthless and dishonest dealers; but more often than not their reason was sheer greed.

Chinese art   The Chinese, having been ancestor worshippers for much of their history, were accustomed from a very early period to copy works of a previous generation or age. The bronzes and jades of the Song period (AD 960–1279) onwards were manufactured in an archaistic style. Great artists of the Tang, Song, Yuan and Ming periods were copied as exactly as possible, and where original silk or paper had rotted, or been damaged and been repaired, the repair was faithfully reproduced in the copy. Even the greatest of scholars in the field of Chinese painting have disagreed and argued as to the authenticity of a particular painting. The Chinese philosophy on the subject has also been somewhat different from the European one. They will exhibit copies in their museums as if they were the originals with perhaps a small note to the effect that what is on show is a copy.

Chinese dealers used to feel that if the prospective purchaser could not see the difference he might as well have a copy. As a result many collections of Chinese works of art have their quota of doubtful or wrong pieces. From the reign of Kangxi (AD 1662–1722) it was common practice to put the marks of Ming emperors not only on copies of Ming wares but also on original works not intended for use in the Imperial household. Almost identical pieces exist, some with fifteenth-century marks and some with eighteenth-century marks.

As with European forgeries, the chief specialists in the field usually know when particular pieces were made and have their means of telling the difference. When an item cannot be properly determined it is usually sold for a much lower sum of money, and occasionally collectors have seen their investment suddenly increase by an enormous amount when they have proved a piece to be genuine. Unfortunately the reverse has also happened.

Many ceramics designs were, and are, produced in imitation of an already existing and popular style. A collector of porcelain, in particular, must become familiar with the histories of the different factories and different techniques of production and the continuing fashion for certain styles to be able to identify pieces correctly. This sort of detective work is one of the things that keeps porcelain collectors happy for hours and causes discussion to continue long after closing time. For example, when the secret of porcelain in Europe was first discovered by Böttger at Meissen in 1710 he took castings and copied Oriental porcelain in the collection of Augustus the Strong. Most of the Oriental pieces copied by him are not particularly rare or valuable, but Böttger's copies are few in number, and consequently have great historical and financial value. It would be disastrous to confuse them.

European ceramics

Perhaps the greatest copier of porcelain was the firm of Edmé Samson in Paris, who carried out their business from 1845 for over 100 years. At first they specialized in making replacements for dinner services, but soon branched out into making close copies not only of the products of the famous European factories such as Meissen, Sèvres and Chelsea, but also of Chinese famille rose and famille verte. Some of these copies can be told at a glance; for instance, the Chelsea and other English pieces are made in a shiny hard paste quite different from the soft paste of the originals, though forms and decoration in the best examples are virtually identical. In certain cases moulds were taken from originals, but owing to natural shrinkage these pieces are always smaller. On the other hand certain copies of Meissen with the Samson mark either ground off or partly or completely hidden by ormolu mounts have deceived even some well-known specialists. When the Meissen piece is a figure reputedly of the 1740s or 1750s it normally has an unglazed flat base of off-white, slightly buff colour, while the copy has a similar base which is nearly white. The trouble is that occasionally a perfectly genuine example will also have a white base.

Copies of the famille rose and famille verte made by either Samson or Herend in Hungary have also deceived many experts; the designs are somewhat stiffly drawn, but so are some of the originals, and the glaze when pooled is somewhat more blue while the originals have a greyish tinge. A large bowl by Samson has spent many years as the centrepiece of a major collection of Chinese porcelain in a museum whose director was one of the great world authorities on the subject. In fairness, however, neither Samson nor his type of porcelain were known to either the director or his staff as their expertise was founded purely on Far East studies. The lesson to be drawn is that only by studying every type of imitation do the tell-tale give-away features become detectable. Ceramic collectors are better provided for in this field than most, and many museums and exhibitions have useful comparative displays, possibly because there is less scholarly stigma attached to the labels 'copy', 'fake' and 'forgery' in the ceramics field. Japanese Kakiemon and Imari are good examples of styles that have been widely copied, and there are excellent permanent displays which trace this progress in the Rijksmuseum in Amsterdam and in the Smithsonian Institute in Washington D.C.

The Imari style originated in southern Japan during the second half of the seventeenth century, and was copied first in China and then in Europe as factories were founded in Meissen, Vienna, Chantilly, Chelsea, Bow, Worcester and

Original and imitations. *One example is Japanese Kakiemon; the other three are European-made ceramics decorated in the Kakiemon style. From left to right they are: a Japanese Kakiemon dish of c.1690. Centre: (on stand) a Chelsea dish of c.1752, and a Meissen shell-shaped salt cellar, of c.1735. Right: a Chantilly saucer of c.1735.*

elsewhere. Even today one of the most popular Crown Derby designs is based on an Imari original. In many cases these were not made to deceive but to supply a market demand for a particular style. Some of the copies are so good that experts argue as to their origins. In a few cases the Japanese porcelain was imported in the white and then decorated in Holland and Germany with Kakiemon or Imari designs.

Most of the misattributions in porcelain and pottery have taken place from ignorance rather than deliberate fraud. Certain factories have captured the public's fancy at different times, and other less popular sources have then produced pieces masquerading under the names of their better-known rivals. This is an obvious source of honest confusion, as are the changes in ownership and direction of factories. For example, the Derby factory took over the Chelsea Porcelain works in 1770, and in the late nineteenth and early twentieth centuries most early Derby figures and wares were called Chelsea. The Capodimonte factory moved from Naples to Madrid in 1759 when the King of Naples, Carlo III, became King of Spain. Its mark was that of the Bourbon family, a fleur-de-lys. The next King of Naples, Ferdinando IV, founded another factory in 1771 whose most common mark was a crowned N. When the Doccia factory in Florence decided to reissue some of its most popular eighteenth-century models in the later nineteenth century it decided to use this crowned N mark. Under the misnomer of Capodimonte an enormous quantity of Doccia and less good nineteenth- and twentieth-century porcelain has been sold to the public.

Furniture Old furniture, by its very nature, can be expected to have been damaged, repaired, restored and reconstructed. Unlike ceramics or silver, wood is extremely vulnerable to heat and damp, and can be attacked by insects and rot. Unlike painting and sculpture, furniture is generally made for use and so will naturally show signs of wear, or damage from misuse.

It follows from this that any piece of antique furniture which is in pristine condition should raise justifiable suspicion. It is not impossible, simply unlikely. Indeed, if a collector wants an unblemished piece it would be more sensible to buy from one of the modern craftsmen who produce reproduction furniture to the very highest standards of design, material and workmanship, providing the price of the latter is not higher.

From the outset, therefore, the serious collector of furniture needs to establish some careful guidelines about what is personally acceptable, since the borderline between authentic and fake is much vaguer in the furniture field than any other. European collectors take a much more flexible view of the degree of restoration that is acceptable than their counterparts in the United States, perhaps because they have a longer and more varied tradition of furniture making and adaptation. What is the status of the commode in the Wallace Collection in London (see illustration), originally made by the great craftsman Riesener in 1780 and then entirely reconstructed by an unknown English cabinet maker some time after the Revolution, in a reduced form, with a replacement marble top? It is a particularly striking example of the sort of adaptations that furniture undergoes, and emphasizes that the phenomenon is not new or confined to pieces of lesser quality. The answer, perhaps, is that most collectors would rather have an adaptation that has some age and history to it than one executed yesterday.

Furniture collecting and furniture making are greatly influenced by fashion. There is nothing unusual in this, but it has its own particular consequences.

Commode by J. H. Riesener (*London, Wallace Collection*). *The commode was probably made by Riesener in 1780 before the French Revolution, but entirely reconstructed in a reduced form some time after 1789. The two panels with off-centre handles indicate they have been cut down, and an internal examination shows that the carcase and marquetry panels come from different pieces.*

When eighteenth-century chests on chests went out of fashion and became inexpensive, it became common practice to adapt the top and bottom halves to make separate chests of drawers which were much more saleable. Careful examination will probably reveal the alteration, since both will have had tops added, and in the case of the top half, feet. The top half may have narrow angled corners, a feature sometimes found on a chest on chest but rarely, if ever, on a genuine eighteenth-century chest of drawers. Some pieces are marriages between parts of two separate pieces – a table top added to a pedestal, for example; or the top may have genuine age and the pedestal be a modern reproduction. Mouldings are often added to mask adaptations. Carving that has been added subsequently is often mean in appearance since the original wood was not designed to take it, while added inlay or marquetry is often excessively elaborate.

Provided these types of features are openly admitted there is probably little harm, and the collector who wants furniture for use may well prefer a piece that has been sensitively and openly adapted to fit a particular use or size. The feature only becomes a problem when such considerations are genuinely or dishonestly overlooked and the piece of furniture is consequently offered at the wrong price. There is no simple answer other than to become familiar with styles, techniques of construction and the social history of furniture when certain pieces were first made or came into fashion. Armed with this, and a sharp eye for such things as plugged holes in drawer fronts where handles have been changed, veneers which do not match in grain and colour, oddly placed screws or poor workmanship, the collector can decide what is acceptable to him, and what goes beyond the line.

Deliberate fakes and forgeries do of course exist, although, as in most fields, the spectacular examples are aimed at those collectors who have both money and gullibility. Lower down the scale attractive pieces are made from old timber and reproductions are artificially distressed to give the appearance of age. In the 1950s some wonderful fakes of mid-eighteenth-century tripod tables and urn stands started to appear on the market, sometimes marriages between genuine tops and bottoms, but with a regularity which aroused suspicion. The demand for small eighteenth-century walnut furniture has always exceeded supply. But genuine ageing is one thing that cannot be reproduced. Furniture which has been well cared for acquires a deep and unique patina from generations of polishing. Chair arms and stretchers become worn by generations of hands and feet, and drawers which have been opened and closed over many years embed their own pattern of movement. No machine can exactly reproduce these features, and no forger or faker has that length of time to play with.

Gold and silver   European gold and silver objects should bear a hallmark which officially guarantees the metal's standard of purity according to the laws of the country of manufacture. Other marks, such as date letters, or maker's marks, may be included. English law and its enforcement were especially strict – one of the historic reasons for the popularity of English silver. The United States has never introduced an official system of hallmarking, although many silversmiths have placed their mark and indicated the standard of their metal on their work.

Collecting antique silver is a relatively new activity. Secular silver was traditionally considered first as a store of wealth – hence the importance of hallmarks – and only secondly for decoration or use. Thus it was not uncommon for pieces to be melted down or remodelled if economic circumstances or changing fashion required it, and much fine workmanship has been lost this way. When Louis XIV had to pay for expensive foreign wars, and Charles I fought for his throne, they and their supporters melted their gold and silver objects to produce coinage to pay their armies. Until the Second World War most silver sold at Christie's was sold by weight (i.e. bids were taken in shillings per ounce), the finer pieces commanding a premium because of their aesthetic and historic qualities.

No other objects carry with them this official stamp of authenticity and origin, and the highest prices are commanded by pieces with clear original hallmarks. Sets such as tableware, which might naturally have been made over a period of two or three years, command a premium if their hallmarks are all of one year. While craftsmanship, style and sheer beauty alone do count with a few cognoscenti, the hallmarks and the names of certain silversmiths such as Paul de Lamerie and Paul Storr in England, or Paul Revere in America, put exceptional prices on pieces made by them.

Silversmiths in England could be prosecuted for selling unmarked silver, and at times were required to pay duty on their pieces. This led to the practice of 'duty dodging'. It was not uncommon for even the best silversmith, when using old or damaged pieces, to take out a piece of silver with hallmarks on it, insert this piece into a new object and so avoid paying duty. Up to a very short time ago, it was illegal to sell such pieces publicly unless they were re-hallmarked, and as a result a 'duty dodger' would be worth only a fraction of an identical piece which had its correct marks. Goldsmith's Hall would even seize such a piece, and if the standard of the silver fell even slightly below sterling (92.5 per cent), then whatever the craftsmanship or age of the article, it would be melted down. The Victoria and Albert Museum has a magnificent ewer by Lamerie which they saved from such a fate. The law has recently changed and 'duty dodgers' over 100 years old can now be collected legally.

Plain seventeenth- and eighteenth-century pieces were not very fashionable in the nineteenth century and were sometimes embellished by being chased or repoussé with flowers and other designs. Tankards were also turned into jugs by having spouts added. All these things spoil the original conception, and as collectors now look for purity, such alterations of the pieces considerably reduce the value for the specialist collector.

Antique silver acquires a wonderful patina from use and regular cleaning quite different from the quality of new silver. Familiarity with silver objects will enable a collector to recognize it, and it cannot be produced artificially. Gold, on the other hand, does not show a patina of age, and even the greatest scholars are wary of gold artefacts from antiquity unless they have been excavated with the most stringent precautions by reputable archaeologists. One of the first such forgeries was a 'Scythian' gold tiara made in 1896 by a Russian goldsmith from Odessa called Rouchomovsky in good faith for a man called Hochmann, who got two runners to sell it to the Louvre. More recently gold and silver artefacts from the Middle East have appeared regularly in the market and have been treated with suspicion, though among them there could possibly be a few unrecognized genuine articles.

Sculpture and bronzes

The young Michelangelo is reputed to have made a sculpture of a fawn in imitation of the antique, and according to the sixteenth-century art historian Vasari then to have broken a tooth to make it look more authentic. Whether the story is fact or fiction it highlights the point that many sculptors learned their trade by copying other work. A sculpture that has stood out of doors for several generations may look more ancient and worn than one which has been better

A 19th-century enamelled terracotta bas-relief by Giovanni Bastianini in imitation of Luca Della Robbia (1399/1400–1482) (*London, Victoria and Albert Museum*).

protected from the weather, so that only the specialist who knows what particular feature to look for can then tell whether a piece is Greek, Roman, Renaissance or merely an eighteenth- or nineteenth-century copy, and even then he may be wrong. One of the most famous pieces of sculpture, the Apollo Belvedere, was held up by experts for over 400 years to be a pure example of Greek art, and as such had great influence. It is now known to be only a Roman copy.

Bronzes present an even greater problem, since very few sculptors actually cast their works themselves, and in the case of certain sculptors like Rodin and Renoir many of the works were cast posthumously. Apart from the patina of age, a casting of a famous Rodin bronze ordered through the Musée Rodin today should be of equal beauty to one of the originals.

The collector can take some comfort from the fact that any sculpture requires a great deal of time and skill to complete, regardless of the cost of materials, so that only a few pieces are actually worth faking or forging. Below a certain price, therefore, any work can be worth buying as decoration regardless of its authenticity. Fakes and forgeries are likely to be made only when the forger knows in advance where he can sell his work for a large profit. Sculpture is not now a fashionable collecting field, and individual pieces are not chased after with the same enthusiasm as paintings. There are no van Meegerens in the history of recent sculpture collecting (as far as we know!), and the cost of materials and labour, with the lack of over-eager collectors, explains why. The story in the nineteenth century was completely different. In Italy in the middle of the century an Italian sculptor by the name of Giovanni Bastianini followed the fashion of the period and went back to the Renaissance for the inspiration of his work. This soon inspired some dealers to pass his work off as Renaissance; after they had discovered their mistake, some of the purchasers nevertheless continued to buy his work in its own right because of its importance in the field of nineteenth-century neo-Renaissance sculpture.

A generation later the Pinelli brothers headed a group that faked the large Etruscan terracottas, and their work formed the centrepiece of the Etruscan rooms of the British Museum for 60 years from 1876 until 1936. The Louvre, the Metropolitan Museum of New York and even museums in Rome were also caught out.

Scientific tests

Scientific tests can reveal certain facts, and may prove convincingly that a work is a fake or forgery, but it is important to realize their limitations. The position is summarized with admirable precision in the *Oxford Companion to Art*: 'A generalization which can be made is that the chance of successful detection by technical means is directly related to the number of variables in the materials and technique. To take a striking illustration of this fact from outside art: owing to the large number of moving parts in a typewriter no two machines are alike, and the attempt to forge a script on another machine can always be detected. In paintings the components such as the support, ground, paint layer, and their constituents provide a fair number of variables which can be specified technically and compared with data from genuine material. In the case of sculpture in stone, on the other hand, the single material is simply carved and little technical evidence is to be expected.'

All ancient pottery can be tested by *thermoluminescence*, a method invented by Professor E. T. Hall of Oxford in the 1960s. The crystalline particles in all ceramics absorb radioactivity from the small traces of uranium, thorium and potassium which are present in the material. This 'bombardment' induces changes in the crystal structure. When heated the crystals revert to their original state, but on doing so generate a pulse of light (hence the term thermo-luminescence). These changes can be measured, and a rough estimate can be made as to when the objects were last heated. As all ceramics have to be fired when made it is possible to tell whether they are old or new. This system also works with the ceramic core of bronzes. But if two objects are of the same age the method obviously will not reveal if the object is made by X or Y.

An *ultra-violet light* shows up all surface repainting or repatination to an experienced eye, though of recent years some restorers have deliberately made their restorations react to ultra-violet rays in the same way as the original. *X-ray photographs* of an object or painting will reveal the underlying structure or the original painting underneath, particularly where materials like white lead pigment have been used. It can also reveal hidden restoration. *Infra-red photography* can reveal hidden underdrawing in a painting, since materials such as black charcoal readily absorb infra-red light. Analyses of metal or paint, *carbon 14 testing* of woodwork, and other scientific tests will help the specialist determine whether an object or painting is genuine and make the work of the forger and faker more and more difficult and expensive. Except for an ultra-violet light most of these tests are expensive, and so are of practical use only when the price of the doubtful object is high.

Quality   The collector or dealer has usually to rely on his or her experience, knowledge and eye when determining the authenticity of something he or she wishes to buy, and relative quality is one of the major factors in determining authenticity, for it tends to speak for itself. Moreover, recognizing quality in the end matters more. Two perfectly authentic fifteenth-century Chinese blue and white plates can vary in price by ten times when one is brilliant and apparently unused, and the other is of more ordinary quality and has obviously been well used at some time in its life. Most specialists would be sure of the latter, as one of the most difficult things for a forger to do is to reproduce convincingly the effect of generations of use. The dish would be either too shiny or too evenly worn without the random scratches and slight mishaps which to the trained eye confirm the age of a piece. The mint plate, being potentially so much more valuable and easier to copy, is a more tempting subject for the forger. But the other factors which make it more valuable can also be those which make it more difficult to copy. In the fifteenth century a really brilliant blue was hard to obtain and certain faults, among which is what is known as 'the heaped and piled' decoration, are now considered a plus. Even eighteenth-century copies are too studied when reproducing this. While the originals were made by simple artisans copying a master design, they still managed a surety and a firmness of drawing which even the most gifted of

copyists find so difficult to reproduce. Recognizing quality and authenticity is one of the things which makes dealing or collecting so exciting — especially if you suspect that others have overlooked the beauty in an object or picture hidden under grime or bad restoration, or that they have failed to spot the object which, because of its rarity, has been dismissed as wrong.

Between items of unquestioned authenticity and the obvious fake or reproduction there is a group which the best collectors and dealers would not touch, not because they have anything overtly wrong with them, but because the trained eye feels there is something peculiar. Sometimes it is because the old artist or craftsman has had a bad day; sometimes because the item is wrong. Fakes often seem to be too good to be true. This is because fashion can fix in the mind's eye the ideal work of a certain period, and it is this inaccurate excellence (which often has a touch of contemporary fashion in it) that the faker produces. Most specialists, if they rise to the top of their field, will go through several stages of thinking they know all the answers and then none of the answers, and finally some of the answers. All dealers, auctioneers, museum officials or collectors of renown make mistakes. Any of them who are shown goods all the time will see numerous objects or pictures which they cannot positively identify. None of this should deter the collector. Providing he has an eye to distinguish the relative quality of a work he wishes to buy, or goes to a reputable dealer or auctioneer, there are still many opportunities to furnish a house or apartment with objects, furniture and pictures of beauty, at a price that is often much lower than buying new objects. If, in these circumstances, the authenticity or attribution of an object causes many hours of pleasurable discussion, who can possibly complain?

Goya: Doña Isabel de Porcel (*London, National Gallery*). (*Far left*) *the painting after cleaning and restoration;* (*left*) *a mosaic of X-ray photographs showing extensive underpainting which reveals the artist's changes made during the execution of the painting;* (*right*) *a photograph taken under infra-red light which shows another alteration.*

6

INVESTMENT, PRICE AND VALUE

Cartoon by Marc published in The Times.

I
n general the only sensible advice to give to someone who is thinking of
investing in art or antiques is 'Don't'. Unless you are very rich, very
knowledgeable, very lucky, and have a great deal of spare time to devote to it,
you are unlikely to have much success. The difference between the art market
and the stock market cannot be emphasized too strongly. In the art market, for
instance, you must not expect a quick return on an investment, and if you do
happen to be good at making instant or short-term profits on antiques, then you
should be thinking of becoming a dealer rather than a collector.

However, if you can afford to buy the very best in any field and to keep it for
long enough, then you will almost certainly do well. This was the policy behind
the British Rail Pension Fund buying in the 1970s. They came under heavy
criticism at the time, although their critics did not always differentiate between
their policy and their methods. They were probably right to allocate a small
(relative to their total funds) and strictly defined sum to the operation and to
allow a time span of 50 years for the realization of any profits. On the other hand
their method, taking the advice of just one auctioneer (whose primary duty is to
the vendor) rather than establishing an independent advisory group, was seen by
many to be very ill-advised, both in terms of their financial responsibility and
vis-à-vis the workings of the art market.

There is a certain Alice in Wonderland quality about the words used when
talking about investment. The sentence 'Art is a good investment' usually means
'*Some* works of art *have been* a very profitable *speculation*'. There is nothing
wrong with speculation, but if anyone argues strongly the case for art investment
ask him what return he would reasonably *guarantee* for works of art. It is not an
unfair question, when a stockbroker or bank can put together a spread of
financial investments which have a quantifiable annual return or cash-in value on
a specific date.

In the late 1960s and early 1970s the financier Jim Slater, whose name was a
byword for shrewd investment in the stock market, applied his investment skills
and techniques to some of the nineteenth-century artists whose work was then
beginning to come back into favour after generations in the wilderness. In
particular he concentrated on the paintings of F. W. Watts, who was a follower of
Constable, buying everything that he could find. His activity helped to raise
prices further, and there seemed little reason for them not to continue upwards.
But it is in the nature of such art world booms that in the early stages there will be
hiccups and backslidings as the market pauses to assess and assimilate the new
price levels. It is also the accepted wisdom of the art trade that in a new field of
this kind no attempt should be made to re-sell an item or a collection in under
about ten years. Mr Slater rather grimly points out that it takes this long for the
dealers' mark up to be covered.

It is also true that a young market will be most affected by outside financial
fluctuations and political events, and this was the case when Mr Slater's other
business affairs went awry, and he was forced to re-offer his paintings at too early
a stage. The general uncertainty in the financial climate was paralleled by a
temporary falling-off of interest in the Victorian picture market, and the result
was that he just about broke even rather than realizing the profit that he might
reasonably have expected had he been able to hold on.

He says that his great mistake in the early days was to buy indiscriminately,
taking anything by Watts irrespective of quality. As Watts was very prolific, this
landed him with many inferior examples as well as a number of gems. However,
he also stresses the advantage for a novice in the field of concentrating on a single

Investment

artist or a small group, and thus being able to keep all the relevant facts and price levels constantly in mind.

Obviously it is a great satisfaction to a collector to know that he has bought well from the financial as well as the aesthetic point of view, and rising prices in his field are a pleasant psychological boost – almost a personal compliment to his taste and acumen. Obviously, too, as his taste is refined and his experience grows, he is likely to want to trade up, to sell earlier and now less satisfactory purchases in order to pay for better examples. This will be easier in a rising market, and to this extent any good collection can be seen as an investment, or at any rate a more or less self-financing operation after the initial stages. Even when you are trading up, however, you should never part with your first ghastly mistake. Keep it constantly in view as a reminder of what enthusiasm can lead to when it is not harnessed to adequate knowledge.

The best collections are those in which the collector is most intimately concerned as a connoisseur. They are also the soundest financially, and the total value of such a collection is likely to be much greater than the sum of the prices of the individual parts.

The greatest drawback to the cold investment approach is that there is no real interest in the objects. If you are merely filling a vault with canvases, you will not accumulate them with the same rigorous standards as if you were going to live with them on your walls even for a few years. You will also have less opportunity to improve your eye and knowledge in the most natural way, and thus will be less likely to understand what you should be buying in and for the future.

It is of course quite possible to give a suitable amount of money to a good dealer and instruct him to spend it wisely for you, but then you would be in the same position as someone who hands the whole decoration and furnishing of their house over to an interior decorator. The result may be immediately impressive, but it is ultimately soulless. It is also no fun.

Ideally, then, collecting should always take precedence over investment. It is all too easy for the investor to acquire second-rate works by first-rank names, where the true collector will be buying the best examples of second-rank artists and craftsmen, and financially there can be little doubt which will do better in the long run.

In 1978 the *Economist* magazine wrote an authoritative report on the financial performances of the stock market and the art market. It concluded that no meaningful comparison could be made. The art market was so fragmented, so subjective, and so influenced by unquantifiable factors such as fashion, degrees of restoration and aesthetic choice, that no helpful investment advice could be proposed for it. Indeed, anyone who has studied the historic fluctuations of prices knows that even in a booming market, the wrong work by the wrong artist purchased at the wrong moment can be a financial disaster.

All this said, it is still perfectly possible to buy cannily as well as pleasurably. As in most other markets, timing, both of buying and selling, is obviously of paramount importance.

Case histories   John William Waterhouse (1849–1917) was an admirable painter, and his pretty and slightly naughty nymphs are now deservedly popular, but like so many of his contemporaries he was almost totally disregarded for many years. In 1895 he thought well enough of his *Ophelia* to send her to the Royal Academy as a temporary substitute for his still unfinished diploma painting, which should have been presented on his election as an Associate Member. In 1913, after a few years

John William Waterhouse:
Ophelia (*sold by Christie's 26
November 1982*). *The painting
made a record price for the artist of
£75,000 ($112,500*).

in a distinguished Scottish collection, *Ophelia* was sold for 450 guineas ($2,250), but by 1950, when she was bought by Lord Hayter, she made a mere 20 guineas ($56). Lady Hayter parted with her in 1968 at 420 guineas ($1,058), a handsome profit doubtless, but this sale was just too early to catch the Victorian revival in full flood. By 1971 the picture had reached 3,000 guineas ($7,560) and when it returned to the saleroom in 1982 it was knocked down to a Japanese dealer at £75,000 ($112,500). Thus a perfectly timed buy and what could have been one of the greatest investments of all time were thrown away by the unfortunate timing of the resale.

Excellent timing in both buying and selling was shown in the case of *Contradiction – Oberon and Titania*, a crowded and meticulous fairy painting by the mad parricide Richard Dadd, which was sold at Sotheby's in March 1983 and for a short period held the auction record for any Victorian work. In 1964 the vendor had bought it for £7,000 ($19,600), and he had held on, despite the temptations of the intervening boom years, to see it realize £550,000 ($825,000). A contributory factor here was the popularity of Dadd's only other major painting, *The Fairy Feller's Master-Stroke*, which is in the Tate Gallery. His oil paintings are scarce, although watercolours appear in the salerooms fairly frequently. Three months later a Christie's sale also contained an oil painting by Richard Dadd called *Titania Sleeping*. This was an earlier work, and painted when he was sane. As only the work of the mad Dadd raises extraordinary interest today, this work failed to sell at £32,000 ($48,000), another lesson to anyone who thinks that names alone are as important as aesthetic qualities. The star of the same Christie's sale was Tissot's *Garden Bench*, a group portrait of his mistress and her children, which now became the record holder for a Victorian painting by selling to the London dealer Christopher Wood for £572,000 ($858,000). A salutary footnote, however, was the fact, not surprising to saleroom experts but not revealed by the headline writers, that two minor works by Tissot were unsold the same day, failing to reach their reserves of under £10,000 ($15,000) each (see below, pp. 138–41).

Charts which plot the variations in price of individual works of art are often published, and Gerald Rietlinger's pioneering book *The Economics of Taste*, although published in the early 1960s, remains an unequalled mine of information. Spectacular examples of price rises are not difficult to find, one of the most famous being the £2,310,000 ($5,544,000) paid by the Metropolitan

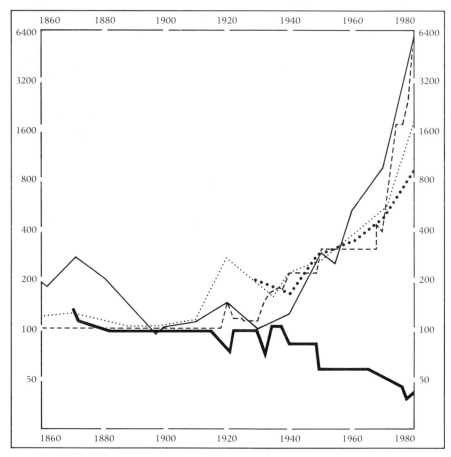

General financial trends, 1860–1980 (*1900 = 100 for all indices shown*)

– – – – – – – – – ·	Average market price of gold in £ sterling (1980 is approx. 70 times 1900 index).
————————	Average rents and land values in England and Wales (1980 is approx. 60 times 1900 index).
· · · · · · · · · · · · · · · · ·	Index of UK consumer prices 1980 is approx. 20 times 1900 index).
• • • • • • • • • • • •	Index of US consumer prices (1980 is approx. 10 times 1900 index).
▬▬▬▬▬▬▬	$/£ annual average exchange rate (1980 (£1 = $2.328) is approx. half the 1900 index).

The Financial Times Industrial Ordinary Share Index was started in 1935 with an opening index of 100 (all-time low 49.4 on 26 June 1940; all-time high 543.6 up to December 1980). The Dow Jones Industrial Index when reconstituted on 1 October 1928 (on a basis comparable to today's) opened at 240 (all-time low 41.22 on 2 July 1932; all-time high 1,051.70 up to December 1980). Sources: Bank of England; Barclays Bank; Jones Lang & Wootton.

(*Left*) **Queen Anne black japanned bureau bookcase** (*sold by Christie's 17 October 1981*). *Prices at auction: 1957–£1,575; 1973–$95,000 (£39,583); 1981–$946,000 (£516,939).*
(*Right*) **Ivory-inlaid ebony cabinet in the Italian Renaissance style designed by Alfred Lorimer** (*sold by Christie's 15 October 1981*). *Cost price (new) in 1867: £4,000. Prices at auction: 1885–£525; 1981–£15,400 ($28,798).*

Museum in New York in 1970 for Velázquez's portrait of his mulatto servant, Juan de Pareja. The second Earl of Longford (whose descendants sold the picture) had bought it at Christie's in 1811 for just under £152 ($760). But it is not really possible to make meaningful financial comparisons over long periods, because not only have tastes and currencies changed beyond all recognition, but increasing scarcity has altered the importance given to what is still available. However, properly understood, a study of the prices of the past can be of great benefit to the collector, investor or dealer. They provide a starting point for anyone looking for fields which may be undervalued today. Since almost nothing is actually unfashionable nowadays, the preferences and tastes of our ancestors can be a pointer to artists and objects which may none the less still be lagging behind their fellows.

To take an obvious example, the prices paid for English portraits by Duveen's American clients in the 1920s and 1930s may well never be equalled. The $600,000 (£160,000) paid by Henry Huntington for Gainsborough's *Blue Boy* in 1921 must be something like five times as much as the £130,000 ($364,000) made by the glorious *Mr and Mrs Andrews in a Park* (now in the National Gallery, London) in 1960, and some four times the £280,000 ($714,000) made by *The Gravenor Family* in 1972. However, the great Duveen was not just an unrivalled operator, and not all his clients were gullible nouveaux riches with more money than sensitivity. The post-Duveen reaction against English portraits was far too severe, denying much merit even to the greatest painters such as Gainsborough, Reynolds and Lawrence, and anyone who had stocked up with good examples during the 1940s and 1950s and had been able to hold on to them, would have done very well indeed.

Another example from the same period is perhaps still more relevant. The first thirty years of the twentieth century saw a remarkable flowering of talent among British etchers. Their inspiration derived from Rembrandt, and more immediately from Whistler, but once they had mastered the technique men such as Seymour Haden – who was Whistler's brother-in-law – David Young Cameron, James McBey and shortly afterwards Arthur Briscoe and Gerald Leslie Brockhurst were masters of their art and artists for all time. Since their etched work was limited, available and for a short while booming in price, during the late 1920s it was treated like the stocks and shares which shared those qualities, and then, with Wall Street and the City, the market in etchings crashed. The peak of the boom was 1925–7, and the total collapse coincided with the onset of the Great Depression two years later.

It is instructive to follow the saleroom history of one fine print, *Clewlines and Buntlines*, by Arthur Briscoe, who was a latecomer to the scene but nevertheless something of a genius. An impression of the etching set his record at £100 ($480) in 1926. It had sunk to £26 10s. ($106) by 1944 and to £15 15s. ($62.50) by 1948. The nadir was in 1955, when a trial proof inscribed by the artist to the noted collector Malcolm Salaman appeared at Sotheby's and attracted a humiliating bid of £2 ($5.60). If the buyer on that occasion were to re-offer this impression some thirty years later it would surely make four figures, and the latest buyer would

(*Left*) **J. J. Tissot (1836–1902): Bunch of Lilacs** (*sold by Christie's 26 March 1982*). *Prices at auction: 1877–£347; 1887–£163; 1895–£50; 1975–£7,350 ($16,170); 1982–£81,000 ($148,230).*

(*Right*) **Watteau: Champs Elysées** (*London, Wallace Collection*). *The painting was bought by the Marquis of Hertford, one of the great 19th-century collectors. The Wallace Collection in Manchester Square, London, is his memorial. He bought the painting for £945 at auction in 1848 and was criticized for his extravagance by the influential* Art Journal *which wrote, 'It would be the climax of imbecile judgement to say that such a picture was worthy of the sum.'*

still prove a wise investor.

This boom and collapse were perhaps the closest that the art market has ever come to the dealings of the City and Wall Street: it was the one occasion on which an investor could say, 'an example of a work of art by so and so has just made so much, therefore my example, which is in almost exactly the same condition, is worth almost exactly the same price.' True, but then in the depressed years that followed all too many of them forgot that they still held works of art rather than intrinsically worthless share certificates.

The years from the end of the Second World War to the early 1960s were a remarkable period for the judicious collector. Great bundles of prints and drawings could be had for a few pounds. The art world provided people with harmless hobbies, but it was not the big news it had been in previous decades and was soon to become again. At that time a print collector could have formed a wonderful and comprehensive cabinet of modern British etchings very cheaply indeed, and if he was far-sighted, he would have laid down a duplicate set for resale when times improved, as they have through the 1970s and into the 1980s, with only two short-lived declines in prices interrupting the general upward swing.

A very different field, in which the expenditure of a few hundred pounds or dollars and a suitable amount of scholarship in the 1960s would have produced excellent dividends in the following decades, is that of medieval Islamic gold and silver coins. Coins and medals of all types have the advantage of telling the collector exactly what they are – provided that he can read the relevant script or language. It is also very much a matter of common sense to work out what

(*Left*) **Andrea Previtali (c.1470–1528): A Young Lady.** *Black chalk on grey paper* (*sold by Christie's 24 June 1980*). *Prices at auction: 1891–£1($5); 1902–£80($392); 1936–£357($1,785); 1980–£26,000($59,800).*

(*Right*) **Nicholas de Largillière: La Belle Strasbourgeoise** (*Strasbourg, Musée des Beaux Arts*).

extraneous factors will make one example a much sought after rarity and another comparatively commonplace. Thus a Damascus gold dinar of 77 AH (after the Hegira; i.e. AD 699) was sold in Switzerland in 1982 for £109,000 ($190,750), a remarkable price, since dinars of 78 and 79 AH made £260 ($455) and £210 ($367) respectively. In about 1965 it would have been possible to get any of them for perhaps £150 ($420). The significance of 77 AH is that it was the year in which the use of representational images was banned in Islamic art.

Prices and values

Specialized knowledge is not the only factor which may turn an interesting speculation into a sound investment. Early information as to what the trade is doing can also be vital. Is anyone planning a major exhibition of an underrated artist? Is a *catalogue raisonné* about to be published, and if so is your example in it? Is a major collection in your field about to be sold? Any of these things can push prices to new levels. Political stability or the lack of it can also affect what other people are likely to buy. The rich in countries without any strong collecting tradition or great artistic heritage are likely to buy anything to do with their homeland (or their tax-haven) and its past, when times are good. If they are uncertain about the future, they will put their money into things which have an accepted international appeal and resale value, such as Old Master paintings and drawings, jewels and stamps. For similar reasons people living under unstable regimes will often collect small and easily portable items. The most interesting collection which I saw recently in one newly independent African country was of several hundred nineteenth-century button hooks.

A wise collector with a bent towards speculation will try to avoid following fashion. Obviously it is better to anticipate it. When a market booms he should be in a position to use it to dispose of his lesser examples if he is inclined to reshape his collection, and, keeping the best, to add fresh, higher-quality works to the collection or move on to a new field. It is the nature of fashion to change, and one wonders, for instance, about the financial acumen of all the people around the world who have spent large sums in acquiring poor Renoirs during the years when any Impressionist paintings have been assumed to be gilt-edged. Like many

prolific geniuses Renoir produced a considerable body of humdrum hack work. Whatever the state of the market or of the fashion, the collector should only buy the very best that he can afford and that is available.

Oscar Wilde's definition of a cynic as someone who knows the price of everything and the value of nothing can be applied accurately to all too many people involved in the art and antiques business. It is often easy to forget that a price is only relevant to one object on one particular occasion, and that even then there is no necessary correlation between price and aesthetic value. In 1963 *La Belle Strasbourgeoise*, a lovely portrait of a pretty girl by Nicolas de Largillière, was sold for £145,000 ($406,000) to the City of Strasbourg. The following year a previously unknown but equally genuine second version by de Largillière was offered at £70,000 ($196,000), and for a considerable time it found no takers. The existence of two versions of the same subject obviously affected the price, as did

Turner: Tintagel Castle, Cornwall (*sold by Christie's 18 November 1980*). *Prices paid at auction were as follows: 1877–£399; 1888–£215; 1946–£163; 1980–£16,000 ($38,400).*

the fact that the most interested potential buyer was now out of the market, but was the intrinsic value of either or both also affected?

In 1983, a major auction house offered a painting entitled *Ladies and Gentlemen Embarking for the Isle of Cythera*, which was attributed to Watteau. At the time, some experts felt that the picture was unquestionably a Watteau, though a great many others raised questions about the authorship. The painting was bought by a dealer who paid £120,000 ($180,000) for the work, which was more than an attributed painting usually brings, but much less than an autograph Watteau. The dealer then spent several months researching the painting's history and studying the composition and style. Armed with new scholarly and stylistic information, he sold the work to the German government as an unquestioned Watteau for DM3,000,000 (£658,000 or $987,000). When the painting was sold at the much higher price it had not changed, though the documentation regarding it had. The actual image, of course, was neither more nor less appealing; the only difference was that its place in Watteau's oeuvre had been substantiated.

Psyche Showing her Sisters her Gifts from Cupid (see p. 22), catalogued as by Carle van Loo in the Mentmore sale of 1977, fetched £8,000 ($14,000), but since it was subsequently shown to be an important and well-documented early Fragonard and was later sold on to the National Gallery at many times that figure, what was its actual value? A price is the figure at which something is offered or sold, its value is what it is worth to a buyer or owner, and the two may have nothing whatever to do with one another. The good dealer is the one who knows the value to others of what he has to offer and prices it accordingly. On the other hand, the enthusiastic collector must always beware of assuming that what is valuable to him will necessarily have an equivalent price.

This is why it is often unwise to put too uncritical a reliance on saleroom reports, auction records, price guides and price lists unless you have a personal knowledge of the objects involved and the circumstances under which they were

Meindert Hobbema (1638–1709): Wooded Landscape (*sold by Christie's 18 April 1980*). *Prices at auction: 1849 £452; 1870–£1,660; 1886–£1,617; 1980–£95,000 ($212,800).*

sold. Just because one outstanding work has made a staggering price, one cannot expect the same sort of money for a run-of-the-mill example by the same artist – although naturally other prices may be boosted along with it. In most cases lists of auction prices give too little detail to provide an exact comparison with what is in front of you. Was it in perfect condition? If not, was it the sort of thing that would clean or restore well? Had it been seen on the market recently, or shown to numerous dealers by a greedy owner? Where had it come from and what was its history? Even with something as straightforward as a still-life the subject-matter may have been much more, or less, attractive than in yours. Little, if anything, of this can be gleaned from a price list or index.

However, such things can be invaluable to the professional who knows what he is about, and even to the amateur they can be useful if treated purely as an aide memoire. They can give you a reasonable price range from which you can begin to form a judgement when something is offered to you or when you are deciding on how much to bid.

Booms and recessions

It is sometimes surprising how easily many art and antique dealers allow themselves to become depressed by the changing circumstances of the trade. Like farmers, they often seem to prefer to look on the dark side. In a period of recession they appear to be at a loss to know how to react, and this is especially so if the recession follows a few good years in which security has taken the edge off their critical eye.

There are two ways for a dealer to face a lean period in his market. If he has established enough capital he may decide to sit tight and wait until times improve and he can turn a profit on the book price of his stock. If he is hungrier, or perhaps more of a dealer by nature, he will turn as much of his stock as possible into cash, even if it means taking a loss, so as to be able to buy new goods at lower prices. If done with flair and if interesting goods are on the market this should leave him in a stronger position at the end of the recession than before it. A clear-headed collector should also be ready to turn a recession to his advantage, since it can often provide him with his best opportunities of buying well. But he must be quick, or discreet, since his very activity can help to make prices rise again.

It was very noticeable in the early 1980s, when galleries were closing all around, that many of the surviving dealers were complaining lugubriously about the unavailablity of high-quality goods, and as a result taking much less part than usual in auctions. It was true that there were fewer sales than usual, and that in general they were of a lower standard than in previous years, but at the same time astute private collectors, and perhaps investors, were still attending them and carrying away the best that was being offered. Once the trade had noticed this it regained some of its confidence and buoyancy.

Ideally, then, a good collector, like a good dealer, should buy in a recession, so long as he does not compromise over quality, and should use a boom to weed out and trade up. Of course he cannot afford to stop buying entirely as soon as prices start to rise, since this is likely to bring out some of the best things which he must have if the collection is to be any good. However, in most cases, unless one is trying to be comprehensive, leanness is a virtue in a collection; three superb items are better than thirty worthy but second-rate examples.

To ride the market properly it is obviously essential to keep yourself informed about the current movements of prices in your field. Some market observers feel that the auction market is cyclical, operating in a three-year swing upwards before dropping for a year, climbing to a slightly higher plateau for two years, and then rising again for three. The astute collector can make good specific assessments on his own rather than follow the wisdom or misjudgements of others. One of the best ways of doing this is to spend six months or so viewing every available sale, but buying little or nothing. When anything interests you, make a note of it in the catalogue, giving details of particularly attractive features and any imperfections, and then put your own estimate on it, preferably without consulting any list issued by the auctioneers. Then, if you are able, go to the sale itself and try and work out who is buying what and why. If you are to be any good as a collector you should be fairly accurate in your estimates, and you will certainly know whether you are in fact going to be able to afford your chosen field.

If you cannot attend the sale yourself, you can telephone the auctioneers later for the results of the lots which most interest you, or subscribe for the price lists which the larger houses issue a few weeks later. Sample as many different auctioneers and areas as possible. Naturally you should also be going to all the relevant dealers' exhibitions and visiting specialist shops, and thus be ready to take advantage of any occasion when a dealer has been left behind by a trend, as well as the instances when auctioneers do not know what they are handling.

Given the limitations of space and editorial interest saleroom reports in the newspapers may be very useful to you. Many dealers subscribe to the *Antiques Trade Gazette*, which reports weekly on international and local sales.

Inevitably you will be on terms of rivalry with the trade, especially in the saleroom, but remember too that a dealer can be an invaluable ally for the collector, acting as his eyes and ears as well as a supplier and mentor. It is, after all, in the dealer's interest that you should leave his shop as a satisfied customer, to return again and again, rather than to fleece you in your early days of innocence.

Part II

LOOKING AFTER

A COLLECTION

7

CONSERVATION

Dealer in Antiques (*to wavering customer*): *'Half-a-crown too much for it? Why there's sixteen bobs' worth of rivets in it!' Punch, 1 March 1911.*

Conservation means caring for an art object, and is rather like caring for a child. Pride of ownership is not enough. A cherished object deserves the best conditions, and it has needs which must be ministered to if it is to survive. Adverse conditions such as extensive dryness, damp or too much light are just as harmful to a work of art as to a new-born baby.

Restoration means putting right something that has gone wrong through accident, decay or neglect. Thus a worm-eaten pad foot may need replacing, a broken plate may need mending, or a print that is badly stained may need cleaning. Restoration should only be carried out by qualified experts. If you were ill or had been smashed up in a car accident you would demand the best attention from trained professionals, not a makeshift job from an amateur. Works of art demand the same sort of consideration.

This chapter is not concerned with restoration, therefore. Its subject is conservation, and conservation begins with good housekeeping. If objects are properly conserved and looked after, restoration should be necessary only in exceptional circumstances. Nor is it written for people with a collection of rare objects of museum quality, or for those who wish to live in a museum atmosphere. Rather, the advice is for those who collect as part of their way of life (which is probably busy and without much help), who wish to live with their objects, and who will, on the appropriate occasion or day to day, use their fine silver, china or furniture, and want their paintings, watercolours or carpets to enhance the rooms they live in. In a way such collectors have an additional responsibility, for we should always remember that the works of art we treasure are ours for our lifetimes only, and it is our duty to hand them on to succeeding generations in as good, if not better, condition than when they came into our possession. If you have the slightest doubt about what to do, please seek expert advice. Damage once done cannot be undone, and the aesthetic and financial loss you incur will be out of all proportion to the cost of the professional care and attention which would have prevented it.

It is important to realize that however conscientious you are about looking after objects and works of art, they are constantly at risk of deterioration from three main sources: from light; from air; and from other materials with which they may be in contact. This may sound so fundamental as to cause any collector to despair, but it need not do so. Provided you understand the particular risks which affect the type of object you collect, you can sensibly take certain simple precautions to ensure that the risks are kept to a minimum, even though you may not be able to eliminate them altogether. Overall you should try to create and keep a well-balanced and stable environment in the room or rooms where you keep your collection or valuable objects, ensuring that there is as little fluctuation as possible in temperature and humidity, and that light is kept at a low level when not needed. The best practical advice is to use the rooms where you keep your collection. Unused rooms have a tendency to become damp and stagnant. Using the room keeps the air moving and enables you to keep a constant eye on adverse conditions and act as soon as the atmosphere becomes too humid or dry, or the light becomes too bright. However, do remember that modern central heating systems controlled by time clocks, although efficient and economical, are not always helpful to good conservation. They cause rapid changes in environment by warming a room up quickly; and equally by allowing it to cool rapidly when they switch off, which is probably for the early hours of the morning when the air is at its coldest and dampest. If you can, set the controls and use thermostats to even out the changes and minimize them as much as possible.

The more valuable or rare the objects you collect then the greater the precautions should be, and ultimately this must mean making a decision on the cost of creating a suitable environment relative to the value of the object and the risk of deterioration. If the cost is too great then perhaps you should consider lending it to a museum who would be willing to look after it.

Light   Light causes damage by producing chemical changes. Organic materials such as textiles and paper are obviously most at risk, and the only materials that are not are metal, stone and ceramics. All light will cause damage, and the more powerful the light the more rapid the chemical change will be. The ultra-violet component of light is the most damaging, and daylight and fluorescent light are especially dangerous in this respect. The ordinary tungsten lights found in most houses are relatively free of ultra-violet light. It is possible to buy filters which absorb ultra-violet light, and depending on circumstances it may be necessary to think of using them. The longer the exposure to light (whether filtered or not), the faster the fading. Light can be excluded locally by using curtains to cover display cases or pictures, and of course rooms can be kept dark when not in use. Remember too that lights are localized sources of heat.

Air   The main dangers in the air are excess humidity and pollution. The damaging effect of moisture in the air is interlinked with air temperature, so that what you need to be aware of is the relative humidity of the air. Air can hold less water at a lower temperature than at a higher, and relative humidity is (roughly speaking) the ratio of actual humidity to saturation at a given temperature. The important thing is to keep relative humidity at a well-balanced and stable level. Fluctuations in relative humidity and temperature can be very damaging, especially to objects made from moisture-sensitive materials such as wood, leather, textiles and paper. The fluctuations cause them to expand and contract, and the cumulative effect can be serious. Rapid changes must obviously be avoided at all costs. Relative humidity can be measured with a hygrometer, and the standard advice in the

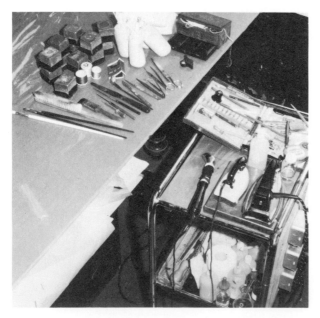

A typical range of equipment used by the textile conservators at the Victoria and Albert Museum. The science and techniques of conservation and restoration are rapidly developing areas of knowledge, and the illustration gives some insight into why restoration is a matter for experts.

museum world is to stabilize relative humidity (RH) at about 50–55 per cent. Museums also aim for a constant temperature of about 20° Centigrade (68° Fahrenheit). Humid conditions encourage the growth of mould on organic materials and the corrosion and rusting of metal objects. Chemical reactions and breakdown can occur faster in warm conditions. Over-dry conditions can cause flaking, cracking, warping and splitting. Remember too that there can be pockets of high humidity or temperature in an otherwise well-balanced environment, for example on an outside wall, or in the vicinity of a window or radiator.

Foresight and vigilance should be the watchwords. If it is cold and damp inside, but warm and dry outside, then open the doors and windows to improve ventilation. Allow sufficient room for air to circulate and help it on its way with fans if necessary. If the air becomes too dry place suitable bowls of water in the room so that moisture can be taken up by the dry air. Cold outside walls and solid floors are places where condensation is most likely to occur, so that objects are best kept away from them.

Pollution is a particular problem for people living in towns and near factories, and for people living near the sea where the air contains high levels of salt. Industrial pollution usually contains a high degree of tar and acid which will fall as unsightly dust, and may then cause a chemical reaction. Airborne acids are also absorbed by organic materials along with moisture. Textiles are particularly at risk in such circumstances, and salt is especially damaging to metals. Pollution is a major problem, since to keep things out of contact with polluted air often means keeping them out of sight as well, which a collector may find unacceptable. Keeping objects in cabinets, and placing glass over pictures and textiles, obviously helps. Regular cleaning is no answer, since cleaning itself causes deterioration and may well involve other risks.

An object may be made of different materials which react unsympathetically together, or it may be badly made because the artist or craftsman has used unsuitable or inferior materials. There is really nothing that a collector can do

Other materials

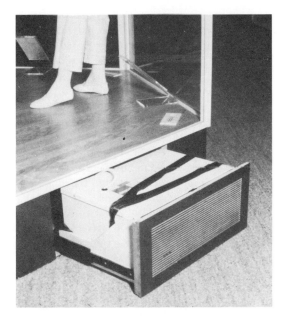

A dust filtration unit built into a costume display cabinet at the Victoria and Albert Museum. Few private collectors can take such precautions, but there are many simple steps they can take to ensure that objects and works of art are well cared for.

about this, although a good restorer may be able to stabilize the object to some degree. Where a collector should take particular care, however, is to see that objects are not placed in contact with potentially damaging materials. For example, if prints are mounted, a suitable acid-free mount must be used; if objects are being stored in a box, use one made of inert plastic, since cardboard, wood (and plywood in particular), and the glue used in the box may cause a harmful reaction; make sure that a display cabinet has not been painted or varnished inside with a material that might cause damage; do not wrap an object in a cloth that contains potentially harmful dyes or dressings. As always, if you are in doubt, seek advice, and leave well alone rather than take a risk.

Under the headings that follow more specific advice is given about the more popular fields of collecting.

Silver   Silver in its pure state is a surprisingly soft metal. In practice it is always alloyed with other materials, such as copper, and Sterling Standard silver is 92.5 per cent pure. But even alloyed, it is still comparatively soft, and in principle any rough handling is likely to damage it irreparably. Silver tarnishes very readily, reacting with hydrogen sulphide in the air to produce a surface layer of silver sulphide. Slight tarnish is not seriously damaging, although the sulphide layer will eventually become quite thick and uneven, leaving disfiguring pits on the surface of the metal when it is cleaned off. It is important to realize exactly what is happening when one 'cleans' silver. By removing tarnish, one is not taking off dirt, so much as removing the top 'layer' of silver and exposing a new layer beneath. Every time silver is cleaned, therefore, it is diminished. There has always been a popular tendency to over-clean silver, and this results in due course in the original surface of the object being completely lost. If in doubt, therefore, do not clean.

When not in use, and whenever possible, silver should be kept out of contact with the air, and should therefore be stored in sealed airtight bags, either designed for the purpose, or made of inert material such as plastic. If a piece of silver is kept for purely decorative purposes, it may be worth considering having it lacquered by an expert. This technique has been enormously improved and is now quite undetectable to the naked eye. A very fine layer of clear plastic is deposited on the surface to create a barrier between the silver and the air. This means that silver need only be cleaned occasionally with soap and water. It is particularly recommended for intricate silver. Modern lacquer is destroyed if abrasive silver cleaners are used.

The best way of keeping silver clean is to use it regularly and in rotation, washing each item separately in hot soapy water, then rinsing thoroughly and drying with a soft dry cloth. Do not put silver in a washing-up machine, as the harsh detergent and rubbing together of pieces will cause severe damage. A long-term silver cloth is useful, but keep it carefully in its own bag, away from harmful dust. Dry teapots and coffee pots thoroughly inside and leave the covers open. Ornamental silver, such as candlesticks, tankards, cups and salvers should be cleaned with long-term foam, and provided the atmosphere is clean and dry, will keep for many months. Use the softest available toothbrush to remove polish from crevices and mouldings. A particular word of warning which is often not heeded is: never tie spoons and forks together with rubber bands. Rubber bands react with silver and produce a depth of oxidization that is almost impossible to remove.

Knives need particular care. Solid silver knives can be washed in hot water

Crests from two different silver salvers of the early eighteenth century. In one the engraved design is as crisp and fresh as when first executed, and is a magnificent specimen of Rococo design; cleaning and polishing have reduced the other to a mere ghost.

without problems. However, only relatively few knives are solid silver, and they are usually fish or dessert knives with silver blades. Bone and ivory handles are loosened and discoloured by steam and hot water. Most silver knife handles are loaded with resin, and this expands with heat, causing stress and possibly damage. Non-stainless steel blades should be cleaned immediately after use, scoured if necessary and then thoroughly dried, as old non-stainless steel oxidizes very readily when damp and is extremely difficult to clean afterwards.

Badly tarnished pieces can be cleaned by using a large piece of aluminium foil in a bowl of very hot water, in which is dissolved a handful of washing soda. The tarnished silver is immersed and allowed to touch the aluminium foil and left until the tarnish disappears. (There is a chemical reaction which results in bubbling in the water.) The silver should then be rinsed thoroughly in clean hot water, and dried with a soft cloth, or first treated with a long-term silver foam. Sheffield plate should be cleaned like solid silver, remembering, of course, that abrasion removes the thin layer of silver that covers the underlying copper. Items like candlesticks should be treated with particular care, as they are often filled with plaster of Paris. Plaster of Paris will take up water and expand if allowed to get wet, and may then cause the Sheffield plate to burst.

The contents of showcases can be protected to some extent by using a patent silver keeper in the case. Patent silver keeper either slowly gives off what is known as a vapour phase inhibitor, an organic substance which forms a protective coating, or, alternatively, absorbs the hydrogen sulphide, preventing it from reacting with the silver. Silica gel crystals can help to reduce humidity, but the humidity level has to be very low to prevent any tarnishing. Beware of velvet-lined showcases, since some velvets are dressed with sulphur compounds containing the sulphur which will cause silver to tarnish.

Silver gilt

This is silver with a fine deposit of pure gold on the surface. Gold is inert in the atmosphere and does not oxidize. Silver-gilt, therefore, does not generally need to be cleaned in the same way as silver, and indeed over-cleaning will merely result in the gradual elimination of the thin layer of gold. Paul de Lamerie's advice was just to clean silver-gilt with soap and water, and this is still best.

Ormolu   Ormolu is bronze gilded with a layer of gold and is most frequently found on furniture mounts, porcelain mounts and decorative metalwork such as clocks, candlesticks and sconces. It can be cleaned by swabbing gently with a wad of cotton wool wrung out in warm water to which a few drops of ammonia have been added. Any traces of ammonia should be removed afterwards with cotton wool swabs wrung out in clean water. However, it is very easy to overclean ormolu, and the greatest care must be taken.

Other metalwork   The main enemy of most metals is humidity. Silver is in fact one metal which deteriorates less than others through humidity. Lead is also less vulnerable than most, but it will corrode quickly in the presence of organic acids, which cause the surface to become covered in white powder. The organic acids in wood are particularly harmful to lead, and it will corrode if enclosed with virtually any type of wood. Gold is the only metal which does not deteriorate.

All metal objects should be kept in as dry an atmosphere as possible, remembering, however, that what may be good for metal may be too dry for other objects. The relative humidity of 50–55 per cent mentioned earlier is a good compromise which suits a mixed collection of different types of objects.

Brass, copper, iron and steel can all be cleaned with good-quality proprietary products, and decorative metalwork can be lacquered after cleaning to give a film-like covering which will exclude air. Steel looks particularly good after it has been lacquered. Blackleading, which is the traditional finish for cast iron, is perfectly safe.

Pewter, which is an alloy principally of tin with the addition of small amounts of lead and/or copper, raises an interesting aesthetic question. Some schools of thought consider it should remain unpolished, but when pewter was in daily use as plates, spoons, jugs and tankards it was scoured and polished. As it is a soft alloy any cleaning should be done sparingly, but there is no reason to suppose it is in any way correct for pewter to be left unpolished.

Bronze sculptures   Only pure mineral wax should be applied, and then extremely sparingly. Do not use modern adhesive labels to mark sculpture, as chemicals in the adhesive can adversely affect the patina, leaving an indelible imprint.

Ceramic and glass   Ceramics and glass are at risk from excess light and humidity only in the most exceptional circumstances. Damage usually occurs through inappropriate or unwise cleaning, which is discussed below, or through careless handling (see Chapter 8).

If the collection is displayed in glazed cabinets it requires virtually no attention at all. Once a year, however, it should all be carefully washed and dried, and the opportunity taken of rearranging. Rather than carry pieces to another room it makes more sense to lay out towels on the floor and bring washing-up bowls to the place where the pieces are kept. Ceramics and glass should be washed with a non-ionic soap (rather than a detergent which can harm the glaze), rinsed and dried on soft linen tea towels. A soft toothbrush can also be used for cleaning. Before washing, examine each piece very closely to ensure there are no previous repairs, unfired decoration or delicate gilding. Many old repairs were made by using water-soluble adhesives. Unfired decoration and later gilding, applied with size, can easily be removed with careless washing in water. Fragile and delicate pieces should not be completely immersed, but merely swabbed gently with a cloth wrung out in soapy water, dipped in clean water and finally dried carefully.

A Meissen parrot of the 18th century showing (a) a bad repair – the neck has been bonded the wrong way round and the head should look to the right; and (b) damage occurring in manufacture – there is a fire crack along the mould seam in the breast.

This treatment must also be applied to damaged or repaired pieces. More robust items can be washed in the usual way, but always take the greatest care and do not be hurried. Do not use a washing-up machine. They use harsh detergents and subject pieces to long and continuous treatment with hot water. Overglaze colours and gilding are soon worn away by such processes, and the heat may damage the glaze and ceramic body.

Glass on display in cabinets will need a yearly wash and dry polish to restore its lustre; a little vinegar in the rinsing water helps to produce a better finish. Glass chandeliers should be cleaned with the utmost patience; any undue haste can cause chipping and breaking. The drops should be washed with a leather wrung out in water to which some methylated spirit has been added. This causes the water to evaporate more readily. A final polish should then be given with tissue paper. If you can dismantle the various swags for cleaning do so – but one at a time so that you are not left with a mass of unrelated drops. Picture glass, mirrors and lantern glasses should be washed with a leather wrung out in warm water to which a little vinegar has been added. Drying and polishing should be done with a second leather.

Glass can be sensitive to moisture if the material from which it has been made has become unstable. Some glass can 'weep' or 'sweat', creating a sticky surface, and 'crizzled glass' displays a very fine surface crazing due to a chemical change in the material. Such glass should be kept if possible in dry conditions with a relative humidity of about 40 per cent.

All repairs should be entrusted only to a competent restorer. If you are unfortunate enough to have an accident with a piece of ceramic or glass from your collection and require an expert to undertake the repair, it is most important that every single piece of the item should be recovered. Apart from the minute fragments, every piece should be wrapped separately in tissue paper to avoid further damage. Do not try to piece together any of the breaks, as any contact will tend to cause further damage. Avoid touching the fresh breaks with your fingers. Attempt to keep the broken edges clean, pack the object carefully and get it to your selected restorer as quickly as possible.

If you have a piece of ceramic which is so badly broken as to be of no value you may be tempted to do a repair yourself rather than have no piece at all. Avoid epoxy resins, wonder glues and rubber-based adhesives, which are all difficult to break down if a mistake is made. Glass should be repaired by sticking the pieces together with a patent adhesive, but an invisible repair is virtually impossible to achieve. Glass breaks with a clean, smooth fracture, and there is no roughness to help hold the broken pieces together. Rim chips can sometimes be ground out, and repolishing can be carried out on scuffed glass door stops, but these are tasks for the expert.

If you have pieces with old repairs examine them carefully and regularly. They may have been repaired with animal glues on which mould may grow in humid conditions, and these may break down completely in over-dry conditions, leaving an object which will fall to pieces when picked up or moved.

Pictures   Nearly all pictures are made from organic materials, and these are particularly vulnerable to excess light and humidity, as well as pollution and contact with other materials. It is essential therefore that they be kept in an environment which provides the most suitable well-balanced and even conditions that can be sensibly achieved. At risk are not only the pigments or inks which an artist has used. The supporting materials, paper, cardboard, canvas or wood, must also be considered as these can deteriorate as fast if not faster than the materials used to create the image.

Good-quality paper has a long natural life in a well-controlled environment. Unfortunately, however, many papers contain acids and other undesirable materials, and in a poor environment will deteriorate rapidly. Humid conditions encourage the growth of mould and encourage foxing – brownish yellow spots on the paper. Conditions which are too dry cause paper to become brittle. Canvas is also at risk in the same way. Wood panels are especially vulnerable, as they expand and contract with changing humidity and temperature. This causes considerable stress and strain in the wood, which may eventually crack, warp or split, causing irreparable damage, probably with paint loss from the surface. Paper and canvas also expand and contract, but with less risk of damage.

Light can cause paper to become brittle and discolour, paper made from wood pulp turning brownish yellow (like newspaper). Paper made from linen or rags, on the other hand, will bleach in strong light. Strong light also causes chemical change and fading in pigments and inks, especially in watercolours.

Works on paper are very fragile, and should on no account be displayed in a room where there is too much daylight, or they will fade irretrievably owing to natural ultra-violet radiation in the light. If a room tends to be bright have the windows fitted with some form of blind. Even partially lowering them during the day brings down the light level considerably. In addition, it is advisable to introduce a thin sheet of ultra-violet filtering perspex behind the glass in the picture frame. This will help protect against both daylight and the ultra-violet content in some forms of artificial light. Do remember, however, that perspex, unlike glass, scratches quite easily. Do not hang watercolours in direct sunlight or near windows, near fireplaces which are going to be used, over radiators, or in draughts; all of these can cause a lot of unnecessary damage.

Paintings should never be hung near or above any heat source, nor in direct sunlight. A correctly hung picture will tend to lean slightly forward at the top, which will naturally reduce the amount of dust settling on it. Dust gilt frames carefully but do not attempt to clean them further; if they require other treatment seek professional advice. If there is the slightest risk of the wall on which a painting or print hangs being damp, think again or at the very least fix thin slices of cork to the lower edge of the back of the picture frame; this will help the circulation of air behind the picture.

Glass enclosed frames do help to provide a stable local environment for pictures, and can enhance the appearance of watercolours, prints and drawings when a suitable mount is used. Whether or not to glaze oil paintings is not always an easy question, aesthetic considerations arguing against it, and conservation in favour. Size and expense may well be the determining factor.

If a glass enclosed frame is used, the glass or perspex should be sealed into the frame. Ideally this should be done with archival framing tape, which will prevent dust entering from the front. The glass or perspex should never touch the surface of the work. The rear of the painting must also be sealed with a backboard and tape. Most softwood backboards (and plywood) are liable to attack by the common furniture beetle (woodworm), and are susceptible to changes in humidity. They should therefore be replaced with a piece of hardboard; and for additional protection, line this with a sheet of ordinary kitchen foil. The back of the picture itself, if mounted correctly, will already be protected by the back of the acid-free mount. The new backboard should be sealed to the frame with brown gummed tape; do not be tempted to use self-adhesive tapes, which do not last.

It is important to keep the back of a picture frame clean, and once a year it should be carefully dusted. At the same time, keep a watchful eye for woodworm infestation, and if this is spotted treat immediately with a suitable insecticide, but take great care that this does not come into contact with the surface of the painting. The frame will normally be of softwood, and once it becomes infested the outbreak can spread to the stretcher of the painting, or to the panel if this is the means of support. If a painting on panel does become infested it will require

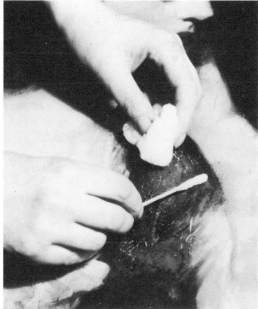

(Left) A panel painting where paint has flaked and curled as a result of neglect. Such extensive damage is virtually irreparable.
(Right) A portrait of Countess Dysart by John Hoppner (c.1758–1810) during cleaning at the Victoria and Albert Museum. The damaged area in the centre shows bad cracking which is the result of unsound techniques used by the artist, rather than neglect by subsequent owners.

fumigation, which is best carried out by an expert; do not attempt yourself to inject insecticidal fluid into the panel.

Any cleaning of the front of an oil painting should be carried out by an expert. Folk-remedies, such as cleaning with cut potatoes or onions, are not only ineffective but can be dangerous. Do not be tempted to use commercial picture-cleaning preparations or chemical solvents. The latter can be disastrous in the hands of amateurs. To have a picture cleaned, restored or relined professionally can be expensive, but it is no bad thing to compare it with the cost of having a car serviced. You will realize that in nine cases out of ten it is reasonable enough, and the restoration will last much longer than a car service. Sometimes, in fact, only minor work need be involved in keeping a painting in good condition, and this need not be costly. The same approach should be adopted with prints, drawings and watercolours. Much damage has been caused by owners attempting minor conservation work themselves, and it is simply not worth the risk.

However, the surface of an oil painting unprotected by glass may be lightly dusted with a wad of clean cotton wool; only do this if you are quite certain that the paint layer is secure. Dirty dusters with rough particles adhering to them can cause unnecessary scratching.

All watercolours and prints should be mounted on acid-free board with appropriate hinges, and the work should be entrusted to an expert. Most modern mounting boards used by commercial framers are *not* acid-free, nor are old mounts. If you are in doubt go to a reliable conservator for advice on mounting. The mount should comprise a window-cut front and also a back mount, thus sandwiching the picture safely between the two leaves. An original mount may be re-used but only if lined with acid-free board.

Miniatures usually have their own glazed and backed purpose-built frames. It is very unwise to attempt to open them. If there is evidence of mould or dust inside, consult an expert. Where miniatures on bone or ivory are concerned, special care must be taken to avoid the slightest drying out or heating, as they cannot easily be repaired once they are curled, warped or split.

Books   'The free circulation of air is probably the most important single factor in the climatic conditions for the safe storage of books' (A. D. Baynes-Cope, *Caring for Books and Documents*, British Museum Publications, 1981). In the absence of obvious structural faults, such as a defective damp course or a leaking roof, good ventilation keeps dampness at bay, without allowing the atmosphere to dry out.

There should be no difficulty in recognizing a well-ventilated room suitable for the storage of books. It should, however, have a sound *inside* wall, where the shelving can be located out of direct sunlight. Radiators or other sources of heat should not be in the immediate vicinity. It is also important that the wall should not conceal any potential hazards, such as plumbing (a burst pipe would cause untold damage). Like most objects, books expand or contract with changes in temperature, and if this occurs too often and too extremely, unacceptable stresses will be inflicted, leading to permanent damage. Ideally books should be kept in a room which is on the cool side.

Books are meant to be handled (incidentally, the natural oils in the skin of clean hands are an excellent conditioner for leather bindings), and a well-bound book should not suffer if removed gently from the shelves and opened carefully, avoiding any sudden or violent movement.

Some experts prefer open shelving because it ensures good ventilation, but glass-fronted cases, provided they have some openings or air holes, should not be discounted. Glass helps maintain temperature and relative humidity at even levels, and is the best protection against dust, polluted air and unwanted handling. Ordinary glass, however, only partially filters out harmful ultra-violet light, and a glass-fronted case is no exception to the rule that all shelving should be out of direct sunlight, especially as the glass will act as a heat trap (like a greenhouse). Once on the shelves the books should be well supported, both from below (sagging shelves force the tops of the books together) and from the sides, allowing as little movement as possible without packing them too tightly. It greatly helps if they are shelved according to size, an arrangement for which there is ample historical precedent. If possible leave a gap between the books and the back of the shelves to allow a free passage of air behind them. Large books, especially tall folios, are seldom adequately supported when upright and easily topple over when a neighbouring book is removed. They are best, therefore, kept horizontally, but never in a pile, one on top of the other, otherwise damage will easily result whenever any but the uppermost is removed.

Good housework is the surest way to avoid insect and rodent infestation and regular dusting of books is an essential part of their conservation. The tops of the books can be dusted away from the spine, with a soft clean brush, a feather duster, or a vacuum cleaner in reverse; it is essential to keep the book tightly closed, otherwise the dust will simply be brushed inside. However, even if the books are dusted in front of an open window, the disadvantage with normal dusting is that although the dust is removed from the object itself, it will settle elsewhere. A vacuum cleaner, with a nozzle attachment, used in the normal direction, will actually remove the dust altogether and will not harm the books if used carefully. It is vital to put a piece of muslin as a filter over the end of the nozzle which will rescue any parts of the binding (such as labels) that are, or become, detached; it will also reduce the suction. Awkward corners and crevices in the shelves provide ideal places for insects to lay their eggs and breed, and should be cleaned with a stiff paint brush, or, better still, a vacuum cleaner with a narrow nozzle.

Foxing, spotting and mould are well-known enemies of books. As with animal infestation, the risk of this danger can be minimized by observing the atmospheric conditions already described and a sensible amount of housework. Again, an atmosphere which is pleasant to live in is more likely to promote adequate conservation than seldom-used rooms with damp or stagnant air. It is possible to fumigate books heavily infested by insects or mould, but the necessary materials are potentially dangerous, the techniques tedious and time-consuming, and the efficiency of any treatment is difficult for the layman to gauge. Such tasks are therefore best left to the expert. Better still, avoid acquiring such obviously defective books in the first place. Nevertheless, whatever the apparent condition of new acquisitions, it is always a good idea to dust and check them thoroughly for infestation, a procedure which can be combined with collation. Serious problems of damp, rot or infestation, whether of buildings or books, should be immediately referred to specialists. Local libraries or record offices, who usually have much experience in these matters, should be able to point you in the right direction if other inquiries fail.

Dried-out leather bindings can be brought back to life with a suitable dressing. The British Museum publishes a formula which can be made up by a chemist (caution: it is inflammable and toxic), but opinions vary on the best ingredients, and professional binders have their own preferred mixes. The British Museum formula is *not* suitable for vellum and parchment bindings. Ideally you should discuss dressings personally with an expert, and ask for a practical demonstration and supervision of your first attempts at application. Do not apply the dressing too generously; the leather will be saturated and if the dressing penetrates to the paper of the book the resulting damage will be to all intents and purposes irreversible. Too little is better than too much. The individual will, with experience, devise his own techniques, but a good method is to dip a wad of cotton wool, or clean soft cloth, into the liquid, wipe away the excess smear on to clean paper (not newspaper), to make sure the dressing has been evenly taken up, and then lightly apply to the corners of the book, working inwards in a circular motion, paying particular attention to the joints, which are usually the part of the book which most requires treatment. Let the dressing dry thoroughly by standing the book upright with the covers just enough open for it to support itself. The drying process takes about 48 hours; before replacing the books on the shelves polish them with a clean duster. Waxing is sometimes suggested, but is not advisable, principally because it effectively seals the surface of the leather, preventing it from breathing.

On no account should any bindings, plates or pages be repaired with adhesive tape, which rapidly deteriorates (and can never therefore provide a permanent repair), leaving a residue which it is usually impossible to remove properly. Loose boards may be tied in place with archival tape until the book is repaired.

The treatment of spotting and foxing is a controversial subject and should be left to the expert for appraisal and possible treatment; never attempt treatment or any form of washing yourself. Do not leave books lying around in direct sunlight, which causes not only fading or discoloration of the bindings but also distortion of the boards and embrittlement of the paper. Do not insert extraneous material (for example, catalogue descriptions or newspaper cuttings) into your books: the bindings were designed to contain the pages of the book only and will be distorted if used as portfolios. Always leave a book as it is rather than risk damaging it out of ignorance, and never hesitate to consult an expert.

Parchment and vellum are highly reactive to changes in relative humidity and temperature. Single documents are best housed between sheets of acid-free tissue in archival storage boxes, or in acid-free mounts if displayed. Illuminated parchments should be protected from the harmful effects of light, and treated as watercolour paintings or miniatures. If the skin support is allowed to dry and curl up, the painted illumination will flake away.

Furniture   Furniture is particularly susceptible to damage from uncontrolled humidity, temperature and light. Wood is an organic material. It expands and contracts as it undergoes changes in temperature, and absorbs and loses moisture with changes in humidity. Also, it dries out and becomes brittle with age, however ideal the conditions in which it is kept: the wrong environment will simply speed up this natural ageing process.

It is also important to bear in mind the way furniture is constructed. Movement in the timber through expansion and contraction will cause stress and strain in the individual timbers themselves (causing panels to crack or split, for example); the movement will also cause stress in the joints where individual members are brought together. If metal nails or screws are used, these can corrode in humid conditions and affect the timber in which they are placed. The wrong environment may also cause adhesives to break down. Furniture made from solid hardwoods such as oak and mahogany are least at risk. All veneered furniture needs particular care, since clearly there can be considerable movement between the timber of the carcase and the thin veneers which cover it, and fragile veneers will then become detached or split and crack.

However, if furniture is kept in a well-ventilated atmosphere away from extremes of heat, light and humidity there is no reason why it should not have a long life and require very little attention. The main damage to furniture comes from central heating. This dries out the atmosphere, and creates localized sources of considerable heat. Excessive dryness can be combated by the use of simple humidifiers which are manufactured to hang on radiators, or by placing bowls of water in the room. It is also possible to buy electric humidifiers which are designed to keep a strict and accurate control on humidity. The method used is not important so long as a properly balanced and consistent atmosphere is maintained. Furniture is relatively bulky, and its arrangement in a room is not always easy. However, it cannot be stressed too strongly that any piece of furniture of any aesthetic merit or financial value must never be placed near a radiator or hot pipe. If a sacrifice has to be made, sacrifice the convenience and beauty of the arrangement of the room, not the piece of furniture. It would be far better to sell the piece and buy something else that can be placed away from the source of heat rather than see it deteriorate.

Direct sunlight can have the same effect, and bleach the wood and ruin its original surface. Again, there are two simple remedies: place furniture away from direct sunlight, and if this is not possible, use blinds to filter the light when the room is not in use.

All furniture should be checked for woodworm from time to time. The surface evidence of infestation is small holes, but these do not necessarily reveal the full extent of the damage underneath. New holes usually appear between April and June, due to the life cycle of the beetle which causes them. The female beetle lays eggs in cracks and crevices in the wood. When the eggs hatch the larvae bore into the wood, to emerge two years later leaving the tell-tale exit hole. Look carefully for signs of fresh wood dust and powder, which may also appear if the area is lightly tapped, as this is a sign of active woodworm which should be dealt with immediately. Pine, fruitwood, beech and walnut are especially prone to attack, as

An expert restorer applying size with a hypodermic syringe to fix flaking gesso on a 17th century chair. Such techniques must only be carried out by trained specialists.

are the soft or whitewood parts of furniture, such as blocks supporting feet, backboards, knuckle joints on card tables or gate-leg tables, and the seat frames of chairs. A considerable amount of antique furniture can be found to have had slight woodworm in its early life, but this seems to have disappeared with the drying out of the sap, and is long since dead.

Woodworm seems to flourish in a still atmosphere, so that a good circulation of air helps to keep it at bay. If active woodworm is detected it can be treated with one of the preparations on the market as directed, but liquid treatments can damage finishes on furniture and a reputable restorer should be consulted.

Any new acquisition should be thoroughly checked for woodworm, and any infestation should be dealt with before bringing the piece into your collection. It is also worth considering the atmosphere in which the piece has been when you acquire it. To take an extreme example: if you bought a piece which had been standing in a damp stable for some period of time, it would be most unwise suddenly to introduce it into an atmosphere which was warm and dry by comparison, which even the most perfect 'museum' atmosphere could well be.

Furniture with a wax finish should be polished no more frequently than every few weeks or so. In between polishes a dust with a clean dry cloth is sufficient. The purpose of polishing is to enhance the wood's appearance, and to build up a protective surface. To be properly protective the surface needs to harden between polishes, which is why over-frequent polishing is not advisable.

There are a number of good wax polishes on the market, and a reputable furniture dealer will be able to offer advice, and in all probability will sell a suitable product. Spray polishes are not much use since they do not feed the wood, and often contain harmful additives such as silicon.

It is easy to make up a polish of natural beeswax and turpentine which will produce a very good finish. Place the beeswax in a jar and cover it with genuine turpentine for a few days. (You must use genuine turpentine, not substitute.) The beeswax will dissolve to produce a mixture which should have the consistency of thin cream. More turpentine can be added as required to obtain the right consistency. Dust the furniture first to remove any grit which might scratch, and apply the mixture *sparingly* with a soft cloth. Rub hard to start with and then gradually ease the pressure. The final polishing off should be done lightly with a clean soft cloth. The beeswax and turpentine mixture has a good shelf life.

This treatment will soon build up a good finish, and over many years furniture that has been well looked after and regularly polished will acquire a wonderful patina. On no account allow anyone to persuade you to strip furniture of this patina. It is gained only by hard work and many hours of labour. Nor are there any short cuts. Electrical and mechanical buffing machines do not give the same finish since they work at speed, generating heat, and the heat melts the wax, leaving a sticky surface which is neither good for the wood nor capable of building a fine patina.

Furniture which has been French polished has a hard, high-gloss finish which is quite different from the patina achieved by wax polishing, as well as being harder and more protective. French polish is applied to furniture in the workshop by a complex and skilled process and thereafter needs no more than dusting with a soft dry cloth. Waxing is not necessary.

Gilded furniture and painted furniture need only gentle cleaning with an ordinary duster or feather duster. Polish should never be applied. Oriental lacquer needs special care since it is particularly susceptible to damage from central heating and sunlight. Unwise exposure to either will cause the lacquer to crack and bubble, and the result is disastrous. To clean lacquer a gentle wipe with a soft dry cloth is all that is necessary. Do not apply wax or cream.

Whether or not to clean brass handles is a matter of personal choice. Plain brass can be brightened with a suitable metal polish, but the polish will stain surrounding surfaces if it gets into contact with them. Never use wire wool on metal surfaces under any circumstances. Cleaning ormolu is discussed above.

Marks, scratches and stains on furniture are a problem. It is easy to say that prevention is better than cure, but accidents do happen, of course. The most frequent causes of marks are the wet bottoms of glasses and vases, and from hot objects like teapots or coffee pots. If it is a superficial mark on the wax surface, polishing should take care of it in time. If the mark has penetrated the patina and stained the wood it is a job for a trained restorer. The remedies which recommend using wire wool and other miracle cures should not be used by the amateur. In any case furniture which is several hundred years old cannot look like new, and there will inevitably be some blemishes on the surface. These should be accepted as part of the character of the piece in question.

Furniture which is in bad condition must be entrusted to a restorer of experience and repute. The restoration of antique furniture is definitely not a field for amateurs. Even apparently simple repairs can be full of pitfalls, and the damage caused by inexperience may be very difficult to redress. If a piece of furniture seems to be of no significant aesthetic or financial value the relatively high cost of restoration may tempt you to try a repair or stick back a loose veneer. Before you do so, however, think twice, and if necessary obtain a valuation of the piece and an estimate for restoration. You may find your judgement on pieces and values is incorrect, and that a professional restoration *is* worthwhile. Even if it is not, never use glues based on epoxy resins, or the new instant glues. You should only use adhesives that are reversible, and these glues are not. Eventually you or someone else may want a proper restoration carried out.

Textiles, like wood and paper, are organic material, which means that eventual deterioration is unavoidable and inevitable. However, some surviving textiles are known to be at least 5,000 years old, and from the number of historic textiles around us today, we know that they are able to survive in good condition for hundreds of years.

Textiles

The most effective way of preserving a textile, whether it is historic or modern, is by preventing damage. Although certain techniques should only be carried out by trained conservators, there is much that the private owner can do in his own home to protect objects made partly or wholly of textile.

Damage to textiles can be caused by chemical reactions, such as those caused by light, atmospheric pollution and humidity; and by mechanical action, such as micro-biological attack, handling, and normal wear and tear. The precautions against damage therefore involve the conditions in which textiles are kept and the methods by which they are looked after.

The ideal environmental conditions in which to keep organic materials have already been discussed at the beginning of this chapter. These are the conditions that ought to apply in all museums and galleries; but, although desirable, it is not always possible to maintain such controls in the home. However, there are many practical steps that an owner can take to protect textiles from environmental damage.

The lighting of textiles is obviously important to a display; and yet light, especially natural daylight, is one of the major causes of deterioration, leading to loss of strength and flexibility in the fibres, and to the fading of dyestuffs. It is therefore advisable to display textiles out of natural daylight, and certainly in a position where no direct sunlight falls on them at any time of day. Exposing textiles for only short periods will further help to reduce the effects of light. This can be achieved by hanging curtains in front of them; by positioning them in a dark corner with a spotlight for occasional viewing; or by rotating them with others kept in storage.

The temperature and relative humidity of the atmosphere are other major factors. Fibres absorb moisture: the higher the relative humidity, the higher the moisture content in the textile. Ideally, textiles should be kept in RH 50–55 per cent, and in even temperature. A textile kept in relative humidity above 60 per cent is liable to fungal attack. At the other extreme, if the atmosphere is too dry (below RH 45 per cent), the physical characteristics of the fibre will change, and the textile will become stiff and brittle.

Practically speaking, textiles are best kept in rooms where the relative humidity and temperature remain constant and can be controlled, and not, for instance, in rooms that are seldom used, as these can be too cold and damp. They should not be sited above radiators or by draughty doors and windows, where there will be significant fluctuations in temperature. Draught also makes textiles susceptible to airborne pollution. Sulphur dioxide gas is an increasing atmospheric hazard, and acidic conditions cause particular degradation in cellulose fibres like cotton and linen. Only full air conditioning can remove sulphur dioxide from the atmosphere, and this is expensive and not always practicable. The effects can be reduced by displaying objects in frames, or by placing them where there is little circulation of air.

Having provided the most favourable conditions for a collection of textiles, the owner can take other steps to ensure that they are looked after with the greatest care. Handling should be kept to a minimum, and when it is necessary, accidental

The vacuum cleaner being used to surface clean this tapestry is separated from the textile by using a nylon monofilament screen.

damage can be reduced by a few simple precautions:

the object should be fully supported when it is moved;
no undue strain should be placed on the textile;
hands should be clean and dry;
cigarettes, food and drink should be kept at a safe distance;
wrist watches and jewellery should be rcmoved;
pins, adhesive tape and adhesives should never be used for temporary repair;
all chemicals should be avoided;
adequate precautions must be taken to protect textiles when redecoration is taking place.

Regular surface cleaning is essential for textiles in use and on open display. Dust collects on textiles, just as it does on furniture, although it is not so obvious. A soft bristle brush should be used on fragile objects such as woven silk or velvet upholstery, a vacuum cleaner with a nozzle on more robust ones such as tapestries or rugs, with a piece of net secured over the nozzle to prevent loose fibres being taken up into the vacuum cleaner. No other method of cleaning, such as spot cleaning, washing or dry cleaning, should be undertaken without the advice of a professional textile conservator.

Regular surface cleaning will not only reduce the effects of everyday pollution, but will also provide a constant check on the condition of the object. It will show up the fungal growth caused by damp, the brittleness brought on by over-dry conditions, the weakness that results from exposure to sunlight or from mechanical strain, and the first signs of insect attack. Appropriate remedies can be taken at an early stage.

It is better to treat insect infestation, such as moth or carpet beetle, by surface cleaning and by gently shaking the object outdoors (if it is strong enough), rather than by applying commercially available products, such as mothballs, which

In storage, three dimensional textiles should be padded out with acid-free tissue paper. Flat textiles should be rolled rather than folded.

cause harm to any living organism, insect and human alike.

The entire textile must be examined when checking and surface cleaning, including areas that remain undisturbed by routine housework because they are difficult to get at – pelmets, hangings that fall behind furniture, the underside of upholstered chairs are all potential danger spots for insect attack and mechanical strain. All checks should therefore be undertaken in an organized and, if possible, supervised, manner, ideally twice a year. They should also be carried out on any textiles kept in store, although it is important to remember that handling itself causes damage and should be kept to a minimum.

Wise and careful choice of materials used alongside textiles in storage and display will help to increase their life. In storage, textiles should be separated one from another using acid-free tissue paper, which can also be used to pad out three-dimensional textiles to prevent creases forming. Acid-free tissue can be bought easily in local shops.

Ordinary paper and cardboard have a high acid content and are to be avoided in any form, whether as backing to frames, linings to drawers, or in any other way. Specially manufactured cardboard boxes that have a low acid content can be obtained, and these make good storage containers. Acid-free card is also available, and can be used for mounting textiles for display. All these products need replacing after a time, as they do gradually lose their acid-free quality.

Hidden dangers lie in traditional materials used for storage units and display cases. Oak, for instance, releases acetic acid that will damage textile fibres in the long term, and so oak chests are not a safe place to store the household linen. Many adhesives are potentially harmful, even some of those sold as being suitable to use with textiles; over the years they will decompose and cause irreparable damage. Certain plastics also decompose and release harmful vapours, and the commonly used polythene storage bags can trap moisture, causing the formation of individual pockets of humidity.

The siting of storage for textiles should be carefully chosen. The most common stores, attics and basements, are the least suitable, as changes in temperature are at the most extreme at the top and bottom of a building. Outside walls should also be avoided, and storage units kept in the middle of a room. (Similarly, textiles should not be displayed on outside walls.) Ease of access to the store room enables objects to be moved in and out with the least damage, and in the individual storage units also allows good circulation, which prevents pockets of humidity forming.

In storage, large flat textiles should be rolled on to a roller slightly larger than the textile itself, and separated from it by a layer of acid-free tissue. Textiles need to be rolled in the direction where they are strongest. For carpets and tapestries this usually means in the direction of the warp, and for any textile with a pile, such as rugs and velvet, with the pile outermost to avoid crushing. An outer protective covering of pre-washed calico is put over the rolled textile, and the rolls preferably slotted on to purpose-built rings, rather than placing heavy rollers on top of each other.

Small flat textiles can be stored in acid-free boxes, again with a separating layer of acid-free tissue, so long as folding and over-crowding are avoided throughout.

Large three-dimensional objects, such as costumes, whether on display or in storage, need purpose-built supports. Costumes that are strong enough to hang should be provided with a coathanger that has been padded to suit that particular costume. This is quite a straightforward task, and it will immediately improve the appearance by giving a shape to the garment. (Instructions for preparing padded coathangers can be found in *The Care and Preservation of Textiles* by Karen Finch and Greta Putnam, published by Batsford.) Stored costumes can be further protected by making a loose bag of pre-washed calico to hang over them.

When any textile is displayed or stored, its own weight should receive as much support as possible, for a lot of damage is caused by strain. Velcro is recommended for hanging large flat textiles such as tapestries, the soft side sewn on to the textile across the top to distribute the weight evenly, the rough side attached to the wall, preferably on to a wooden batten cut to the correct size, which can be raised or lowered on a hoist. In this way the textile can be taken down for cleaning or storage with the least possible strain.

The framing of textiles, if carried out according to certain basic principles, is one of the safest methods of display, because it provides full support to the textile and protects it from its surroundings by providing it with its own micro-climate. It can also be the most attractive way of showing a textile, through the careful choice of backing material and frame. On the other hand, if carried out by inexperienced hands, framing can cause irreversible damage. The choice of suitable materials is crucial, and also the method of mounting. A guideline to framing textiles can be found in *The Complete Guide to Needlework Techniques and Materials*, consultant editor Mary Gostelow, published by Phaidon Press.

The provision of adequate storage conditions will help to slow down the damaging processes which affect textiles. If, in their use or display, a change in condition is noticed, action should be taken straight away, before the damage becomes irreversible. Repairs should only be carried out by experts.

If textiles are displayed by wisely chosen methods in controlled environmental conditions, their owners can enjoy the rich contribution they make to any home, secure in the knowledge that everything possible is being done to protect them from damage.

A padded hanger will keep a coat or dress in shape and ensure that no one point takes all the garment's weight.

8
HANDLING
WORKS OF ART

May: 'Mamma! Mamma! Don't go on like this pray!!' Mamma (who has smashed a favourite pot): 'What have I got to live for?' May: 'Haven't you got me, Mamma?' Mamma: 'You, child! You're not Unique!! There are six of you – a complete set!!' Cartoon by George du Maurier, Punch, 19 July 1911.

Hands are extremely sensitive and useful instruments. Properly controlled they can reveal a great deal of information and yield enormous pleasure; incorrectly used they can do untold damage. Many works of art reveal their innate qualities as much to the touch as to the eye, and some more so. Handling is especially important for collectors who are learning to know and recognize objects and gain confidence in assessing quality and genuineness. And physical touch gives a sense of immediacy to almost any work of art, even if its appeal is primarily visual rather than tactile. Handling a precious or beautiful object seems to make all the senses more alert and implant it more firmly in the memory.

Size, texture, weight and temperature are all qualities that are revealed through the fingers and hands, and with practice they can all be judged extremely finely. It is said that some blind people have developed their sensitivity of touch to the point where they can distinguish between different colours; there are, apparently, minute differences in the radiation emitted from blue as against red, for example, which can be detected by the fingertips. Most sighted people are lazy about their sense of touch, usually because the eye produces a quick answer, although it may often be less reliable.

Hands can, of course, do damage which the eye can never do. Clumsy fingers drop precious objects, snap them, crush them, tear them. Fingernails scratch; the palms of hands sweat, and sweat is a horribly corrosive and staining substance. But there are some parts of the hands or face which are highly responsive to touch and yet are less potentially damaging . The back of a hand will gauge temperature or texture and does not sweat; so will the cheek. Porcelain experts are sometimes seen 'kissing' an object. This is not an excess of aesthetic passion. Lips are very sensitive judges of texture and temperature, and the kiss may indicate much about the ceramic body, and whether the part kissed is a well-disguised restoration, invisible to the eye, but differing in texture and temperature from the real thing.

Both the novice and the experienced collector should take every and any opportunity to handle works of art, although this is admittedly not easy. Museums and public collections, which are the most obvious places of study, must of necessity have a general 'hands off' policy. Indiscriminate handling by vast numbers of people would soon do irreparable harm to their collections, and it is obviously not possible to refuse admission to visitors because their hands are dirty or because their fingers are encrusted with rings.

Opportunities for handling

Any collector might well consider building up a collection of fragments — broken pieces of porcelain or pottery, pieces of timber and veneer, samples of paper, pieces of material and so on — purely to learn what they feel like. The fragments can probably be begged or traded for a small favour, but their instructive value can be enormous. Better still, handle them blindfolded until the hands become totally independent of sight! Learn to assess weight, and to anticipate the weight of a given volume of material, since this is one of the most difficult things to fake or imitate. For example: different woods have very different densities as well as textures and appearances, and a block of solid oak is quite different from a block that has a soft-wood core covered with an oak veneer.

Private collectors will usually allow fellow enthusiasts to handle objects, although they will be understandably wary until convinced that you know how to handle objects correctly. Some museum curators will also be helpful if convinced that you have a genuine need, and are engaged in serious research.

Dealers and auctioneers actually invite inspection and handling of the objects and works of art they hold for sale, and they give the collector the best opportunity of all. But there is a warning to note. They will hold you responsible for any damage or breakage that occurs. Accidents do happen to the most careful of people; elbows get nudged, feet slip, sleeves brush small objects off a ledge. If you are going to handle objects of high value regularly, you should probably take out an insurance policy to indemnify yourself against such occurrences.

Aesthetics   Many objects and works of art were made to be handled or demand to be touched. All objects designed for use ought to feel and handle well in addition to pleasing the eye. For example, a teapot should be well balanced with a comfortable handle, a glass should feel good in the hand, a knife and fork sit comfortably in the palm and allow the index finger to apply easy pressure. Chair seats and arms should be at the right height and accommodate the appropriate part of the anatomy, unless there is some reason for making them deliberately uncomfortable, such as the hard hall chairs on which servants were required to wait.

Small bronzes positively demand to be handled, and the temptation to caress almost all good sculpture is not a wicked impulse to be suppressed, but a sensitive aesthetic response. It would be astonishing if an artist who worked closely and physically with materials like marble, wood, clay or bronze would want others to be indifferent to the tactile qualities with which he or she had been so preoccupied. The same is true of cabinet-makers caring for the physical qualities of wood or making drawers or cupboards that open and close with smooth-running precision.

There is a danger that the 'hands off' policy, which museums and public collections must follow for security reasons, could entirely eliminate one of the most important qualities of many works of art. Perhaps this is one of the reasons for the relative unpopularity of sculpture in recent years, since saying to people 'you can look at the sculpture but not touch it' is like saying 'you can look at the paintings but only on days when the light is poor'. What chance does untouchable sculpture have, then, in a public gallery against paintings which are lit with endless care?

Paduan bronze oil lamp (sold at Christie's 8 December 1981). This mid-16th-century lamp (height 10.5 cm), known as 'The Pelican in her Piety' was, like many sculptures, made to be handled with pleasure. There is a relief on the underside of the base which can only be seen when the piece is handled.

There have been praiseworthy attempts by some museums to put on exhibitions for the blind, where the specific purpose is to allow sculpture to be handled, but such opportunities rarely exist for the sighted visitor. Curators do, of course, have the satisfaction of handling works of art all the time, and it would be a welcome development to see them making more facilities for handling objects available to reputable collectors, individually and in groups, rather than closing entirely this vital area of investigation and pleasure. It is an unfortunate and still insufficiently recognized fact that whereas modern methods of communication and information have brought knowledge and awareness of works of art to a greater audience than ever before, most of that audience is conscious only of a reproduction or illustration; it has little or no experience of two of the most important qualities of works of art: physical presence and physical feel.

Before handling an object an inspection for obvious defects and a few moments' thought are essential. Genuine accidents may be inevitable, but carelessness is unforgivable. Every object has physical strengths and weaknesses, and it is only common sense to avoid handling that part which is physically most vulnerable. A collector who knows his objects will know where the strengths and weaknesses are likely to be.

Safe handling

The first rule is to handle only one object at a time and to ensure that both hands are free for the task. If a shelf in a display cabinet needs cleaning it is both time-wasting and dangerous to try to lift an object with one hand while using the other hand to dust where it was standing. The safe procedure is to remove all the objects from the cabinet, one at a time, until the surfaces of the shelves are cleared for a thorough dusting. When removing objects from a cabinet it is important to have a clear space on which to deposit them, so that they are not crowded together or touching other things. This precaution applies also to metal objects. Slight knocks may easily indent delicate silver pieces or scratch the patina of bronzes.

The second rule is to wear sensible clothes. Garments with flowing sleeves and endless folds may look beautiful but they all too easily knock things over, and watches, bracelets, bangles and rings can be equally dangerous.

Ceramic collectors need to handle pieces with particular attention. Never lift up a teapot by the handle. Remove the lid and hold the vessel by putting the finger inside and gripping the outside wall with the thumb. This holds firmly and securely any teapot or jug. The same rule applies to all precious porcelain pieces, which should be held by their bodies and not by their delicate handles. Porcelain figurines should never be held by the arms or legs but cradled with the body resting comfortably in the hand. A cup should be picked up separately from its saucer, and again not by the handle. These precautions are necessary because handles and limbs protrude from the body of the piece and are the most delicate parts. They may have been weakened by an invisible crack developing after a slight knock, or occasionally they are not properly luted to the body at the time of manufacture. Because such faults can take years to emerge, the incautious collector may be unpleasantly surprised to be left holding the handle while the cup or pot ends up shattered on the floor.

Ceramics and glass

Don't overcrowd cupboards – allow enough space between piles of plates and individual objects so that there is no risk of breakage. The plates of each spare service should be in separate piles, but ideally not more than twelve to a pile. Each size should form a pile on its own. In this way the surface decoration is protected

from plates being slipped in, which causes scratching. This is particularly so if there are too many plates stacked together. Handpainted and gilded plates should have a circle of chamois leather, natural felt, or even newspaper between them to protect the decoration.

Glass has to be handled rather differently. Usually the strongest part of a glass object is its base or foot. The safest way to handle a drinking glass, for example, is to hold the stem firmly but lightly with the thumb and first two fingers, while supporting its foot with the other hand. It is ill-advised to try to show off one's dexterity by clutching a bunch of glasses in the manner of a wine waiter at a restaurant. Knocking the rims together may cause chips, and these unsightly faults can only be remedied by grinding down the glass, which inevitably leaves an unbalanced appearance. Heavy-footed bowls should not be lifted by the rim alone, but gently tilted on one side to create enough space to insert a hand underneath, while the other hand holds the bowl from inside. This avoids putting heavy strain on a delicate rim, since the main weight is supported by the hand underneath while the other hand is used gently to steady the piece.

Ceramics and glass objects, because they are so liable to damage from impact, should always be placed on a firm surface covered with a soft material. If you have to move the pieces in your collection from one place to another, a padded carrying basket should be used. This will eliminate the possibility of accidentally dropping any. If more than one piece is to be carried in the basket ensure that generous packing is provided between each item.

Paper   Paper is more delicate and fragile than might be supposed, and prints, drawings, watercolours, maps, valuable books and manuscripts need special care. Always wash and dry hands thoroughly before handling works on paper. This reduces the likelihood of the combination of dirt and sweat staining the paper. Always

(Far left) The correct handling of glass. The example held is an English four sided pedestal stemmed baluster goblet, c. 1710. (Left) Sculptures need very careful handling as they are often made in sections and can pull apart under their own weight if unsupported. For example, a heavy marble base could pull and break the relatively fragile legs of this piece of its weight was not taken up by the hand.

(Right) Prints are best stored flat in a solander box, and should be handled lightly at the edges.

hold a sheet of paper in two hands. This will minimize the amount of pressure put on the paper by the fingers and thereby the amount of sweat left on the sheet. It also helps to reduce the chances of creasing the paper: holding a sheet of paper in one hand almost always causes a crease of one sort or another.

When a print or drawing is not housed in a display frame it should be kept flat in a proper folder and protected from abrasive contact by an inner cover of acid-free tissue paper. Mounted prints or drawings should be stored according to size, with the largest one at the bottom and stacked mount to mount, again with a piece of acid-free tissue in between each one. Mounted sheets should be stacked flat (and *not* on their side), one on top of the other. When viewed, each mount should be moved sides and face up. *Never* turn them over. Turning over can easily result in the sheet catching in the mount opening, causing at the least bad creases, and more seriously, tears.

Careless handling or careless storage is a common cause of creases and tears and discoloration at the margins of etchings, maps, and engravings, often to such an extent that the paper margins have to be trimmed back to the plate mark. Discerning collectors usually avoid these mutilated goods, so loss of margins means loss of value.

Furniture

Furniture is frequently handled and put to use even when it is collected primarily for the enjoyment of its design and the quality of its wood. Protective devices should be used with discretion, however. Attractive sideboards are all too often deprived of beauty by having their tops covered with plate glass to prevent scratching and marking the wood. But the glass itself can easily be scratched or cracked, and even if it remains intact dust and grit eventually accumulate under it. Cleaning necessitates lifting the glass top, and this can cause unsightly scratches on the surface of the wood. Less fussy forms of protection suffice, such as felt pads or linen mats, and these can be easily obtained.

Never force drawers or doors or try to close them with one hand or a knee. If you are moving furniture remove the drawers as well as their contents, and also the contents of cupboards. Firmly hold the furniture by the carcase — i.e. its framework. Always make sure that glazed or mirrored doors are secured shut, and lock the doors of cabinets. Do not ask a piece of applied moulding or a hinge to bear the weight of the whole piece. And do not drag or push furniture along the floor. What seems a short cut rapidly ends in disaster.

Legs are designed to carry the vertical thrust of weight and are easily broken by the shearing force of pushing and pulling. Chairs should be moved by gripping them with a hand on each side of the seat rail and lifting them well clear of the floor. Drop-in seats should always be taken out. The dangerous habit of sitting on a chair and rocking on its back legs is foolhardy for the occupant as well as damaging to the chair. Armchairs also should be used only in the way they were made to be used, that is sitting on the seat and never on the arm supports. These are the least strong parts of the construction and easily loosened or broken by such misuse. Sitting on the arms of wing chairs can be a particularly costly mistake, because it is necessary to remove the upholstery before the resulting faults can be put right.

Sculpture

Sculpture also needs careful handling, especially when large, as the sheer weight of its material can lead to damage, and marble, being a crystalline stone, is surprisingly fragile. Marble portrait busts or statues should never be lifted by the neck or any undercut extremities, as this risks fractures at vulnerable points. They should also ideally not be rocked or pivoted on a hard floor when being moved, as this may chip the edge of the base. If dropped a piece will shatter. Adequate manpower should be available for any lifting. Hands should be clean too, as marble stains easily and is hard to clean.

Bronzes, while they possess greater tensile strength than marble, may have hidden casting flaws along which they are liable to fracture if roughly handled. Dents to noses, fingers, toes, etc., are easily caused and greatly reduce the value of a piece. With pigmented or gilt wood carvings the same care in handling, storing or display should be given as with a panel painting. The wood expands or contracts with changes of relative humidity, and loosens the surface layer of gesso and paint, which will then flake easily. It is particularly prone to adhere to the hand if the object is carelessly grasped.

Oil paintings

Oil paintings on canvas are relatively robust, but like all works of art need careful handling. The safest place for them is hanging on the wall, providing the fixings are secure. With small pictures, it is better to use two loose rings or screw-eyes fixed to opposite sides of the frame and hang on 'X' hooks or double 'X' hooks, than to rely on picture-wire or cord. It is not only a safer method of hanging but it also ensures that pictures always remain straight. If you are hanging heavier pictures and want to be sure that 'X' hooks will bear the weight, drive a screw through the centre of each of the hooks. Any picture of considerable weight should be hung professionally. This is a wise precaution because you run a considerable risk in hanging a picture insecurely; it could fall at any time, and while it may escape serious damage itself, the frame will most certainly not do so. Furthermore, furniture and decorative china are also at risk.

If paintings are to be stacked (for example, if you are decorating or spring-cleaning a room) make sure they are stored in a safe place, away from activity, and away from a dusty atmosphere or one with paint fumes. Paintings should be stacked upright or on their sides on an old eiderdown or folded blanket, back to back so that rings, hooks, nails and other projections cannot damage other paintings or frames. Stack the largest paintings at the back. Do not place too many together, and put sheets of cardboard, foam rubber or old blankets in between the paintings for protection. If you are taking paintings out or putting paintings into the stack do not cut corners. Remove or replace each painting one at a time, lifting it carefully well clear of the stack. Do not pull them along the floor or allow one to fall against another.

Paintings on panel must be handled with particular care as panels are very fragile, especially when old, and can crack or split very easily (see also Chapter 7).

When carrying a painting on canvas hold it by the stretcher, and avoid touching the paint surface. Always carry it with the paint surface towards you. Large paintings should be handled by two people, or more if necessary. Make sure that the painting is securely attached to its frame. If it is not, it may be better to remove it altogether rather than risk the two becoming separated at the wrong moment or remaining as a trap for someone else. Forward planning and caution must always be the principal rule.

Summary

More than for almost any other aspect of collection, safe handling is a matter of common sense. If you can demonstrate by example to fellow collectors that you are aware of the dangers of careless handling, are willing to handle objects with care and confidence, and are grateful for the opportunity, most of them will be quite willing to allow you to do so. By the same token check first that visitors to your collection know what they are doing, and if they pass the test, then by all means share with them your pleasure in handling works of art.

An oil painting on canvas correctly carried by the stretcher, with the frame well supported. Behind are oil paintings correctly stacked according to size.

9

DISPLAYING
WORKS OF ART

'Fichtre! . . . Épatant! . . . Sapriste! . . . Superbe! . . . ça parle! . . .'
Lithograph by Honoré Daumier.

More ingenuity has gone into the display of works of art in the last half-century than at any previous period. Nevertheless, it remains a shadowy subject about which very little has been written, and on which it is almost impossible to give specific advice since the best solution is so often the outcome of particular circumstances and taste. However, it is probably helpful to have some idea of the context and traditions of display as well as some general guidelines.

In the first place display is interlinked with interior decoration. Interior decorating, among other things, means creating an environment suited to a particular activity and way of life. Works of art, if they are included, may play a secondary role, blending into the overall decorative scheme without drawing attention to themselves. A conscious display is different, and usually both private collectors and professional interior decorators wish to set out works of art so that they will be noticed and gain interest by their arrangement. It may involve devoting a whole room or gallery or building to the purpose, but it can also be achieved through a single piece of furniture (a cabinet for example), or through objects arranged on a table top or prints hung on a wall.

Ideas about display and interior decoration must overlap, but by realizing that there can be a distinction the collector need not be intimidated into presupposing that some grand scheme or huge expense will be necessary to make the best of a collection. Some decorative schemes have become works of art in their own right – the Villa Farnesina in Rome for example, or work by the Adam brothers. On the other hand some collections have not been displayed at all, but kept in a box under the bed and produced only for the owner's fellow enthusiasts. They have not necessarily suffered from this secretive treatment.

The Mediterranean tradition

The great asset which is special to those European countries bordering on the Mediterranean, and which is denied to Northern Europe, is sunlight. It has a warmth and glow quite different from the cold grey light of the North, and by intensifying visual appearances as well as encouraging an outdoor life-style, it produces some of the most attractive conditions for display. To the Northern eye this light often comes as a staggering revelation – one only has to think of the effect on the paintings of Turner, van Gogh or Matisse. These features were exploited most effectively in the central feature of the Roman house, the atrium – a court open to the sky, around which the house was built. All the principal dwelling rooms opened on to it, providing an ideal place for the display of sculpture, which was the Romans' first love, and which looked at its best in this well-lit and relaxing environment. Walls were often richly painted with frescoes, the styles and themes ranging from *trompe-l'oeil* decorations of elaborately coloured marble, to illusionistic scenes of interiors and landscapes which gave the impression of looking out of a window. Still-lifes and fanciful combinations of animal, human and vegetables forms were also popular.

Roman taste in collecting and art was strongly influenced by the older Greek tradition, but for neither is there much surviving detailed evidence about the arrangement of their rooms. Both liked luxury. Both used chests to hold objects, whether of daily use or of value. The chests themselves could be extremely elaborate. The Greeks apparently hung their possessions on the wall, whereas the Romans first introduced large tables with wood or marble tops and elaborately carved supports typically of a creature such as a winged griffin. They also invented the cupboard with shelves, and perhaps these were used to display the quantities of finely wrought silver to which they were addicted.

The early Renaissance also prized sculpture above paintings, and their architecture exploited the attractions of open space and light. Renaissance paintings give us a good idea about the actual detail of display, a particularly good example being Carpaccio's *Saint Augustine in his Study*. Compared with contemporary painting by Northern artists the Mediterranean method of display is seen to be much less fussy and crowded.

From the Renaissance onwards there was a strong cross-fertilization of artistic ideas between Italy and Northern Europe. Northern princes of the sixteenth century were keen to proclaim their enlightenment by adopting Italian attitudes, and in the eighteenth century Palladian and neo-classical architecture and decoration were based consciously on Italian prototypes. The prospect of an Italian style house nestling in the wet green English landscape has become so commonplace that the novelty and absurdity of it become forgotten. Yet a house such as Holkham Hall in Norfolk was exactly that, and the magnificent sculpture gallery deliberately adapts the Mediterranean tradition to the totally different environment of a landscape exposed to the east wind and the North Sea.

Modern architects have used and developed the tradition. They have produced curiosities like the Getty Museum at Malibu in California which is a replica of the Villa dei Papiri excavated at Herculaneum and attempts to show how the Romans might have displayed their treasures. They have also used modern materials and a functional aesthetic to build small museums such as the Maeght Foundation in the south of France, or the Miro Museum in Barcelona where light, water and courtyards lend a special magic to works of art.

Vittore Carpaccio: The Vision of Saint Augustine (*Venice, Scuola di San Giorgio degli Schiavoni*). *Carpaccio's painting contains much information about Renaissance collecting and attitudes to display. Books and small antique bronzes are prominent, indicating their importance. Paintings are not included.*

Sculpture Gallery, Holkham Hall, Norfolk. *The house was built in 1734 by Thomas Coke (1697–1759), the first Earl of Leicester, in collaboration with Lord Burlington and William Kent. It took 30 years to build. The Sculpture Gallery was designed to house the collection of antique sculpture bought in Italy during 6 years of the Grand Tour, which Thomas Coke undertook between the ages of 15 and 21. The design of the house is an adaptation of Palladio's Villa Mocenigo.*

Without long hours of sunlight, and based on a more indoor life, the Northern tradition has been to create richly decorated and crowded interiors. Thus in many palaces and houses darkness not lightness can be the main impression, although there was one most attractive feature which is hardly ever seen today: candlelight. The static and rather brilliant quality of electric light cannot compare with the warm flickering blaze of candle-laden chandeliers, which gave an alluring significance and attraction to the reflecting surfaces of glass, mirrors, silver and gilded wood. Many settings which are held out today as historically correct need an imaginative leap to visualize them under candle-lit conditions.

Collections of paintings were often massed on walls, sometimes in special galleries built for their display, and there are a number of galleries still laid out in this manner. Corsham Court in Wiltshire is an outstanding example, being untouched since its creation in the mid-eighteenth century. When there is a large sale Christie's and Sotheby's auction rooms are still inclined to look like old picture galleries. There is also now a fashion among museums to re-create traditional displays, and there is no doubt that individual paintings which might look weak in isolation can benefit enormously from a crowded company.

The Northern tradition

Spencer-Churchill Collection, Northwick Park. *The photograph shows the display favoured by George Spencer-Churchill for small sculptures.*

George Spencer-Churchill, who died in 1965, was one of the last collectors in the ninteenth-century style; as well as inheriting a number of fine pictures he delighted in rescuing dark and forgotten paintings. In his picture gallery at Northwick he would be horrified if the re-arrangement due to a new purchase were to leave a rectangle of wall visible. He would spend hours working out how best to cover every inch. The centre of the gallery had cases crammed with Greek vases, while upstairs in his library, shelves at dado height had their entire surfaces covered in small bronzes and other antiquities from both East and West. He wanted his guests to look at his collection piece by piece yet in its entirety, and was not the slightest bit interested in blending his collection with the interior decoration of the house.

Specially designed rooms and pieces of furniture, often of considerable elaboration, are a particular feature of the Northern tradition. There are many examples of beautiful coin, print and porcelain cabinets, and many Central European rulers had a treasury where they collected all kinds of objects and vessels made out of precious stones and metals, and mounted hardstones and rarities such as coconut cups and nautilus shells. The idea of a porcelain room started in Holland in about 1670, and was adopted by many of the German princes, a spectacular example being the Johanneum created by Augustus the Strong in Dresden between 1717 and 1721. Oriental porcelain in the seventeenth century was a luxury for the rich, and the walls of a porcelain room would be festooned with brackets and shelves as well as inset with niches. Special pedestals and stands were designed, and every available surface was crammed with porcelain. At this time there was very little discrimination in quality, for the main interest was in the colouring (most of the porcelain imported before 1700 was blue and white) and the emphasis was on shape and size to fit a particular spot.

Throughout history we have tended to despise the taste of our forebears, and Macaulay writing in the mid-nineteenth century found this type of thing quite hideous. Commenting on the way Queen Mary had decorated at Hampton Court in the late seventeenth century, he wrote, 'In every corner of the mansion appeared a profusion of gewgaws, not yet familiar to English eyes. Mary had acquired at the Hague a taste for the porcelain of China, and amused herself by forming at Hampton Court a vast collection of hideous images, and of cases on which houses, trees, bridges and mandarins were depicted in outrageous defiance of all the laws of perspective. The fashion, a frivolous and inelegant fashion it must be owned, which was thus set by the amiable Queen, spread fast and wide. In a few years almost every great house in the Kingdom maintained a museum of these grotesque baubles. Even statesmen and generals were not ashamed to be renowned as judges of teapots and dragons; and satirists long continued to repeat that a fine lady valued her mottled green pottery quite as much as she valued her monkey, and much more than she valued her husband' (*History of England*, Chapter 9).

The Oriental tradition

The Chinese themselves have a long and distinguished record of collecting, and were probably the first to show restraint in the display of paintings and works of art. Their paintings are kept rolled up in scrolls, or if of small size kept in albums. The usual decoration for a Chinese collector today is very sparse, and almost certainly few, if any, of his better pieces will be on view. Pieces and paintings appropriate to a particular festival or season will only come out for the occasion. If another connoisseur visits the collector he may be asked what he is particularly

Modern Japanese display. *The Japanese tradition is simple, spare and elegant, in contrast to the 'clutter' of much Western display.*

interested in, and with due ceremony the requisite boxes will be brought out, each piece lovingly unwrapped, examined and discussed and then equally lovingly put back. The scrolls will be unrolled and held down perhaps by a scroll weight which is a great work of art in its own right.

The Chinese place great emphasis on the absolute purity of their works of art; a piece of porcelain must be without the slightest chip or crack, a jade must be flawless, undamaged and of the purest translucent colour. The importance is not on the distant visual effect, but on being held in the hand and examined closely.

Taste in Japan is even more guided by tradition than in China, and Japanese houses and apartments are normally quite sparsely decorated. Only since the industrial boom of the last fifteen years have the Japanese collected non-Eastern art, with the exception of their taste for Impressionism, which caught on with a select coterie at a very early period. The Japanese also venerate everything that is necessary to the tea ceremony. The teabowl must be of a certain proportion and the juxtaposition perfect. This, combined with the importance of pieces actually used by famous tea masters of the past, has a great influence on Japanese decoration and design. The artist potter is of equal renown to the artist in Japan, and certain potters have themselves even been designated 'National Treasures'. High prices are often paid for Chinese works of art similar to those which came to Japan at an early period, or which either were used by a famous exponent of the tea ceremony or are of exact proportions for the same ceremony.

Modern approaches

The main tendency in public and private has been to abandon crowded and fussy displays in favour of a sparser and more selective approach. There are a number of reasons. Taste changes, and there was a strong reaction against the overcrowding of the nineteenth century. By the turn of the century Chinese and Japanese ideas had become widely fashionable. Technological change, especially sophisticated electric lighting, has made it possible to isolate works of art and present them with the spot-lit glamour of film stars. Museums with vast collections have developed ways of presenting an eye-catching and informative package around selected objects. The increasing scarcity of works of top quality has meant the need to isolate and make the most of what is available.

Specialization and improved scholarship have not escaped the art world, or left methods and displays unaffected. Increasingly there have been comprehensive exhibitions devoted to single artists or themes, with a full scholarly catalogue and immensely elaborate displays by top designers. One of the most spectacular and successful examples was the exhibition of the Treasures of Tutenkhamun, which travelled the world for several years during the 1970s and was seen by an audience of millions. Specialization has also produced a new profession, the interior decorator. The big names have produced their own style and designs which are instantly recognizable, although the client who uses them risks the loss of individuality for the assurance of a certain standard of 'correct' taste.

Many modern ideas about display reflect the awareness by collectors and curators of their responsibility to conserve the objects in their care, to share them with others, and to educate. Praiseworthy as this is, it is as well to be aware that there are dangers. Many works of art have been wrenched from their natural setting and thrust into an environment which is elaborately planned and highly didactic but wholly unsympathetic. For example, religious pictures designed to hang high up in a dark side chapel of a church lit by flickering candlelight are not helped by being hung at eye level in a blaze of spotlights in an anonymous whitewashed gallery. Yet it happens all the time.

64 Old Church Street, London SW3. *This room, designed by Erich Mendelsohn and Serge Chermayeff, shows an approach to display very characteristic of the mid-20th century.*

There is an increasing enthusiasm for period settings, and twentieth-century scholarship and research have produced some impressive results. There is no doubt that many works of art gain in significance and interest by sharing an appropriate setting rather than by being isolated like a laboratory specimen. Yet here too there are pitfalls. A proper acknowledgement and conservation of the past and its traditions are important, provided they do not develop into a desire to stop the clock entirely. It is not possible to re-create the past exactly. An 'authentic' period setting which rigorously excludes anything from a previous age takes purity to the point of unreality. No painting can be restored to look precisely as it did when it left the artist's studio. Claims to do so are often a euphemism for over-cleaning.

Lavish custom-made displays can be very enjoyable and exciting, but they are only one of several options, and most private collectors have neither the means nor the inclination to design even a whole room to fit an existing collection. In general a simple idea carried through with conviction is infinitely better than an elaborate one which is half-hearted. The great advantage of the private house is that it is not a museum with its obligation to accommodate a stream of unknown visitors and attendant security problems. Attitudes to display can be much more relaxed and informal. Nor is perfection always a virtue. A faultless porcelain dish of the Song dynasty can be dull and without life, while a distortion in the firing

General advice

can turn it into something memorable. It is like a computer playing a piano sonata with no mistakes, while the virtuoso might make several and at the same time lift the performance into the realms of the sublime. In the same way a technically incorrect display can show a degree of artistry which illuminates the object and shows the character of the collector. There are collectors who have holes in their carpets, cobwebs in their sitting rooms and the most primitive of living conditions, and yet are surrounded by works of art of great beauty crammed higgledy-piggledy into a showcase or tacked arbitrarily to the walls, which look wonderful in spite of the disarray. False ceilings or concealed spotlights do not necessarily show off works of art and pictures to the best effect. An ordinary room with strategically placed standard and table lamps, which leave attractive areas of light and shade and hint at greater beauty beyond, may be quite sufficient and more effective.

Space is an all-important consideration. Large pieces of furniture crowded into small rooms look uncomfortable and oppressive, just as small paintings isolated on a large wall merely look abandoned and unwanted. Small paintings, prints and drawings are best kept in folios or grouped together to form a well-thought-out design.

Today's ideas of the use of space are far less bound by fashion than those of even twenty years ago. A cluttered effect has come into fashion again. A reason for this is that there are still a number of people who love buying and soon find themselves surrounded by pictures and objects of fairly mundane artistic quality. The abstract theorist will say that they ought to get rid of them all and with the money buy a single item of greater quality which can be shown off starkly and simply, and for some this is the answer. Others, however, like to have the clutter and the memories of how and when each piece was acquired and who owned

Oriental porcelain on a pyramid stand (*Berlin, Schloss Charlottenburg*). *A typical display of the early 18th century.*

them before. They can be arranged according to category, size or colour, or a combination of all of them, but they need even greater thought in display than the masterpiece. The owner must decide which pictures, drawings or prints he wants at eye level when standing or when seated, and which need to be looked up at. If he collects furniture it is difficult if not impossible to crowd without either destroying its appeal or making the interior look like a furniture dealer's showroom.

It is important to choose the right coloured background with the right texture. The framing of a picture can make an enormous difference to its decorative appeal, and today if it has lost its original frame a reproduction of the type of frame it was likely to have had is normally suggested, though some people like to hang certain types of paintings on the wall unframed. Drawings are even more difficult as they are usually mounted as well as framed, and fine mounts can add enormously to their appeal. They should never be placed where direct sunlight can fall on them, as this will turn the paper brown and fade the colours. It can be dangerous to place any painting in strong sunlight. When there is an open fire in a room any picture not covered by glass is likely to get dirty and dark, particularly if it is hanging over the fireplace. Glass protects the picture, and today it is possible at a price to get special glass which partly protects it against the harmful rays of the sun. On the other hand, glass often reflects light, and it is sometimes very difficult to see any picture thus protected. If the wall concerned is very sunny and unsuitable for normal pictorial art, china plates, dishes and other flat objects can be put on the walls in the same way, observing like rules regarding background and colour. Several large houses have fascinating designs on the walls of a hall made from groups of early firearms and other weapons. With imagination the same can be done with many different kinds of collections. China and other ornaments can go on open shelves or decorate the tops of tables, brackets and other furniture, or be placed in cabinets which are objects of beauty in themselves. Some china, glass and other ornaments lend themselves to a crowded display, others need space around them, while others again can be grouped together. The traditional way of arranging them is by size and by compatability of colour, and if a shelf or surface is deep enough, they can be spaced forwards or backwards, and some raised up on wood, fabric or transparent plastic stands to give an interesting variation in height. Bowls usually look better if displayed at eye level or above, unless the interior decoration is the more beautiful or if they serve a practical purpose on a table top. A haphazard grouping of objects can also look very beautiful if arranged by someone with a good eye who knows how to place each piece in relationship with the other.

Poor condition can be disguised by standing the object at a certain distance or height from the viewer – worth considering when the price of a damaged piece is only a fraction of the perfect piece. Restorers today, without spraying and heavy repainting, can often make a piece even with quite ugly damages look very presentable.

Mirrors hung in the proper places can add depth to a room, and in more intimate surroundings can reflect the other side of an object put in front of them. Porcelain rooms such as that of Queen Mary at Hampton Court often had mirrors to emphasize and exaggerate the profusion of riches.

Museums need to have labels so that visitors can know what they are looking at. Depending on the current taste in the museum these labels can be placed next to the objects or pictures, which detracts from the visual appearance but makes things easier from the education standpoint. Discreet labels on the walls look better but are sometimes more difficult to match with the object. A private collector does not normally label his objects, though some pictures have small plaques on the frames with the artist's name and sometimes the title of the picture. Small objects such as coins which are kept in cabinets often have labels underneath. It is, however, useful in a large collection to be able to identify every piece, and a small collecting label with a number referring to a catalogue is usually considered the best method of getting over this problem. Whether a collection is eventually sold, given to a museum or passed on to a descendant, it is useful to posterity if all information known to the collector from the previous history of the object, his own researches or the opinions of other specialists and collectors to whom he has shown his treasure can be documented.

Colour matching is important. Glass seems to reflect the light better if placed against a soft dark background; even old-fashioned black velvet looks very good. Blue and white porcelain is very difficult to mingle with other coloured objects, but shows up well against a yellow background. The reason? Blue and yellow are colours which react against each other in the eye, the yellow intensifying the perception of the blue. To be properly effective, however, the correct tone of yellow must be chosen, and its area carefully controlled so as not to swamp the blue. It is worth acquiring a book which outlines the basic scientific principles of colour perception and mixing, since it will show quickly why certain combinations do work and others do not. Also, do not forget to study paintings to see how artists use colour and composition. An artist who really understands colour rarely produces a riot, but uses a restricted range and exploits one or two colours to the full. For example, Constable shows how a small, and often overlooked, touch of red can bring vitality to a large area of green that would otherwise be dead; Monet shows how a carefully selected cool blue can bring out the quality of a warm red; Matisse shows how areas of white are important to let colours 'breathe'; Velázquez uses wonderful colour harmonies such as a silvery grey and soft salmon pink.

Fussy wallpapers, which can be very effective in modern settings or even period ones when there are few objects and fewer pieces of furniture and pictures, can be disastrous as a background to a collection unless chosen by someone with great feeling and flair. The more colour there is in the pictures and objects, the less there should be in the background. A plain pile carpet pulls a room together when there are a lot of things of different shapes and colours in the collection, while scattered Persian rugs and carpets on a polished floor look better in a fairly sparsely furnished room.

As mentioned earlier, strategically placed lamps can show a private collection off charmingly, but a great amount of thought should be put into the lighting of a collection. Having decided how to display it, the collector must decide where the light is going to fall both by day and by night, whether concealed strip-lighting in a cabinet can be properly concealed yet not cast any ugly shadows, or whether certain pieces should be moved round in order to catch the light on one side and leave an unimportant facet left in the shade. Some people have very elaborate lighting on all their pieces, with dimmer switches and all the remarkable appurtenances of modern science, and have made their collections as memorable to the visitor as the Tutenkamun Exhibition, but others have forgotten that in the daylight many modern lights look extremely ugly. One only has to go to certain London West End theatres to find the balconies or other fine architectural details ruined by batteries of unconcealed lights. Lights over pictures can be ugly too, and if badly adjusted only reflect their own light; a special spotlight which is shaped to the picture or object it is meant to show off can be the most effective way of illumination, but it is important to hide the spot itself, and to make sure that paintings are not damaged by the heat which will also be projected by it.

If you feel the need for advice from a professional decorator, take time to find one who is sympathetic to your collection and to your taste. Also, do not be led astray by someone else's elaborate display. Many decorators are particularly skilled at making things of purely decorative value look like collector's pieces by the skilful use of materials, colour and lighting. The advantage of taking the advice of a professional decorator is that if the collector wishes to be bold, the decorator often knows when he can break the rules, or go close to doing so, and yet still be successful.

Ultimately the essential principle must be to respond visually to the object you wish to display. What are its prime qualities? Shape and form? Texture? Colour? Subject-matter? Craftsmanship? Historical associations? Once the response is identified it is relatively easy to devise an appropriate display. If the initial response is insensitive or confused no display, however elaborate, will solve the problem. A collector who has the courage and enthusiasm to follow his own eye in his acquisitions needs only to extend the eye a little further to make an effective and individual display.

Calke Abbey, Derbyshire. *The drawing room is decorated and arranged exactly as it was in 1856, and has remained, like most of the house, untouched since the mid-19th century. The curious and reclusive history of the house and its owners has thus provided a unique documentation of taste and display.*

10
INSURANCE AND SECURITY

Protection from Burglars, for Ideal and other Homes.
Punch, 25 February 1920.

I nsurance is very much a matter of personal choice. Anyone who is concerned about financial investment will want the maximum realistic cover, which is expensive for works of art and antiques, and trying to find the lowest quotation is emphatically not the wisest course. Those who collect mainly for pleasure can lighten the burden prudently in a number of ways.

Having decided in principle to take out insurance, the next step is to find a suitable broker. It has to be said that comparatively few brokers understand the specialized field of fine art insurance, and it is advisable to consult the leading auctioneers or trade associations for the names of recommended brokers (see Appendix 2). This is all the more important in North America, where some brokers offer fine art insurance policies which may be less expensive than standard homeowner's policies.

Should you insure?

The first stage is to decide the nature of the cover required, that is to say the kinds of 'risks' to be covered. Since most collectors will keep their collections at home they will probably think of extending their existing 'Householder's Comprehensive', or 'All-In' policy. The words 'Comprehensive' and 'All-In' need some qualification, since the policies cover only certain specified perils such as theft, fire, explosion, water damage, or storm damage. In the event of a claim the policy holder has to show that the loss or damage has occurred as the direct result of one of these perils or 'risks'. It is not sufficient, for example, to say that something has disappeared and therefore it must have been stolen. Actual evidence, even if only circumstantial, is required before a claim will be met. Insurance companies will ask if the police have been informed, and in the United States a police report from the investigator is a necessary piece of evidence.

Another type of insurance is called 'All Risks'. This represents the maximum cover you are likely to obtain and it is less of a misnomer. It will cover you in addition against accidental breakage and disappearance, but like any other insurance it should be emphasized that it will not cover 'inherent vice' such as the progressive deterioration of certain early glass or the deterioration of tapestry through atmospheric conditions. An appropriate aphorism is 'insurance covers the unexpected and the unforeseen, but not the inevitable'. 'All Risks' cover for ceramics – which are easily breakable – is particularly expensive, and it is possible to reduce the cost by having cover for 'All Risks excluding breakage'.

Extending a 'Householder's' policy may seem to be the simplest method of providing some cover, but your insurers may not be willing to accept the added risk of a valuable collection at the same rate of premium. Generally speaking it is better to have a separate 'All Risks' policy for a collection. In the United States, the average homeowner's insurance policy has many limitations that work against the collector. Under many such policies there is a $500 limitation on claims for precious metals which includes silverware and items of numismatic interest, as well as a $500 limitation on jewellery, both new and antique. Further, many homeowner's policies work on a formula basis whereby the contents of the home are valued at 50 per cent of the house's value regardless of what is in the house. These factors make the homeowner's policy unsuitable for almost any collector. Certain companies within the United Kingdom have similar restrictions.

Type of cover required

Decide precisely *what* you are going to insure, and make a comprehensive list of items involved, say those worth more than £50 each, giving as much detail as practicable. Items below £50 can be included in a lump sum as one item, although you would be advised to list them individually for your own purposes, and such a

What to insure and for how much

list might be needed to justify a claim. If a collection consists of small items, such as stamps or coins, you may be required to list them all anyhow. If you can relate your list to a photographic record, so much the better. Such a record is always of interest to the true collector, and in these days of modern single-lens reflex cameras and fast colour negative films, which dispense with the need for special lighting, the provision of such a record is neither difficult nor expensive. Keep your original purchase invoices as these will be helpful in the event of a claim.

Attention to these seemingly irksome details will assist the prompt settlement of any claims, as will a professional valuation of the articles. Valuations for insurance purposes are normally carried out by the leading auction houses or by professional valuers, or appraisers, among whose number are certain antique dealers. Such valuations are accepted as the basis of any claim provided copies have been lodged with your insurers at the inception of the policy and approved by them. The standard valuation fee in the United Kingdom is about $1\frac{1}{2}$ per cent, with a reduction in rate for values over, say, £50,000, though in the United States fees are most often charged on an hourly basis. You will find further information on this subject in Chapter 11. You may, however, not wish to go to the expense of a professional valuation for a small collection, in which case a detailed record with photographs and bills of sale is important. Always explain to your insurers at the outset how you have arrived at the sum insured.

On what basis should you value your possessions? The maximum valuation is the full market price, or replacement cost, of an item, that is what it would cost to replace in the 'retail' market. This is the basis of many insurance valuations. Many collectors, however, are satisfied in the event of loss to recover a lesser amount, such as the sum they would realize if they sold the object or collection in the open market. It is imperative to discuss with your insurer which type of cover you want since the values of the works of art, the premiums, and the documentation required by the insurer will vary accordingly. Thus, if you wish cover based on the object's original cost to you, you should give the insurer a copy of the receipt for your purchase. If you wish cover based on the object's replacement value the insurer may require a valuation performed by a professional valuer, though you may be able to satisfy the insurer's need for documentation by providing auction prices for similar items. (These prices, however, will tend to be lower than what the similar items would cost when bought from a dealer.) Whether you choose a cost basis or a replacement basis, it is important to reach a mutually satisfactory valuation for your collection – an 'agreed amount' – with your insurance broker before taking out a policy. Thefts and damages are traumatic in themselves without adding a quarrel with your insurer.

You may also want to have the valuations updated every three years or so. At various periods, as with American paintings in the late 1970s, fantastic appreciation occurs, and the value at which your collection is insured should reflect very recent, if not current, market values. The fee for updating a valuation, if you consult the original valuer, is significantly less than for the original work.

Information given to insurers

You will have noted an insistence on giving your insurers as much detail as possible: this is because insurance is based on the principal of 'utmost good faith' – *'uberrima fides'* is the legal Latin phrase sometimes still seen. You must, without necessarily being asked first, disclose all material facts: that is to say anything that could influence the insurer's view of the risk. Examples are the location and

Florence after the flood. *On the night of 3/4 November 1966 Florence, already soaked by days of torrential rain, was struck by a torrent of water and mud which raced at 40 miles an hour. Few precautions had been taken, and virtually no warning given. The personal loss and damage to works of art housed in Florence was incalculable. In many cases restoration was impossible. The cause of the disaster was a combination of misfortune, bad planning, neglect, lack of responsibility, procrastination, and financial meanness – each of them innocuous individually, but fatal in combination. The disaster could have been prevented, and the money that might, with foresight, have been spent on the necessary means of prevention was tiny compared with the cost of reparation after the disaster.*

physical protection of the collection, your past insurance history and details of all persons who have normal access to your home and/or your collection. This is particularly important if they are not members of your immediate family, or if you carry on any trade, consultancy or medical practice at your house which allows access by members of the public. British insurers may in fact ask you to complete a questionnaire called a 'Proposal Form'. This is an important document and will form the basis of the contract between you and your insurers. Answer all the questions truthfully and fully, and give details of any material facts not covered by the form on a separate sheet of paper if necessary. A material fact is one likely to influence acceptance or evaluation of the risk by underwriters. If in any doubt consult your broker. Non-disclosure may nullify the insurance.

Security   Regarding physical protection against theft you may find that before you approach your prospective insurers it pays you to install efficient locks, bars, bolts, or grilles, to make the premises difficult to enter. Even so it is not easy to give a detailed guide because so much depends on the type of building and its geographical location. Expert advice is freely available in the United Kingdom and the United States from the Crime Prevention Officer at the local police station. Elsewhere in the world the police are usually willing to give advice on protection and the advisability of maintaining a valuable collection in your home.

As a general rule, two mortice deadlocks of the highest specification should be fitted to each external door, and window locks should be fitted to all ground-floor and first-floor windows. Examine all doors and window frames to make sure they are at least as strong as the locks. This applies particularly to older properties. Remember that protection should be in effective operation at all times when the house is unoccupied and that vulnerable windows, such as those at basement level and out of sight of passers-by, might benefit from iron bars, internal shutters or a collapsible grille.

The basic principle is to protect the perimeter of the property to prevent an easy entry. No thief likes to spend a long time outside a building trying to get in. Elaborate locks internally are not crucial and can simply lead to extensive damage, for once inside the thief is usually out of sight and earshot with time to spare. However, if a collection consists of small items a good safe is worth buying, preferably one substantial enough not to be manhandled and also fireproof. *Do not leave the keys in the house!*

With these precautions, if you have an otherwise clean insurance record as far as your house and collection are concerned, and if your area is not particularly hazardous, you may find the insurance company will not ask for a burglar alarm. On the other hand, if you seek coverage when you have virtually no protection

The National Gallery goes underground. *During the Second World War pictures from the National Gallery in London were stored for safety in a disused Welsh slate quarry.*

whatsoever it is possible that the insurers will ask for an alarm straight away without considering the alternatives. If you are asked to install an alarm, choose a nationally recognized organization to supply it, a firm with good local maintenance facilities, and one that gives a complete guarantee. The local police or your insurers should be asked for a recommendation. It does not pay to use a small local firm just to save a few pounds. The primary requirement is an efficient alarm that will go on working for many years.

Cover away from home

It is important to understand the geographical limitations of your policy and to make sure that it is worded in accordance with your probable requirements, both present and future. As you purchase additional items for your collection, you may take them home and there they will remain. In this case insurance at your residence is sufficient, plus cover from the time of purchase for the journey home from the shop. Suppose, on the other hand, you are a collector of silver and are wisely keeping some of your collection in the bank, your policy should cover not only your house and the bank but the transit between the two places.

It is also worth pointing out that the policy covering your residence will not normally cover items sent away to restorers or loaned for exhibitions. If you choose to get coverage for such occasions the restorer or exhibitor may require a 'waiver of subrogation (abrogation)' from your insurer before he will take the object into his possession. The waiver states that your insurer is covering the object while it is away from your home, and it may not be issued immediately. Many exhibitors and institutions, and a few restorers, carry their own insurance. If you agree to have your property covered under their policy make sure that they list a valuation for your object on the receipt or in a separate letter. This valuation should be acceptable to you. You may also want to stipulate that they will be responsible for repairing any damage to the object and that you have the right to choose or at least approve the restorer. Another important point is to make sure that their policy does not simply cover 'legal liability only'. The more specific your requests the more satisfactory your recompense in the cases of loss or damage. Transit to and from the exhibition must also be considered, and if there is any doubt whatsoever then consult your brokers, arranging your own cover if necessary. This will be on a 'nail to nail' basis, as the insurance term so aptly describes it – from the time an object is picked up from its normal resting place or hook, until it is safely back again.

Conditions, warranties and average

When you finally receive the policy from your insurers look carefully at *all* the print, both large and small. Take special note of any warranties, conditions and clauses that you think may present difficulties in the event of a claim. For example, there may be a clause excluding the breakage of 'brittle articles'. This clause should be avoided at all costs as 'brittle articles' have never been satisfactorily defined. Many otherwise substantial articles appear, in insurers' minds, to be brittle and proven so to be simply because they have become broken. Another clause that can present difficulties is the 'Pairs and Sets' clause which in effect says that if one article of a pair is lost or broken the insurers will only pay half the value of the pair. This is not a satisfactory arrangement as a pair of articles is invariably worth more than twice the sum of two single items. Even at the expense of paying a small extra premium it is wise to have this clause amended to provide payment for the loss of 'set value'.

The 'Average' clause is one particularly favoured by Lloyd's Underwriters and says in effect that if you are under-insured any claim will be reduced proportionately. For example, if a collection is demonstrably worth £100,000 and it is insured for £75,000, payment will be made for 75 per cent of any claim. Many policies issued by insurance companies do not contain the Average clause, but nevertheless the companies ask the insured to sign a declaration that the sum insured represents the full value. In the event of substantial under-insurance you may find that the company would try to reflect such under-insurance in the claim settlement, rather than reject the claim in its entirety on the grounds of mis-statement, provided they felt that there was no intent to deceive.

The Average clause does not apply to specific items insured individually for an agreed value. This is why it is so important to tell your insurers the precise basis on which you are insuring and how your values are arrived at. Do not forget to revise your values from time to time to keep up with inflation and market trends.

If, after negotiation with your insurers, you cannot avoid having a warranty or warranties in your policy, then pay particular heed to their provisions. The most usual warranty is the 'Protections Maintenance' warranty, which says that all protections provided for your premises must be in full and effective operation whenever the premises are left unattended. It means exactly what it says: namely that every lock must be locked, every window shut and all doors closed. Do not expect any sympathy from your insurers if you forget to lock the door when you depart or if you leave windows open for ventilation. If you have a burglar alarm it must be serviced regularly and checked for satisfactory operation before you go out. If after that the alarm fails to function or the locks do not withstand the attempts of the thieves to enter the house you will not be penalized.

Keeping down the cost of insurance

It is not possible to quote actual premiums. So much depends on the individual articles – are they easily portable by thieves or easily breakable? – and on the crime rate in your area. The premium for Mayfair or Park Avenue is not the same as for the Outer Hebrides or Alaska. Many factors can affect the final bill, but there are acceptable ways of keeping the cost of insurance down. The first and most obvious method is to obtain alternative quotations, but bear in mind that in insurance, as with everything else, you only get what you pay for. Consequently limit such inquiries for alternative rates to reputable brokers experienced in the fine art field. Secondly, you can insure for less than the full total value of the articles: for example, having prepared a schedule of values you can elect to be your own co-insurer for 25 per cent of the risk, leaving the insurers with the remaining 75 per cent, and pay only 75 per cent of the basic premium. Thirdly, you can insure on a 'First Loss' basis, calculating what you feel would be the maximum value you could lose as the result of one burglary or fire. Thus you might take the view that burglars would be unlikely to take all of your porcelain collection and insure only a certain sum. If they take more than this you have no claim for any loss over the agreed maximum, and bear in mind that the chances of total loss by fire are considerably greater. You can exclude the theft risk altogether, but cover in full all other risks such as fire, lightning, water damage, etc. The exclusion of the theft risk reduces the premium substantially.

Another method of saving on the premium is to take a substantial 'excess' (or 'deduction'), in respect of any loss other than by fire. This means that if the 'excess' or 'deduction' were, say, £1,000, you would not receive the first £1,000 of any claim. This is another form of self-insurance, which should reduce the premium slightly.

You can also reduce the cost by keeping part of your collection (particularly silver, jewellery, or coins) in the bank, where because of increased security the

The Underwriting Room at Lloyds. *Lloyds of London is traditionally the centre of the world's insurance market.*

rate charged is substantially less than for a private house. Similarly, the loan of articles to a museum with adequate security can provide the means of splitting the risk into smaller parts and obtaining a lower overall premium.

Insurers will not as a rule give a discount for good physical security since it is regarded as an essential prerequisite for the issuance of a policy, but as mentioned above good physical protection may avoid the need for an expensive alarm system at the outset.

A collector obviously wants to preserve his collection rather than receive compensation, and elementary 'risk management' is a worthwhile exercise. Insurance against theft is one of the first considerations, but the risk of damage by fire and water should not be underestimated. If, for example, you collect prints, drawings and watercolours you should observe the basic rules of conservation, such as hanging them well away from direct sunlight or strong light of any description (see Chapter 7); deterioration from such abuse would not be covered by any insurance. There are other less obvious, but equally important considerations: are they hung or stored directly beneath the bathroom or an area where there are water storage tanks? If you live in an area which has been subjected to flooding in the past, even perhaps some thirty years ago, are you satisfied that you are not keeping valuable books, prints or veneered furniture in a place where these might suffer if your house were to be flooded? Do you have a smoke detector in your house to warn you of a possible fire when you are asleep

Risk management

or otherwise occupied? Have you got suitable fire extinguishers to hand so that you can tackle the blaze pending the arrival of the fire brigade?

Damage caused by excessive humidity or excessive dryness in the atmosphere will not normally be covered even by an 'All Risks' policy unless cover is specifically requested, and such cover will be expensive and difficult to obtain.

From the point of view of 'All Risks' insurance there are further matters to be checked: examine all your picture fastenings regularly to make sure they are not showing any signs of stress or strain. Do not rely on picture wire, as the strongest part is often an iron core which can rust and break in time. Old-fashioned picture cord is less reliable than the modern nylon cord. If any weight is involved chains are much better, and if these can be secured from two points on the picture and two points on the wall so much the better. The fastenings of all shelves should be checked from time to time to make sure they are secure. Be careful that display shelves are not overloaded, as they may pull away from the wall with disastrous results.

Chapter 7, which deals with conservation, will give further guidance on minimizing the risk of deterioration in antiques and works of art. One final word of advice on the subject: do not commence restoration work before obtaining your insurer's written approval.

Claims   It is to be hoped that you will never have cause to claim upon your insurers. If it is a small claim and you notify the insurers at the outset with a detailed explanation as to how the loss or damage occurred, together with supporting evidence to prove the value of the claim, it is unlikely that your insurers will appoint anyone to deal with the matter on their behalf, but in the event of a major claim they will probably appoint a loss adjuster. A loss adjuster is a professional evaluator, and although his fees are ultimately paid by the insurers he is expected to give a fair independent verdict on any claim in the same way as a judge, although paid by the State, is not expected to be biased in favour of the prosecution. If at the outset of the claim you view the adjuster in this light, regarding him as a friend and not as someone sent by the insurers to beat you down, you should have no difficulty in arriving at a fair and amicable settlement. As pointed out earlier, a mutually acceptable valuation made on a properly understood and agreed basis minimizes the potential for disagreement. Of course sometimes differences can arise because you do not fully understand the wording of your insurance policy or the scope of cover granted, or because the adjuster has not been sent the full risk history by the insurance company. At this stage you should perhaps report the difference in opinion to your insurance broker, or to the insurance company if you normally deal with them direct. Every claim has to be settled eventually, and the quicker and more amicably this can be done the better for all concerned.

One point on which a difference of opinion can sometimes arise is depreciation in value following damage, and this particularly applies to objects which by their very nature are unique and irreplaceable by an identical object. For example, a damaged picture can be restored in most cases, but if this is the first damage that the painting has ever received there will undoubtedly be the basis for a claim for depreciation in value. If, on the other hand, the picture has been restored extensively in the past, a first-class restoration at the time of the recent damage may not reduce its value. If you request, when you first take out your policy, that a particular restorer should handle your item in the event of damage, you will be assured that the damage will be properly repaired and the loss minimized. Depreciation in value is a matter of opinion, and if you cannot reach an agreement

Gainsborough: The Duchess of Devonshire (*Washington, National Gallery of Art, Andrew W. Mellon Collection 1937*). *The painting was bought in 1876 for approximately £11,000, a record price for any picture at auction. It was stolen from the dealers, Agnew's, and taken to the United States. Small pieces of it were sent back to Agnew's with terms for its return. 25 years later it was finally traced by Pinkerton's, the private detective agency, and sold to Pierpont Morgan.*

with the adjuster then you should consult a third party: either a dealer or an auctioneer.

Much the same remarks apply to furniture. If there has already been restoration to a piece, further restoration will probably not affect the ultimate sale value. It is all a question of degree, and it is impossible to lay down hard and fast rules. On the other hand, if glass or porcelain is cracked or chipped there is no doubt that the loss in value is substantial, and it is indeed sometimes better for the article to be treated as a 'constructive total loss' and for the insurers to take over the salvage. This means that the insurers pay the claim in full, as though the object had been wholly destroyed. They take the damaged article, dispose of it for what it will fetch and keep the proceeds.

It is perhaps advisable to emphasize that if an article is damaged only the very best and most experienced restorers should be used. Although restoration may be expensive, any depreciation in value is probably lessened. A responsible collector ought to maintain those articles that have given so much pleasure in the very best possible condition, and it is surprising how much additional damage an inexperienced restorer can do which can never be put right at a future date.

A word of caution is necessary here on the subject of depreciation through damage: this is normally covered by policies issued in the United Kingdom and by fine art policies in the United States, but there are some policies issued abroad which do not cover depreciation in value and which would have to be amended to meet this.

Stolen property recovered

A point which sometimes arises in connection with a claim is the ownership of property which was lost or stolen and which is subsequently traced. Normally when an insurance company has paid for a loss ownership is transferred automatically to the insurer, and if the article is recovered the insurer is entitled to sell it for his own account. Of course you may wish to have the stolen property back, and you can probably come to an arrangement with the insurance company at the time of settlement that if an article is recovered within a reasonable period of time, say one year, they will give you the opportunity of buying it back for the amount paid on the claim. You must, however, realize that you cannot expect them to extend this time limit indefinitely, and that if a valuable painting is recovered some five years later they may not be willing to let you have it back for the price they paid for it originally, especially if there has been a substantial rise in the market value in the interim period. It cannot hurt, however, to try to negotiate a clause that allows you to buy back the painting if it is recovered for the amount you received for it plus interest. While such an approach may seem equitable you must remember that under such terms the insurance firm will lose out if the item's value has appreciated, and the collector, not under any compulsion to re-purchase the item, will not suffer financially if the item's value has lessened.

On the other hand, all insurers would be more than happy to negotiate the private sale of the painting to the original owner and would not seek to take advantage of the situation. You, the former owner, may have had the use of their money for a few years and you cannot therefore complain if at the end of the day they appear to have made a 'profit', if only on paper.

In conclusion, the broker or insurer you need is one who knows a great deal about the objects he is insuring; not only will he give you the fullest and least expensive cover but you will also get every possible assistance in the settlement of your claims, which are, after all, what insurance is all about.

11
VALUATIONS

Lady (age seven): 'How much is that, please?'
Stallholder (age nine): 'How much has your mother given you to spend?'
Punch, 28 August 1907

Avaluation is an approximate judgement as to financial worth under normal circumstances. It is not a prediction of what someone may eventually pay. Although the open market of the auction room will form the basis of the judgement, a valuer is not trying to guess what would happen in extraordinary circumstances. All that the fall of the hammer establishes is that on a particular day a certain buyer was prepared to pay a particular price for an object. A month previously he and the under-bidder might have been willing to bid twice as much; a month later neither might have been willing to bid at all, for general reasons such as economic uncertainty, or for reasons entirely personal to themselves. Most objects sold at auction do fall within a predictable price range, but every day there are extraordinary surprises when things sell for much more than expected, or for much less. When an auction price and a valuation do not coincide, it does not follow that the valuation is wrong. The purchaser may well discover in time that his judgement was at fault and he has paid too much; or he may discover that he has bought a bargain.

Most people probably have a fair idea of the value of their house, though it may cover a wide price range. But this general idea can become very fluid and subject to much discussion when, for example, the house owner decides to put his property on the market. If the house is part of an estate of similar dwellings it is easy enough to find recent precedents, though even here factors such as location and condition may make an appreciable difference. If the house and location are unique, matters become much more difficult. Do you wait for an economic upturn and then suggest an excessive price in the hope that somebody will come along, fall in love with the house, and pay it? It is certainly possible to make a valuation on such a basis. If you ask three different estate agents what they think is a sensible asking price, you may get three widely differing views, because there is a strongly subjective element in the answer. If one estate agent personally dislikes the house and what you have done to it, he will find it difficult to put the highest valuation on it. Do you know what your house might fetch if, unfortunately, you were forced to make a quick sale in poor market conditions in order to raise cash as quickly as possible? If your insurance company asked the value of your house, meaning the cost of rebuilding it if it burned down, would you know the answer?

The point of this discussion is to emphasize that although the house does not change, the valuation of it can vary widely according to the circumstances and

conditions put forward. Any valuer, therefore, if he is to give you a meaningful and realistic answer, must be fully briefed as to the purpose of the valuation and the circumstances surrounding it. He will be in touch with general market trends, but he needs proper details to be able to work from these to a particular answer for your case.

Fine art valuations

Fine art valuers face special problems which make their job particularly difficult. The art market is very small and very volatile. General valuers have to keep in touch with many different markets – furniture, Continental porcelain, Chinese ceramics, silver, carpets, and so on – all of which may be behaving differently or moving in opposite directions. Some markets are so small that they may be supported by a single buyer, and that buyer may cease to be active overnight. The valuer has to be a judge of subjective quality, for as pointed out in Chapter 6, two works by the same artist may have values differing by a multiple of many times simply because one is an attractive and popular example, and the other not. Fashion also has a very strong influence on the market. Most difficult of all, the valuer has to make judgements on authenticity. No one asks an estate agent to say whether a house is genuine – it is enough that it exists – but a fine art valuer may have to decide whether a painting is by Rubens, or his assistants, or his workshop, or a contemporary copy, or a later copy, or even a fake or forgery, before he can put a value on it. And if the attribution is wrong it follows that the value put on it is also wrong, regardless of any other consideration.

Types of valuation

Informal valuations can be either verbal or written, and are for the benefit of the owner. Usually they are made in the anticipation of sale, or as an encouragement for the owner to sell. A wise owner should be level-headed about such a valuation, especially if it is accompanied by any sort of pressure to sell. The temptation is obviously to give the business to the person who recommends the highest valuation, but this is not necessarily the best decision. If the opinion is supported by a cheque, that is obviously ideal, but it has unfortunately sometimes been the policy of people who are competing for objects to sell on commission or at auction to suggest an unrealistically high valuation initially in order to secure the business. Once the owner is committed, he then finds that as the object fails to sell, or as the date of the auction approaches, the valuer whittles

(*Left*) **Richard Dadd: Contradiction – Oberon and Titania.**
(*Right*) **Richard Dadd: Titania Sleeping** (*detail*). *Volatile markets present valuers and collectors with difficult decisions. The examples here and overleaf reflect prices between March and June 1983. Dadd and Tissot are both artists whose work had fallen out of favour until relatively recently (see also p. 78).* Contradiction – Oberon and Titania *was sold at Sotheby's in March for £550,000 ($825,000), a record price for any Victorian painting. However, in June* Titania Sleeping *failed to sell at Christie's and was bought in at £32,000 (only later works, painted when Dadd was insane, are currently sought after by collectors).*

(*Left*) **J. J. Tissot: Reading a Book.**
(*Right*) **J. J. Tissot: The Garden Bench.**
The two works illustrated here appeared in the same Christie's sale on 24 June 1983. The Garden Bench *established a new record for a Victorian painting by selling for £572,000 ($858,000).* Reading a Book, *on the other hand, was bid to only £12,000 ($18,000), and two other works by Tissot failed to reach their reserve (see p. 76).*

down the initial valuation with various plausible excuses to a realistic level at which a sale could take place. The poor owner scarcely knows whether to believe the excuses or bear the additional trouble and expense of taking the business elsewhere and starting again. The answer is to take the business to individuals or organizations with a reliable reputation in the first place, not to be seduced by over-optimistic talk, and finally if the suggested value still seems surprisingly high to ask for it to be supported by a cheque or by a firm written commitment to undertake the sale for not less than a certain price within a certain time limit.

Formal valuations are produced in written form and contain a carefully worded certificate stating the purpose for which they are executed. They are usually required for taxation, legal and insurance purposes, and will be used by those institutions and officials as well as by the owner and his professional advisers. Clearly, a great deal may hang on the accuracy and balance of such valuations, and the reputation and authority of the valuer who makes them. They can be made for single items, or for whole collections, in which case they may run into several volumes, since each item is separately described.

Bases of valuation   The cornerstone of the valuer's pricing scale is 'current market value': what an object might fetch on the open market (i.e. at auction) in normal circumstances. Indeed, one statutory definition is 'the price which it [the object] might reasonably be expected to fetch if sold on the open market'. The grey area in this legal definition is to know what 'reasonably' means in the context of markets which are so often volatile, subjective and difficult to predict.

'Current market value', or 'fair market value', is the basis used for most tax calculations, or where there is a division of property in divorce proceedings, or where chattels are distributed voluntarily or by court order between members of a family. It will also be used when a valuation is asked for on the basis of 'willing buyer and willing seller' (or 'willing and knowledgeable buyer and willing and knowledgeable seller'). Given the wide range of prices that a willing buyer might buy at, or a seller sell at, this is one of the most demanding situations for a valuer,

especially if he knows that a sale is likely to take place as a result. Rather than ask a single valuer to come to an answer, each party should obtain their own independent valuation and negotiate over any difference.

Some tax legislation now requires a retrospective valuation, which means that the valuer has to say what the value would have been at a certain date, perhaps as much as twenty years earlier. The difficulties of agreeing this hypothetical figure need hardly be emphasized.

Insurance valuations are discussed in Chapter 10.

Choosing a valuer, and the cost of valuations

If a collection has been formed with the help of a dealer, he is the obvious person to turn to for a valuation, particularly if it is required for insurance purposes. He will not only be aware of current prices in his specialized field; he will also know the scale of profit margin to be included in calculating replacement value. In the case of an inherited collection or a wide-ranging group of works of art it is probably advisable to turn to one of the major auction houses with their many experts, comprehensive records and up-to-date knowledge of international prices.

Most auction houses and dealers will give a free verbal valuation, hoping that if a sale does result they will be rewarded with the business. Formal valuations are not free. As well as being very time-consuming to prepare, the valuer, in the certificate, is putting his professional reputation on the line on behalf of the owner, and a fee is the price for such a commitment. Most British firms calculate fees on a percentage basis, often on a sliding scale, so that if for instance the total value is £50,000, they might charge $1\frac{1}{2}$ per cent on the first £10,000 of value, 1 per cent on £10,001 to £30,000, and $\frac{1}{2}$ per cent thereafter, resulting in a fee of £450. The sliding scale is usually preferable to the fixed percentage basis; in the above example a flat 1 per cent charge on the total of £50,000 would have resulted in a fee of £500. However, the percentage basis can be abused and lead to the inclusion of inflated values and unnecessary details. It can also prove inequitable in a situation where there are a few very expensive items to be valued. As a result some organizations (including Christie's) are prepared to quote on a time basis, and this may well prove a more economical method of having a valuation made. It is therefore advisable to make inquiries about charges and fees before embarking on what can prove to be a costly exercise.

In the United States many appraisers also charge hourly or daily rates, regarding the practice of basing the fee on a percentage of the total valuation as unethical because the appraiser may be inclined to overvalue the collection, thus guaranteeing himself a larger fee. Over-inflated values can result in higher insurance premium payments, a tax-audit if the object is donated to a non-profit-making institution for a tax deduction, or high taxes in an estate valuation.

Is a valuation necessary?

There are certain circumstances where a valuation is required by law (for example where an estate has to be valued after a death), and certain situations where it may be unavoidable (for example where property is in dispute in divorce proceedings). In the United States valuations, or appraisals, may also be required when taking out an insurance policy or when donating an item or collection to a tax-exempt institution, in exchange for which the collector may claim a tax deduction.

Most collectors probably have a fairly shrewd idea of the value of their objects, and if they are active buyers or sellers they obviously should follow their market closely. Thus they are in as good a position as anyone to make an informal valuation, and need turn to the experts for a second or written opinion only if there is a particularly difficult attribution to discuss, a rare piece to value, or if other circumstances make a formal valuation advisable. In this regard practice differs markedly between the United Kingdom and the United States. The general advice given to United Kingdom collectors is to avoid formal valuations unless they are absolutely necessary. They are expensive and they carry risks. A comprehensive written document which details exactly what you own and where it is could be embarrassing or dangerous if it fell into the wrong hands, especially if each item is given a financial value. As has been pointed out, valuing is an imprecise art at best, and the figure arrived at depends on many factors. But once a valuation is committed to paper in formal language it is very difficult to escape from. With hindsight, a valuation may be seen to have been over- or under-optimistic, but it would be a long and virtually impossible task to persuade a government department or insurance company or lawyer or accountant to disregard it. Markets do change very quickly, and a valuation made unnecessarily at what turned out to be the peak or floor of prices could be most unfortunate and expensive.

Despite the risks inherent in having a formal valuation or appraisal, Americans have, by contrast, come to depend on these written documents. Many insurers will not cover fine art or decorative art unless an appraisal is provided by the collector. From the collector's point of view, if there is no appraisal in the insurer's files, making a claim can be even more difficult and prolonged than if an appraisal whose values both the insurer and the collector agreed to is present. Another consideration is that because tax regulations changed in 1982, collectors are no longer allowed to claim tax relief after a theft or loss unless the value of the items listed exceeds $10,000. Even then, only the amount above $10,000 is tax-deductible. Because the governmental agency that reviews such claims, the Internal Revenue Service, is not staffed by art experts, claims made without the benefit of an appraisal are automatically negotiated downwards, regardless of the property lost.

Part III
BUYING
AND
SELLING

12
SALEROOM PROCEDURE

The Auctioneer hits his thumb.
Cartoon from the London Evening News.

An auction is a competition in which the auctioneer puts goods up for sale and the buyers compete against each other until there is a winner. As in all competitions there is a genuine element of excitement and unpredictability which attracts the saleroom *habitué* time after time. Auctions have a very long history. Herodotus describes the Babylonian custom of selling village maidens in marriage at an annual auction. Certainly they were known to the Romans, who used them for a wide variety of public and private sales, including slaves and military booty.

The most familiar system of auction sales today is for the auctioneer to take bids from his audience, calling out the bids as he takes them, and – in fine art auctions – announcing the winning bid by the decisive smack of his ivory hammer. This procedure is, and has been, subject to variations. In the Dorotheum in Vienna they have two auctioneers calling out the bids, and one of them rings a bell. In Amsterdam in the seventeenth century the auctioneer struck a copper bowl with a ring on his finger. There have been 'candle stick auctions', in which the auctioneer set up an inch of lighted candle, the last person to bid before the fall of the wick becoming the purchaser. In a 'Dutch auction' property is offered at successively lower prices until one is accepted.

A saleroom is simply a market place, an open method of buying and selling. Newcomers who sit rigid, listening intently to the auctioneer and petrified that an indiscreet nod or blink may buy them a priceless piece of Ming, need not fear, since the last thing an auctioneer wants to do is knock down a lot to someone who does not want it. His job is to match willing sellers and willing buyers, which is why the publicity offices of the auction houses ensure that specialists and collectors the world over know what is for sale and when.

Thus an auction room is a place to sell and a place to buy, and the procedure can best be considered under these two separate heads.

A seller with a portable object takes it to the auction house where a free opinion and valuation will be given by an expert at the reception area or 'front counter' (although some auction houses, including those in the United States, have viewing rooms where experts will discuss the property with the collector in private). Because the auction market has become enormously popular in North America appointments are almost necessary to ensure speedy service and a meeting with a top-level expert rather than one of his assistants. If the object is considered suitable for sale it can be entered at that moment. A form is filled in which includes details of insurance and valuation as well as a description of the article and the vendor's name and address. In the United States, a separate contract, which is usually lengthy and elaborate, must be signed as well. The vendor should check thoroughly what charges are made by the auctioneer. As well as his commission there may well be charges for insurance, photographs and other incidentals.

Once an article has been accepted, it is stored until either a suitable scheduled sale takes place or enough lots for a specialized sale in a particular category have been amassed, which should not normally be more than a few weeks or at the most a few months. Each object is then catalogued, collated and given a lot number. When the catalogue is printed a copy is sent to each vendor or consignor in the sale, and the rest are sent to subscribers and potential buyers all over the world. Some catalogues include an estimated market price for each lot. Because of the time needed to prepare an elaborate catalogue, this whole process usually takes a minimum of two months and often a good deal longer. The less elaborate

Selling:
basic procedure

Edwin Long: The Babylonian Marriage Market (*Egham, Surrey, Royal Holloway College, University of London*). *This famous Victorian painting illustrates an account by Herodotus of village maidens being auctioned for marriage. The artist made preliminary studies at Christie's saleroom and the figure on the rostrum is based on Thomas Woods, who was then Christie's leading auctioneer. The painting was sold at Christie's in 1882 for nearly £7,000, a record price at the time for a work by a living artist.*

the catalogue and the less research needed to properly identify and describe the article, the less time needed to get it into a sale. If time is an important factor to the seller he should ask the auction house expert when the object will be sold. Major auction houses publish their programmes of specialist sales months in advance.

Once an object has been sold the owner has nothing to do but await the cheque which will be the sale price minus the auctioneer's commission and other charges. The waiting period is from a couple of weeks to a little over a month to allow for collection from the buyer.

Selling: variations on basic procedure

Non-portable objects: if a piece is too large to move, valuers will go to private houses to view and give valuations. This of course also applies to large collections, or indeed the entire contents of a house. In such cases once the valuation has been completed an inventory will be drawn up and arrangements made for packaging and transportation to the saleroom.

If a house is large enough, and if the contents prove to be of sufficient value, a sale on the premises or house sale may be recommended. This is a highly skilled operation, which buyers and auctioneers alike enjoy immensely. Specialists will descend on the house to compile the catalogue and make the necessary arrangements for such matters as car parking, marquees and so on. The work involved is enormous. The cataloguers and the administrative team will be based in the house for a number of days, depending on the size of the sale, and will often be accompanied by photographers and by porters to rearrange things. There is nothing quite like a good house sale to generate excitement in every single department and among a broad range of buyers.

(Above) **A sale at Christie's Great Rooms in St. James's, London, 27 June 1983.** *The auctioneer, John Lumley, is taking a bid at £890,000 on the Miró painting which is directly to his right. The painting was eventually sold for a record price of £961,200 ($1,480,248). Further to his right members of Christie's are watching for bids, or taking bids over the telephone (the painting was in fact sold to a telephone bidder). To his left at a desk are the sales clerks who keep a record of all transactions during the sale.*

CATALOGUE

OF THE

CONTENTS

OF

STOWE HOUSE,

NEAR

BUCKINGHAM;

Which will be Sold by Auction, by

Messrs. CHRISTIE and MANSON,

ON THE PREMISES,

On TUESDAY, AUGUST 15th, 1848,

AND EXTENDING OVER

THIRTY-SEVEN DAYS,

Commencing at Twelve o'clock precisely each Day.

PRICE FIFTEEN SHILLINGS.

TO ADMIT A PARTY OF FOUR, WITHOUT WHICH NO PERSON CAN BE ADMITTED.

[For particulars of Catalogue, see next page.

(Left) **Catalogue of the Stowe House Sale, 1848.** *The sale lasted for 37 days – the longest house sale on record – and dispersed the collection of the Duke of Buckingham and Chandos. Special trains brought crowds of visitors from London. A total of 6,480 lots were sold, indicating a much more leisurely pace than at sales today.*

Regional representatives: most major auction houses have a national and international network of representatives and regional offices. These have general rather than specialized expertise, and they will, if appropriate, obtain an opinion from the experts and arrange for transport, insurance and all documentation so that the object can be sent to the most suitable saleroom with the minimum inconvenience to the vendor.

Reserves: when an article is valued for sale an auction house will usually advise a client whether to put a reserve price on it, which means the price below which the owner does not wish it to be sold, and below which the auctioneer will not sell. All reserves are a matter of complete confidentiality between the client and the auction house, and are not published or revealed in any way even during the auction. You may decide not to place a reserve on the item and ask the auctioneer to sell using his discretion, in which case he will be guided by his own judgement or the estimated market price published in the catalogue. Alternatively you may well say you want to sell at any price. It is always complicated, and generally illegal, for an owner to bid on his own lot where a reserve price has been agreed.

In most auctions other than perhaps fine art sales a large proportion of the sale is sold without reserve or with the auctioneer's discretion. The market usually ensures that most lots do reach their value, even when sold without reserves.

Buying in: if the lot does not reach its reserve price it is 'bought in', and a small commission is generally payable. 'Bought in' means that the auctioneer has acted on behalf of the vendor and bought in or retained the piece for the vendor because the bidding did not reach the agreed reserve. If the vendor is agreeable, the lot can usually be re-entered in another sale with a lower reserve; if not, then it is available for retrieval by the vendor after the first sale.

**Buying:
basic procedure**

If you are interested in buying at auction study the catalogue carefully, including the terms and conditions as well as the descriptions of the objects, and examine carefully the object that you wish to buy. The obvious advice 'look before you buy' and 'read the catalogue' is covered in detail in Chapter 13. All too often the

The Chanel Sale (*2 December 1978*). *The photograph shows the Chairman of Christie's, John Floyd, selling clothes from the collection of the famous couturier, Coco Chanel. The saleroom was suitably decorated for the occasion, with models displaying the clothes as in a fashion show.*

advice is not followed, and the buyer has only himself to blame for not doing so.

Once you have decided to try for one or several lots, you must be prepared. Ask how fast the auctioneer proceeds. Although the average is 80–100 lots an hour, there can be a vast difference. Position yourself in good time in a place visible to the auctioneer and concentrate. You should ensure at all times that your bid has been accepted, and the simplest way to do this is with a positive wave of the catalogue, which will normally be acknowledged.

In the United States and some United Kingdom salerooms auctioneers require buyers to register for and bid with 'paddles' more and more frequently. Paddles are just that – paddles shaped like table-tennis bats, bearing numbers that refer to the client's name, address, and in some instances credit rating. Since one must register for paddles before bidding, it is a good idea to get to the saleroom five or ten minutes early to sign up.

Once you have 'caught the eye' of the auctioneer he will usually continue to accept your bids as well as those of one other. In this way you bid alternately, which is the easiest and fairest way. It does, however, tend to frustrate others attempting to bid, but the auctioneer will have noticed them, and as soon as one of you drops out he will turn to the others to inquire by gesture or a remark if they wish to continue bidding; when he has finally ensured that there are no further bids he brings the hammer down. Bidding is simple provided you ensure that the auctioneer has seen your bid. Even if he is accepting other bids, he will invariably have seen you and will come back to you, and even if he doesn't, before dropping the hammer he will inquire of the audience whether there are any more bids.

On the fall of the hammer the auctioneer or his assistant will inquire your name, and, if you are unknown to him, he will ask for your address as well, though at paddle sales the accounting department will already have this information, so you need only tell the auctioneer your paddle number. This action in itself will establish that your bid has been accepted, and depending on the conditions of sale in the catalogue, this is taken as the completion of the contract of sale. Some conditions lay down that the contract is only completed when the lot is paid for.

View from the rostrum. *The photograph shows a busy sale in a crowded room at Christie's South Kensington. It illustrates the importance of bidding clearly and decisively to make sure that a bid is neither overlooked nor confused.*

Having purchased your lot you may then decide to leave the saleroom and call back later for your purchase, or you may decide to postpone collection until the following day; in either case the auctioneer can ask you for a deposit or indeed for the full payment depending on the circumstances at the time. On some occasions you may even be able to pay and clear your goods during the sale. Once again, read the conditions of sale, and, just as important, any notices that may be posted around the saleroom. The price you are required to pay may include a 'premium' over and above the hammer price, but this will have been stated in the catalogue.

Buying: variations on basic procedure

'On the hammer': tensions can run high when a sale is in progress, and it is amazing how often a regular buyer will act like a complete novice by becoming over-excited if he thinks his bid has not been accepted. Do not be put off by this. Stay calm and remember that the auctioneer remains the arbiter of the possible moods, frustrations or indeed elations of the buyer. It can occur that on the fall of the hammer a bidder suddenly realizes he is too late and calls out; if such a case is genuine the auctioneer has the discretion to re-offer the lot. Sometimes the auctioneer notices a bid just as the hammer falls, in which case he will call out, 'On the hammer', and continue the bidding as if it had not fallen.

Establishing credit: if you are unknown to the auctioneer and intend to bid a substantial sum, you should make yourself known to him before the sale and provide suitable bank or credit references. Remember that the auctioneer is not obliged to accept any bid, and the purchaser's ability to pay is just as important as his willingness to bid.

Commission bids: a large number of buyers request the auctioneer to accept and execute bids on their behalf. These are called *commission bids*, or order bids, and they can be made by post or telephone, or left with auctioneer. Often more than one bid will be received for the same lot, and all bids will be in the auctioneer's book. The auctioneer, for instance, may have two separate bids in his book from buyer A and buyer B of £100 and £150 respectively. These written figures are the maximum amounts that the buyers are prepared to spend. The auctioneer's duty in this case is to assume that bid A (£100) is covered and that bid B is to be executed as cheaply as possible (i.e. one bid over £100). Subject to reserve and no other bids being received, the lot is then knocked down to the highest bidder (i.e. buyer B) for say £110. This is when the auctioneer may use the phrase 'against you all'; it simply means that the lot has gone to a commission bid and not to anyone who has been bidding in the saleroom.

Many people see commission bidding as a conflict of interest, but in fact it is a simple arithmetical exercise, which does of course demand the highest integrity and care. At a recent count at Christie's South Kensington saleroom in London, a total of 2,000 bid requests were made and executed in one week, many of these being on behalf of professional buyers. Often specialists and collectors leave bids with the auctioneers as they prefer to maintain anonymity; perhaps avoiding the danger of rivals competing for the sake of it (or because they may assume that the specialist has spotted something they have missed). Mainly, however, bids are left by potential buyers simply for their own convenience. Incidentally, while 'commission bid' is the accepted term, the auctioneer does not in fact make a charge for this service.

'Wrong footing': Suppose you decide that the maximum bid you are prepared to make is £100. It can happen that the object is knocked down for £100, but is nevertheless sold to a rival bidder. This can be infuriating, especially if you have asked someone else to bid on your behalf, but it is avoidable. It occurs for the following reason. Suppose you (let us call you Smith) are bidding against Jones, who is the only other bidder, and that your absolute limit is £100. If the bidding goes as follows you are fine.

Smith	£60	Smith	£80	Smith	£100
Jones	£70	Jones	£90	Jones	No bid

But if the bidding goes as follows, you are in a dilemma, as Jones has bid *your* maximum bid.

Jones	£60	Jones	£80	Jones	£100
Smith	£70	Smith	£90		

The way to overcome this is to set your maximum bid and add 'plus one', that is one more bid just in case the bidding is on the wrong foot. Thus if you are instructing someone else to bid on your behalf, instruct them to bid '£100 plus one' (or £90 plus one if you cannot afford to go over £100). In this way there can be no misunderstanding or recrimination afterwards. There can, of course, still be frustration; if Smith has agreed to bid '£100 plus one', Jones may still get the prize at Smith's maximum of £110 – this possibility cannot be prevented.

The auctioneer has complete control of the sale, including the discretion whether to accept bids or not, and the size of increments between bids. Usually the increments will be in the region of 10 per cent. In a fast run-of-the-mill sale he is unlikely to vary this, as he wishes to get on with the sale smoothly and efficiently. In major sales with highly priced lots he may well accept smaller increments, in themselves substantial, as his duty is to do as well as he can for the vendor.

Advice on bidding

It is easy to get carried away in the excitement of the salroom. Plan your own procedure carefully. Fix your limit and stick to it firmly. Don't kick yourself if you seem to lose a lot for the sake of one more bid. Your rival may have been willing to carry on. As you gain experience you will learn when to come into the bidding. Sometimes it pays to let everyone else have their say, and then come in at the end as a new bidder.

Bidding in the room can be extremely discreet. Many dealers and collectors may want to conceal their interest from rivals, and may have spoken to the auctioneer before the sale and set up a system of code bidding, although this holds many pitfalls. Regular bidders are well-known to auctioneers, who will be aware of the sort of item they are interested in, and may only need a smile or a blink as an indication of a bid, and a slight turn of the head to stop. Even with unknown bidders an understanding can be built up very quickly with an auctioneer so that he will understand the smallest incline of the head, although the question 'Are you bidding, Sir?' will often be elicited if the bidder is being too obscure or difficult.

Most bidders, whether they have winked, nodded, sneezed, scratched or indeed waved, always assume the auctioneer has seen their bid. In a busy auction room, this is of course visually impossible. The majority of bidding misunderstandings relate to what is described as 'in line' bidding: this is when two or more people are directly in line with the auctioneer's eye, and all of them may be convinced that the auctioneer is taking their bid. In this situation the auctioneer will usually re-offer the lot, so that bidding can continue.

In major international sales bids can be telephoned direct to the saleroom. A member of staff in the auction house will tell the bidder what is happening, and relay the bids to the auctioneer. It is possible to arrange an open telephone line for

this, although it is impossible to predict exactly the time when a lot will come up for sale. If it is known that a sale will attract an extra large crowd of buyers and spectators, a second saleroom with a second auctioneer may be set up to accommodate the overflow. Bids in the second saleroom are made to the second auctioneer in the usual way. The main auctioneer is relayed by closed-circuit television and sound to the second saleroom, and the second auctioneer has a microphone link so that he can relay back the bids he is receiving to the auctioneer in charge, or his clerk. It sounds complicated, but in fact is perfectly straightforward, and with modern video technology it can be a very efficient operation.

The auctioneer's role   By the time the auctioneer climbs on to his rostrum, much work has already been completed, and this is the point which will decide whether or not his advice has been correct. The rostrum is the acid test for the auctioneer and the test of his knowledge. In his catalogue in front of him, he will have a note of every transaction he or his colleagues have carried out with regard to values, and very often with as many as three or more different sets of figures for every lot – the reserve, the estimated market price and commission bids.

The auctioneer is generally the senior expert in the department, and will probably have catalogued many of the lots and know many of the owners and potential buyers personally, so that he can deal with any special difficulties that may arise during the sale. At many auction houses, as each successive lot is called a porter will show the object and the auctioneer will open the bidding. As the reserve is normally somewhere below the estimate issued to the public with the catalogue, the auctioneer normally asks the room for a low opening bid. In New York, the reserve cannot exceed the higher estimate.

Occasionally a lot will fail to reach its reserve. There can be many reasons for

(*Left*) **Constantin Guys: Christie's
Saleroom** (*London, Christie's*). *This drawing
by the French artist Constantin Guys
(1805–92) records his visit to Christie's.*

(*Right*) **Eloquence** *or* **The King of Epithets.**
*The cartoon, published in 1782, shows James
Christie in the rostrum, and the caption gives
an example of the eloquence for which he was
famous. In a busy modern auction there is
little time for eloquence, one of the few changes
in procedure between the 18th and 20th
centuries.*

this; an owner's excessive demands, a cataloguer's over-optimism, a sudden and
dramatic drop in the particular market, or simply lack of interest in the object on
the day. The auctioneer can therefore be confronted with a reserve against which
there is only one person bidding. The auctioneer cannot sell the object below the
reserve, so *he* has to bid on the client's behalf, sometimes euphemistically called
'taking bids off the wall', until the sole bidder exceeds the reserve or until he
drops out. In the latter case the object is bought in on behalf of the owner. There is
much misunderstanding about this practice, which leads many to believe that the
auctioneer is simply 'running' them and trying to raise the price falsely, when in
fact the so-called 'bid off the wall' is simply a bid on the owner's behalf. In the
case of an 'owner's bid' to protect the reserve, most people will not be aware of
the absence of a bidder. If however an auctioneer is inexperienced it may well
seem as if he is talking to a pillar, but this is fortunately unusual, and the principal
aim of the auctioneer is to see to the smooth running of his sale. This is his skill.

There is no doubt that both bidder and auctioneer have the ability to turn a sale
into a very boring occasion; the auctioneer can proceed at a snail's pace, hesitate
and confer too often. If a sale of over 300 lots does not proceed at around 100 lots
an hour, there will not be many left in the audience towards the end. A bidder
may correspondingly hold up proceedings by disputing during a sale or always
bidding just as the hammer is about to fall, thus disrupting the rhythm of the sale.
The auctioneer will always try to strike a rhythm as well as retain a suitable
atmosphere during the sale. Trust is an important element in any profession, and
confidence between auctioneer and client – whether buyer or seller – is of
paramount importance.

The auctioneer has a principal duty, and that is to sell on behalf of the vendor.
This duty means that he has a tremendous responsibility, not just to the seller, but
also to the buyer, and he needs to have every faculty working to carry out his

duties properly. A sense of humour is vital as he can receive the backlash of an individual's frustration. He needs to remain cool, but not aloof, in command without being dictatorial, and should a dispute arise, which fortunately is rare, be judge, prosecutor, defence and jury, sometimes with only a split second for consideration. As a general rule he succeeds. The notable exceptions only go to prove that he is after all human and not, as some would have, an automaton without heart or feeling. A reasonable auctioneer will never refuse a reasonable request from buyer or seller. He is bound, however, as all are, by the rules; although in general he will bend as far as he can to maintain an equilibrium between buyer and seller. After all he is an agent, neither selling nor buying in his own right; and on that basis he should not find himself in difficulties.

The reputation of an auction house ultimately rests on the integrity, probity and expertise of the individuals who run it and work in it. Essential qualities are accuracy, honesty, efficiency, impartial advice to sellers and buyers, total confidentiality in all matters both inside and outside the saleroom, and financial soundness. They are high demands, but any auction house which fails to live up to them will lose business to its competitors, and if the auction houses of a particular country fail as a whole in these respects then either business will go elsewhere or the whole market will be weakened. There is an analogy to be drawn with banks, who are expected to maintain the highest standards. One bank in difficulty or with a bad reputation weakens the whole financial system and can have far-reaching consequences, like the ripples from a stone dropped in a pool — as was shown in the financial traumas of the early 1970s.

In this context it must be emphasized that auctioneers are not — or rather should not be — dealers. The reasons are not difficult to see. By acting only as an agent for the vendor, having no ownership of the goods sold, the auctioneer has no conflict of interest. But if he becomes a dealer as well as an auctioneer, and buys objects for his own account in order to sell them at auction with the intention of making a profit, he makes it very difficult — some would say impossible — to maintain the standard of impartial advice that has traditionally marked the best auctioneers, since he has a very partial interest. Furthermore, if the auctioneer through misjudgement makes losses not profits on his dealings, his objectivity towards all vendors, reserves, commission bids and his whole role as an auctioneer may be prejudiced.

A healthy market depends on dealers and auctioneers playing their respective but separate roles. It is certainly in the interests of collectors that they do so, since he requires overall variety, choice, reliability and a free flow of objects and good advice. Monopolies do not create such conditions, nor do mistrust and bureaucratic regulations.

The procedures and practices described in this chapter are those established by the major London auction houses. The procedures are a result of over 200 years' experience in the auction trade, and are followed in all their overseas offices. In broad terms the same descriptions apply to the general practices at smaller and more newly established auction houses that have developed their own systems, although there will be some minor differences. If you are bidding outside your usual area, take care to verify local procedures, and in particular check on commission and taxation rates, which can vary widely. The main reason for the international dominance of the London auction houses is that they provide — and are seen to provide — an efficient, reliable service with highly competitive rates of commission, backed up by a tradition of sound, independent advice and expertise.

13
READING A SALEROOM CATALOGUE & VIEWING SALES

A peep at Christie's – or – Tally-Ho and his Nimmeny Pimmeny taking the morning.
The cartoon shows the Earl of Derby, a keen hunting man, with the famous actress Elizabeth Farren who was his close friend of many years, and later the second Countess. Her nickname Nimmeny Pimmeny comes from her performance of the character Lady Emily Gayville in General Burgoyne's play The Heiress.

uying at auction can be time-consuming, but good preparation by the proper use of catalogues and viewing can save a lot of trouble and make a long journey very rewarding instead of a waste of time. Try to get a catalogue in advance, read it immediately and see if there is anything you may want. If you decide that there is something for you, do any research you may need, check all references that the catalogue gives you and then view the goods on one of the specified days and times at the saleroom.

You should remember that there are two users of a catalogue: it is not merely a buyer's handbook to an auction; it is also a working document of the saleroom staff and for the auctioneer when he needs to conduct the sale. The quality of his catalogues is crucial for the auctioneer. They are the means by which he communicates with the buying public, and every entry in every catalogue reflects his knowledge and professional skill. This skill is shown in the accuracy of the description, in the correctness of judgements about date, attribution, quality and authenticity, and in the soundness of estimates of value. Skill is also required in 'lotting' items together; this applies not just to pairs of pictures or ornaments, sets of chairs or whole or part dinner services, but also to objects that the auctioneer thinks unworthy of an entry of their own. Thus the following entries might appear in a catalogue:

85   A collection of babies' and children's clothes; and a doll's dress (a lot).

199   A whale oil lamp, the cylindrical stem with central drip pan, touch marks on handle, $8\frac{1}{4}$ in. (21 cm.) high; a bulbous Wine Pot, in late 16th Century style, 10 in. (25.5 cm.) high; a Schnabelstitze, touch marks on handle and base, $13\frac{3}{4}$ in. (35 cm.) high; and a Tankard with touch marks on handle, and interior Tudor Rose, $8\frac{3}{4}$ in. (22.2 cm.) (4)

A

CATALOGUE

OF THE GENUINE

Houfhold Furniture,

Jewels, Plate, Fire-Arms, China, &c. And a large Quantity of Maderia and high Flavour'd Claret.

Late the Property of

A Noble PERSONAGE,

(DECEAS'D,)

The Furniture Confifts of Rich Silk Damafk, mix'd Stuff ditto, Cotton and Morine in Drapery Beds, Window-Curtains, French Elbow and back Stool Chairs, a large Sopha with an Elegant Canopy over ditto, Variety of Cabinet Work in Mahogany Rofe-wood, Japan, Tortoifhell, inlaid with Brafs, &c. Large Pier Glaffes, a curious Needle-work Carpet 4 Yards by 5, Turkey and Wilton ditto, fome valuable Jewels, and Plate, &c. Ufeful and ornamental Chelfea, Drefden and Oriental China,, a Mufical Spring Clock and Eight-day ditto, fome fine Bronzes, Models, Pictures, &c. &c.

Which will be Sold by Auction

By Mr. CHRISTIE,

At the Auction Room, in PALL MALL, on Fryday next, and the Four following Days.

The whole to be view'd on Wednefday next, and 'till the Time of Sale, which will begin each Day at Twelve o' Clock.

Catalogues to be had at the Great Room as above, and at *Mr. Chriftie's, Caftle-Street, Oxford-Road.*

(*Left*) James Christie's first sale, 5 December 1766.
(*Right*) Christie's saleroom in the Palazzo Massimo Lancellotti, Rome.

The ability to lot together appropriate items is one of the most important skills a cataloguer needs.

The accuracy and quality of catalogues vary enormously, and the only general advice one can give is to read carefully and to be alert. Experience is of paramount importance. It is only by reading catalogues and comparing the descriptions with the objects themselves that you can learn to interpret the phraseology and get a 'feel' for a catalogue. In time you will recognize the strengths and weaknesses of different auction houses in your area of collecting, and know when to be suspicious of a catalogue entry. Does the description sound unlikely, for example? Does a vaguely worded entry perhaps conceal the cataloguer's ignorance? Is the object being over-described to make it sound better than it really is? In the end, practice is the only way to acquire expertise in the art of reading a catalogue.

There are two different levels of cataloguing. There is the simple description which most small, local auctioneers use, and the full description used by the major international auction houses.

Catalogue descriptions

The simple description is usually just that, a literal description of an object, and the information given can be *more or less useful*. The two examples cited above are typical. They identify the objects, and where appropriate give the dimensions. Lot 85 could contain almost anything in any quantity. However, a knowledgeable

collector can glean a good deal of information about Lot 199. There are clearly four items only in the lot, confirmed by the figure (4) at the end of the description. Touch marks are the maker's marks stamped on pewter, akin to a silversmith's maker's mark. Thus the wine pot is likely to be pewter as well. A Schnabelstitze is a spouted German flagon. A collector of pewter might well be encouraged to make a journey to view the lot from the description given.

The cataloguer has to communicate with the unseen and unknown buyer, and, if he is unsure about the identity of an object, he must emulate the fly-fisherman and cast a line over the buyer who may not be sure that he will go to the sale. Be on the lookout for this. The lure can sometimes be slight. In 1982 a mixed lot of textiles in a big but hurriedly catalogued house sale contained 'a cerise [cherry pink] taffeta costume'. Although the cataloguer could not identify the costume, he recognized that it was interesting, and so described the colour and material. An eagle-eyed costume collector realized from that information that the costume might be a rare eighteenth-century uniform of an Esquire of the Order of the Bath, and in fact it was.

Watch out, too, for the entry that seems very improbable. The entry 'A German allegorical etching by Jacob Max Ardell' led a collector 100 miles away into the provinces to find out what it meant. The cataloguer had copied a German inscription on the mount which ascribed the print to 'Jacob Max Ardell' – a German misreading of the name James McArdell, an Irish engraver. The print was in fact by McArdell and turned out to be of great art-historical importance.

Only by viewing a sale can such 'finds' be unearthed, and that means a considerable commitment of time and travelling expenses. But victories are rarely won easily, and whereas there is always the chance that a 'find' or a bargain lurks in a catalogue, so can a disappointment. 'A porcelain figure of a monkey playing a flute' might be from Meissen, but it might also be broken or a much later copy. 'A black and white print of an executioner' could be Prince Rupert's mezzotint worth £20,000 ($28,000) or an illustrated page from a Victorian magazine. Only experience of a particular saleroom can tell whether 'a small group of cups, some with saucers – mixed', 'a small stack of novels' or 'a collection of reproductions – various' is likely to contain the old Worcester coffee cup, a D. H. Lawrence or Evelyn Waugh first edition or a Gould bird print. It varies from firm to firm and object to object. And experience will show that subjects such as lace, gramophones, pewter, 'Old Master' prints and maiolica are ones for which few firms have specialists, and consequently mistakes are more likely to occur.

The full description, on the other hand, is much more precise, and is designed to be helpful to the specialist buyer. In a 1981 Christie's print catalogue, the following entry occurred, and it is worth analysing as an example since it is particularly detailed.

after Sir Joshua Reynolds, P.R.A.

Nelly O'Brien (Lady Mary O'Brien) by J. Dixon (C.S., R.26)

Mezzotint, an undescribed state before Chaloner Smith and Russell's first
  states, with the title space not yet burnished clean and with a scratched letter
  inscription just visible lower right 'J Dixon fecit 1772' (as suggested by
  Hamilton), a fine, rich impression, watermark proprietary, published by
  W. W. Ryland, London 1774, with thread margins or trimmed on the
  platemark, a minor thin spot at the lower left corner, a few unobtrusive
  foxmarks, remains of old tape at the reverse edges.

P.506 × 355 mm

Provenance: The Duke of Buccleuch L. 402

'after Sir Joshua Reynolds, P.R.A.' means that the print is based on a painting by Reynolds, who was President of the Royal Academy. 'Nelly O'Brien (Lady Mary O'Brien)' indicates that the subject of the print, and the picture, are usually referred to as *Portrait of Nelly O'Brien*. J. Dixon is the engraver, and the technique used is mezzotint. 'C.S., R. 26' refer to standard reference books on prints. C.S. is Chaloner Smith, and R. is Russell, both authors of books on mezzotints which list 'states'. The next reference, from 'an undescribed state' to '1772', gives some detail of the appearance of the print and the fact that Chaloner Smith and Russell

Nelly O'Brien, mezzotint by J. Dixon, 1772.

do not describe it. This is important, since a print which is of a previously unrecorded or undescribed state is of great importance to the specialist print collector. Hamilton is the name of another author who wrote a book on prints after Reynolds. The entry then comments on quality, the watermark of the paper, the publisher of the print and the date. There then follows a detailed description of the condition of the print. The P preceding the measurements indicates that these have been taken from the plate mark. The print was once in the collection of the Duke of Buccleuch (who possessed prints of only the best quality), and L refers to another author called Lught who wrote a book listing the 'marks' or 'stamps' that many collectors put on their prints.

A specialist print collector will immediately understand the abbreviated references to the four authors, and will have no difficulty tracking them down (see Chapters 2 and 3). Measurements of prints can be made in a number of different ways, and there will be a note in the catalogue explaining the conventions and terminology that are used. This particular entry has in fact an added interest, since a check in Hamilton's book would show that the cataloguer has actually missed something. Hamilton's note describes the Buccleuch impression of the print – the actual one in the sale; i.e. he does not merely make a suggestion as the cataloguer has thought.

This type of cataloguing is usually the most reliable. An ignorant cataloguer cannot give such information, and once you have your basic knowledge, you can recognize the mistakes a non-specialist makes. You will also have your own ideas and areas of knowledge. However, don't be put off by such errors as names misspelt and ranks and subjects muddled up. The average cataloguer is hired for his knowledge of works of art, not because he understands peripheral subjects such as titles or heraldry. The kind of mistakes that you should watch out for are errors in 'provenance', that is the history of an object. It does not matter if a cataloguer gets a family history wrong, but if he does not recognize famous collections like the Lord Hastings for maiolica or the Lord Londesborough for armour, he is painfully ignorant.

Many facts are not mentioned in catalogues. It is rare for imperfections and damages to be listed, but there are exceptions. The condition of porcelain is usually noted. Books are often 'collated', that is, checked as to completeness of text and illustration; serious damage is often noted as 'o.d.s.' (old damages), or 'a.f.' (sold with all faults), or 'w.a.f.' (with all faults). Major restorations are sometimes noted, as are 'marriages' – that is where different parts of a piece have different origins. The condition of coins and prints is given at the main London rooms as this is of great importance to these collectors. But even here goods in multiple lots are not individually described. When test certificates for gem stones and for archaeological items exist, they are always quoted.

Cataloguing conventions

Over the years conventions as to the way objects and works of art are described in auction catalogues have grown up. In some subjects they are complicated and need to be learned. The conventions described here are those used by Christie's salerooms in the United Kingdom and overseas, and thus vary from the similar though slightly different terms used by other auction houses, and from those used in the United States and other countries. Whenever a convention or particular set of terms is used the catalogue will contain a glossary that explains the meaning of each of the terms, and you should always double check this. The most complicated convention applies to pictures, drawings, prints, miniatures and icons. Consider the following catalogue entry:

LOT 123 MANNER OF CONSTABLE
Landscape with ploughman
With signature and date 1823
18 × 26 ins.

Before running off to the saleroom in the hope of finding a hitherto unrecorded masterpiece, it is important to realize that in the cataloguer's opinion Lot 123 was *not* painted by Constable, was *not* signed by him, and was *not* painted in 1823. The catalogue has used the convention which Christie's print at the front of their catalogue in the following terms:

A work catalogued with the name(s) or recognized designation of an artist, without any qualification, is, in our opinion, a work by the artist. In other cases, the following expressions, with the following meanings, are used:

'Attributed to . . .' in our opinion probably a work by the artist in whole or in part

'Studio of . . .' *'Workshop of . . .'* in our opinion a work executed in the studio or workshop of the artist, possibly under his supervision

'Circle of . . .' in our opinion a work of the period of the artist and showing his influence

'Follower of . . .' in our opinion a work executed in the artist's style but not necessarily by a pupil

'Manner of . . .' in our opinion a work executed in the artist's style but of a later date

'After . . .' in our opinion a copy (of any date) of a work by the artist

'Signed . . .' *'Dated . . .'* *'Inscribed . . .'* in our opinion the work has been signed/dated/inscribed by the artist. The addition of a question mark indicates an element of doubt

'With signature . . .' *'With date . . .'* *'With inscription . . .'* in our opinion the signature/date/inscription is by a hand other than that of the artist

Thus if Lot 123 were a painting by Constable the description would read:

LOT 123   JOHN CONSTABLE RA
Landscape with ploughman
Signed and dated 1823
18 × 26 ins.

In practice the description would certainly be much fuller, and there would be possibly several pages of information about previous owners, places of exhibitions, references in art-historical literature, and its general place in Constable's work as a whole.

Prior to 1983 Christie's and Sotheby's United Kingdom salerooms used a different convention, which is given here in full since collectors using old catalogues will need to be familiar with it. The convention was changed to bring it into line with American and Continental practice, and to facilitate a more precise description of some of the more difficult attributions. For example, problems can arise with an artist such as Rubens, who employed many assistants in a large workshop which also included at one time van Dyck and Jacob Jordaens. A painting from Rubens's workshop might have been, but was not necessarily, executed by Rubens's own hand. Different problems arise with artists such as Cotman or Corot, who on occasions willingly put their signature to paintings executed by other artists. The earlier convention is as follows:

The first name or names and surname of the artist
In our opinion a work by the artist.

The initials of the first name(s) and the surname of the artist, or 'Attributed to' or 'Circle of' or 'Workshop of'
In our opinion a work of the period of the artist and which may be in whole or part the work of the artist.

The surname only of the artist
In our opinion a work of the school or by one of the followers of the artist or in his style.

The surname of the artist preceded by 'After'
In our opinion a copy of the work of the artist.

*This indicates that the conventional term in this glossary is not appropriate but that in our opinion the work is a work by the artist named.

'Signed'
Has a signature which in our opinion is the signature of the artist.

'Bears Signature'
Has a signature which in our opinion might not be the signature of the artist.

'Dated'
Is so dated and in our opinion was executed at that date.

'Bears Date'
Is so dated and in our opinion may not have been executed at about that date.

A comparison of the two conventions shows that the new one allows the cataloguer to express his opinion more clearly.

With ceramics the conventions are simpler, but even so they need careful thought. Consider these taken from a Christie's catalogue. Again they are a new convention introduced in 1983/4, differing slightly from the one previously used.

European Ceramics
A piece catalogued with the name of a factory, place or region without further qualification was, in our opinion, made in that factory, place or region (e.g. 'Worcester plate').

'A plate in the Worcester style'   in our opinion a copy or imitation of pieces made in the named factory, place or region.
'A Sèvres-pattern plate'   in our opinion not made in the factory, place or region named but using decoration inspired by pieces made therein.
'A Pratt-ware plate'   in our opinion not made in the factory, place or region named but near in the style or period to pieces made therein.
'A Meissen cup and saucer'   in our opinion both pieces were made at the factory named and match.
'A Meissen cup and a saucer'   in our opinion both pieces were made at the factory named but do not necessarily match.

'*Modelled by* . . .'   in our opinion made from the original master mould made
by the modeller and under his supervision.

'*After the model by* . . .'   in our opinion made not from the original master
mould made by that modeller but from a later mould based on the original.

'*Painted by* . . .'   in our opinion can properly be attributed to that decorator on
stylistic grounds.

Oriental Porcelain and Ceramics

(a)   A piece catalogued with the name of a period, reign or dynasty without
further qualification was, in our opinion, made during or shortly after that
period, reign or dynasty (e.g. 'a Ming vase').

(b)   A piece catalogued 'in the style of' a period reign or dynasty is, in our
opinion, quite possibly a copy or imitation of pieces made during the named
period, reign or dynasty (e.g. 'a vase in Ming style').

(c)   A reference to a 'mark and of the period' means that, in our opinion, the
piece is of the period of the mark (e.g. 'Kangxi six-character mark and of the
period').

(d)   A reference to a mark without reference to 'and of the period' means that,
in our opinion, although bearing the mark, the pieces were possibly not
made in the period of the mark (e.g. 'Kangxi six-character mark').

(e)   Where no date, period, reign or mark is mentioned, the lot is, in our
opinion, of uncertain date or 19th- or 20th-century manufacture.

So, in a catalogue of Chinese Ceramics, 'A large blue and white dish the base with a
Qian long seal mark in underglaze blue and of the period' indicates that the
cataloguer considers this to be the real thing. The following indicates that he does
not: 'A saucer dish painted in underglaze blue with a basket of peonies $8\frac{1}{2}''$
(21.6 cm). Chenghua, six-character mark'. If the entry read: 'A saucer dish
painted in underglaze blue with a basket of peonies $8\frac{1}{2}''$ (21.6 cm), six-character
marks of Chenghua, Kangxi', it would mean that the cataloguer considers it to
have been made in the reign of Kangxi (1662–1722), although bearing the marks
of the reign of Chenghua (1465–87). (See Chapter 5.)

There are a few other conventions and you will soon grasp them in your field.
Some are a shorthand rather than a special code. Most items are dated. British
silver is dated by a mark, but cataloguers date it also by reign: Queen Anne silver
is more valuable than George I. English furniture and French furniture and silver
are similarly dated by reign. Long reigns like those of Queen Victoria and George
III are often divided into 'Early', 'Mid-' and 'Late', that of the latter monarch more
distinctively by the use of 'Regency' for the last two decades, referring to his son
the Prince Regent. It is common to find 'Regency' used also to refer to the Prince
Regent's reign as George IV (1820–37), though strictly speaking this is an
inaccurate use of the term. In America, furniture is dated by decade if it has not
been significantly altered. Some auctioneers now date all furniture to decade.
Most auctioneers use the general periods: 'Baroque', 'Renaissance', 'Empire' or
'Biedermeier', when applicable, as well as dating the item to a decade or quarter
century. In America 'Queen Anne' and 'William and Mary' can apply to furniture
in these styles, although the American Queen Anne style dates from 1730 to 1760.
Queen Anne was on the throne 1702–14, but in the eighteenth century it took
many years for styles to cross the Atlantic.

When Christie's or Sotheby's describe a piece of furniture as being 'attributed
to Chippendale' they mean that it may have been made by him, but there is no
documentary evidence. However, other London houses, including Phillips, use

the term in its old meaning, as 'in the style of'. The word 'style' in furniture applies to the design but not to the date, and you must check the date. A chair in the 'Director' style may be a late Victorian piece copied from a plate in Chippendale's *Gentleman and Cabinet Maker's Director*, published in 1754. If you are in any doubt about a convention, or the meaning of any entry, ask the saleroom staff for an explanation. You will have only yourself to blame if you don't. You must of course also learn the extensive vocabulary used to describe the appearance of antiques, for example cabriole legs, brisée fans, guilloche patterns, encrusted rims, remarques; as well as the foreign words used, for example inro, faience, vignette, Hausmaler and Susani (see Chapter 2).

The more important pieces in sales often have prefixes like 'The property of a Gentleman'. This explains that the piece does not belong to a dealer and has probably not appeared on the market for some years. Variations include '. . . of a Nobleman', '. . . of a member of a European Royal House', '. . . of a Lady', and '. . .

Titania's Palace. *Christie's have sold the entire house and contents of Titania's Palace on two occasions – their most unusual house sale. It is a palace in miniature, measuring 9ft × 7ft × 2ft 3ins, with 16 rooms all fully furnished and equipped and lit by electricity. The palace was conceived by Sir Nevile Wilkinson in 1907 for his daughter, and since 1922 it has travelled the world to raise money for the welfare of children. It was last sold at Christie's in 1977 for £135,000 ($236,250).*

of a Lady of Title'. When the name is used, as in 'The property of the Duke of Omnium', the name will become part of the provenance or history of the piece. Sometimes the named and anonymous are mixed, as in 'The property of a Lady, from the collection of the late Berkeley Paget'. 'Various properties' or no specific heading simply means that the lots which follow come from a variety of different sources. American usage includes more variants like 'Property from the estate of . . .' or 'Property of a Baltimore collector', but rarely includes 'Gentleman' or 'Lady'. The only time when details of the source have to be given is when a pawnbroker sells pledges: he has to give the number of his pledge. It is common to mention that goods are sold subject to a court repossession order if this is the case, especially for cars. In minor sales, owners' names are rarely mentioned. Interesting incidental history is usually recorded in footnotes: thus 'given by the artist to the vendor's father, his barber'.

Specialist sales

The main British and American auctioneers divide their sales into specialized categories. The obvious divisions of Pictures, Furniture, Ceramics, Textiles and so on are often subdivided. Thus there are separate sales for Old Master Paintings, old Master Drawings, old Master Prints, for example, though even they may be mixed as in 'Modern paintings and drawings'. You have to check which type of sale would contain pictures that interest you. With some experience, you will be able to choose your sales from the lists published well in advance of the catalogues. You can then decide to subscribe to the catalogue that you want. This saves you bother, and sometimes money. More importantly, you get your catalogue sooner. Most big auction houses divide their sales into *Important* and *Routine*, the latter now often called *Fine* for no apparent reason. Items are sometimes included in a particular sale in a way which at first sight might seem unpredictable. In fact there will be a good reason, and you should watch out for this. Thus tapestries are often included in furniture sales, since they are often bought by furniture collectors and dealers, and if some important tapestries are put in an *Important* furniture sale, lesser tapestries may also be put in. Your collecting field may also cross a boundary. Fine drawings for book illustrations may appear in drawing or in book sales, sometimes in the same week at the same auctioneer's.

Provincial and continental auctioneers tend to have fewer specialized categories, and often have bigger sales. Unlike the large London or New York houses a small auctioneer rarely has more than six specialist cataloguers. The Continental auctioneer usually sends out one big mixed catalogue every few months.

House sales

A house sale on the premises usually has a great diversity of goods ranging from major tapestries to bed linen and flower pots. As these are often catalogued by a small team, there is always a faint chance that something has been missed; but you will soon find that goods tend to sell for more than their normal price. There is usually a lot of publicity, and if the house is famous or grand there will be many 'trippers' or local residents anxious to carry away, at almost any price, a relic of the Great House.

Estimates

Most large auctioneers publish estimates of probable prices in their catalogues. These are only a guide, and, even if the cataloguer is good, must be treated with caution. If the estimate seems low, look again at the condition. If it seems high, don't be tempted to bid more than your own estimate of the price: the valuer may be over-optimistic. But by the same token do not be dissuaded from bidding. It is said that every sale has a bargain, and it is maddening to miss something by being too timid. Remember also that the valuer may be a specialist in some other, but similar, field and you, therefore, may know more than he does. If you want something badly, be prepared to pay a high price. If it completes a set, it is far more valuable to you than to anyone else. It is easy to be put off by an estimate when the cataloguer does not know what the goods are, or if they are too rare for him to know the value. In 1974 a fourteenth-century Japanese pottery vase was sold in London. It was correctly described, but the estimate was very low – £40–£60. It was spotted by a museum keeper who raised as much as he could. Unfortunately for him a Japanese dealer also saw it in the catalogue and flew over and bought it for £750. In Japan it could have been expected to make about £10,000.

When the auctioneer is unsure of just how much an item may sell for, he may give the estimate as 'refer department', or 'Ref Dep'. This is an invitation to serious buyers to contact the department or auctioneer in question. Although the auctioneer will know what prices comparable things have fetched in the past, the valuation of extremely rare or valuable objects is particularly difficult, and the auctioneers will often prefer to discuss likely prices with serious potential buyers rather than publish his informed guesswork, which might be inaccurate to a large degree and even conceivably put buyers off. With the most valuable objects, the potential buyer will probably want a private viewing and discussion with the auctioneer anyway.

Miscataloguing   The general advice given about estimates applies also to miscatalogued goods. If they are underrated, try to use your knowledge. If you don't want them you

Wine tasting at a Christie's sale, prior to the auction.

probably have a friend who does. If you think an item is overrated, don't bid above your own estimate of its worth. If you believe that something has been wrongly catalogued and you know the auctioneer or expert, he will certainly appreciate it if, in the right spirit, you tell him what your feelings are. If you have bought something and after the sale discover that it is in your opinion not as catalogued you should also approach him. The sale will of course have been governed by conditions of sale (see Chapter 16), and you will have to agree a course of action with him. Make sure that you have all your evidence and that your facts are right, and that you approach the auctioneer tactfully.

Reading the small print

If you are in doubt about anything, you can ask a friend or a dealer for advice. If you ask a dealer, he will expect you to leave your bid with him. He is probably more experienced than you and can sometimes get the goods cheaper. There is more to bidding than lifting your hand. He can tell when to bid quickly to frighten off a rival, and when to bid slowly to tire him out. He will know when he is being 'run up' by someone else who is not a serious bidder and he can shake him off. For this service he will charge a commission of 5–10 per cent. When you have decided to bid yourself, re-read the small print at the front of the catalogue. Find out if there is a 'buyer's premium'. This is a percentage charged by the auctioneer *over and above* the bid price. The conditions often state that a part of the purchase price will be demanded at the time of the sale. This is not normally enforced, but it is best to clear your credit before the auction, so that you can collect as soon as the sale is over. Check storage charges and collection dates. These are more usually enforced, especially with furniture and goods from house sales. If the lots you are interested in are not at the beginning of the sale, find out the speed of the auctioneer or you may be late   or early. Finally, make sure you have packaging materials if you are buying in quantity. There may be a supply of boxes, newspaper and plastic bags, but the auction house will appreciate it if you bring your own, and in any case the goods are usually at your own risk as soon as they are knocked down to you.

Viewing

Viewing sales ought to be a pleasure not a duty. As well as the excitement of seeing the lots previously noted in the catalogue you may well notice things you would otherwise have overlooked, perhaps something outside your normal field of collecting. It may also provide an opportunity to meet other collectors or dealers and exchange opinions and information.

You must check viewing times and try to view as early as possible so you can do any further research you need. As most auctioneers disclaim liability for both attribution and condition, a long and thorough study of the objects is essential, except, perhaps, for the most experienced collector. If asked, the auctioneer will report on condition and will often explain the reason for his attributions, but it is still up to the collector to make his own assessment of these opinions. You must remember that value judgements such as 'good condition' are personal and based on experience, but soon you will be more experienced than many auctioneers. If you see something on view that is likely to get damaged, tell a porter. This is not just courtesy, it could be the item you are interested in that gets damaged next time. Similarly examine all items with care. You may ask a porter to get a drawing out of its frame for you to handle; you may open a watch; you may 'ping' china. Do all these gently, presuming the item to be in bad condition, for you are liable for any damage you do (see Chapter 8).

14
DEALERS

Rembrandt: Clement de Jonghe (*etching*). *Clement de Jonghe was a print dealer working in Amsterdam from 1640 to 1679. His 'address' is constantly found on impressions of prints executed by Dutch artists of the period.*

A story told about Joseph Duveen (1869–1939), who ranks as one of the most successful dealers of all time, concerns an erotic nude by the late nineteenth-century French painter Adolphe Bouguereau. It was not a great work of art, but it had an obvious appeal. Duveen was the man who built up the collections of the American millionaire collectors – Andrew Mellon, Samuel Kress, J. P. Morgan, the Widener family – men and women with an appetite for art and long cheque books but no particular education in the arts. When introduced to a new customer Duveen would show him the Bouguereau and invariably sell it to him. Before long, however, the appeal of the picture would begin to wear thin, and the customer would return seeking something better. Duveen would buy back the now despised painting, sell the customer something of greater artistic merit, and keep the Bouguereau for the next client who needed to be started on the collecting ladder. Thus with infinite patience he educated his customers, guided their taste – sometimes to the point where they could not buy their cutlery without seeking his approval – and made a great deal of money. Duveen did not do anything unusual. He offered a service, and built up a profitable business. It was only the scale of his achievement that was remarkable; the quality and quantity of the works he dealt in, the wealth of his clientele, the detail of his service, his style, and the profits he made. The point of the story is to highlight the fact that all dealers should have the twin aims of providing a service and building a profitable business.

This chapter will be mainly concerned with antique dealers, although most of what is said applies with equal force to other dealers in the arts. All have one thing in common. None of them provides the collector with the necessities of life. Art and antiques make life more agreeable, but they do not cause it to exist. Nor are their services essential as are those of the lawyer, doctor, car mechanic, or undertaker. They deal in unusual objects which cannot be valued by reference to standard volumes, weights or regulated prices. Dealers in contemporary art are in a somewhat unusual position since often they do provide the necessities of life for the artists and craftsmen they represent; and a conscientious contemporary dealer will take time and trouble to encourage and look after an artist so that his work can have the best opportunity to flourish.

Antique dealers

Antique dealers are not a professional group in the sense that lawyers or architects are. There are no exams to pass or minimum qualifications demanded for anyone setting up business. There are professional bodies which require certain standards and discipline members who stray from their code of practice, but membership of them is voluntary. (A list of dealers' organizations and of directories of dealers will be found in Appendices 2 and 3).

This chapter will attempt to summarize the different types of antique dealers and answer some of the questions most commonly asked about them. But it must be stressed that it is impossible to lay down absolute rules, since antique dealers are all individualists. In a recent interview John Partridge, a leading British dealer, expressed his attitude graphically. 'If you're going to be in this business you must choose to be in it. You must have a natural flair and ability with people ... You can't come into it, after all, thinking you're going to make a fortune ... You can make a decent living, it's true, but obviously if I sold all my stock and put the money on deposit, I'd be a lot richer – and a lot more miserable. No, you have to love it, love the people you employ, love the people you meet and love the works of art. You have to be dedicated. You have to be tough minded. You have to be determined' (interview in *The Connoisseur*, January 1983).

Assessing an antique dealer

Thousands of successful transactions between trade and public are concluded every day, but unfortunately dealers only make headlines when there has been some scandal or upset. Recent years have seen a massive 'exposure' of the antiques trade. Stories of dramatic 'rings' – groups of dealers who depress prices by withholding bids by agreement – ruthless 'knockers' who underpay, and general malfaisance have all been gleefully reported on television and in the press, and there have been plenty of books, some specialist but mostly repetitive, which have perpetuated the myths and claimed unjustified inside knowledge of trade behaviour. Of course, everyone enjoys stories of malpractice, and tales of unexpected fortunes found in attics. But these stories do not present a realistic and accurate picture of the reputable dealer, and can lead to unfounded suspicion.

An antique dealer when meeting a new client will have two objects in mind: one is obviously to sell to him; the other is to consider his customer as a potential source of merchandise. The dealer may buy at auction, but unlike the normal shopkeeper he cannot rely upon a manufacturer or wholesaler for his stock. He must always be on the lookout for new sources to find what are known in the trade as 'virgin goods', items that have never been seen on a regular trade circuit. Thus, approaching a dealer is not the prelude to a battle but merely the establishing of contact. And that, for most members of the public, will be through a shop. Assess the location, arrangement, stock and atmosphere of a shop carefully, for most of them express the personality of their owners. Seek out the active or busy ones that have a look of permanence, the ones that move their stock, take an interest in their clients and welcome new ones. You can draw many conclusions from simply entering a dealer's premises. Look around. The man who cares for his pieces usually looks after his clients well.

Mode of reception is revealing, more so than is often realized. An effusive descent and an assault of pattering salesmanship contrast strongly with a comfortable acceptance of your presence and an assurance that if you require assistance you have only to ask. One could be forgiven for wondering whether sharks are not more prone to patter than most.

There are always things to discuss in an antique shop. You can ask about

(*Left*) **Joseph Duveen.** *Sir Joseph Duveen, later Lord Duveen, dominated the international art market in the decades before the Second World War, from his headquarters in New York.*

(*Right*) **Interior of Agnew's Bond Street galleries.** *Agnew's galleries in Bond Street, London, have recently been restored to appear as they were in 1877, and as shown in this watercolour of the period. They were the first purpose-built dealer's gallery in London. Agnew's pioneered modern large-scale dealing in pictures and prints, their stock ranging from modern British painting to Old Masters.*

pieces, periods, timbers, materials, or anything that interests you, and the real enthusiast will be sure to take you up. If you get no response, don't bother.

Don't try to be clever. The half expert displaying his little knowledge is a menace in the dealer's world. Today particularly, with too many volumes of ready-made expertise on every bookshelf, with so many sources of rehashed hearsay on the media, first-hand experience and long-time practice arc still paramount, and there are no substitutes. You need to be very sure of your ground before you can safely assume that you know better than a dealer; a few may be charlatans, but they are unlikely to be in business for long.

Don't expect too much at once. Dealers are not angels, and remember that while you are summing up the dealer, he is assessing you. Your personality, taste, social status, living style and bank balance are all being analysed in the dealer's mind when you first meet. As in ordinary human intercourse, you nearly always get out of it as much as you put in. Many lasting friendships blossom from a casual inquiry about a small piece of silver or even that monumental Victorian wardrobe bequeathed by a great aunt. The great majority of dealers are hard-working, honest people seeking to make a living and to establish a reputation. Some know more than others. Most have a preferred field of interest. Only a few are ruthless money grabbers.

Across the world there are a small number of dealers whose names are household words and whose businesses have existed for generations, being passed on to members of the family or a few selected outsiders. Their customers are frequently the national museums and highly experienced collectors. However, do not be intimidated by their august names and premises. Among pieces of museum quality they stock objects well within the reach of ordinary mortals, selected with great expertise as to quality and authenticity. They will be happy to encourage genuine enthusiasm. They often have specialist exhibitions of interest and importance to collectors. Even displays of the finest things should be treated as reasons for hope, rather than despair.

There are a number of large antique shops or antique departments in big stores, but only the largest of these run the danger of becoming de-personalized by

Types of dealer

Betty Parsons. *Betty Parsons was a New York dealer and artist who was one of the original champions of artists such as Jackson Pollock, Barnett Newman, Mark Rothko and Clyfford Still. She ran a gallery from 1946 to 1982, and consciously sought out new and unknown artists. Works from her estate were sold at Christie's in New York in November 1983 for £1,215,588 ($1,823,380), the proceeds to go to establish a foundation to help young artists and to fund undersea research.*

extensive staffs, and in any case you ought to get the service provided by any top-quality retail establishment. Prices and descriptions are usually clearly marked but degrees of restoration may not be noted, particularly if the firm has an 'interior decorator' bias. A decorator is often more concerned with appearance than authenticity, a fact which need only concern you if you have investment in mind. Ask about price reductions if you wish, particularly if you require several items or intend to spend a fortune. There may be a negotiable margin but it is unlikely, as is the discovery of an out-and-out bargain.

The commonest type of antiques business today is probably run by one or two people; a single enthusiast/specialist, perhaps, or a partnership, or a husband and wife team. Sometimes an assistant or secretary holds the fort, but in most cases contact is made directly with a principal. The speciality of the place will be evident from the stock – for example, furniture, porcelain, glass, paintings. So, as a seller, you are unlikely to meet with enthusiasm for your set of chairs from a porcelain man, and equally as a buyer your inquiry about the price of a painting seen unexpectedly in a glass specialist's may produce a bargain, or an extraordinary over-valuation. Your own knowledge must guide you in such a case, for there is no reason for a dealer to have expertise or knowledge superior to yours in a field outside his chosen speciality.

If you wish to dispose of a specialist item, an inheritance perhaps, or an heirloom on which you require to raise money, preliminary inquiry at a dealer's will give you an idea of what to expect. But, in judging the difference between what a dealer will pay, and what he will ask, remember that his knowledge has been expensively bought and he has to make a profit to cover his overheads. Remember, too, that dealers are plagued by enthusiastic time-wasters who pick

Watteau: L'Enseigne de Gersaint (*Berlin, Schloss Charlottenburg*). *The Parisian dealer Gersaint commissioned Watteau (1684–1721) to paint this picture as a sign for his shop on the Pont Notre Dame. Even if not wholly true to life it usefully illustrates the many aspects of a dealer's service: a large and varied stock, attentive service, instruction, help with practical matters such as packing, and a relaxed and sympathetic atmosphere.*

their brains, note their prices and then take their business elsewhere. This is one reason why so many defend themselves with coded price tickets. The other main reason for this sometimes annoying practice is that thieves tend to steal the objects with the highest prices marked on them.

Not all dealers specialize, although most have an inclination. General dealers stock furniture and the accessories to dress it up. This may include anything from carpets to paintings and chandeliers, usually with a preference for a certain period or even timber. There are oak and mahogany men, walnut enthusiasts, satinwood addicts. There are Art Nouveau and Art Deco merchants, Oriental, Continental and Scandinavian specialists, stockists of every period from medieval weaponry to Victorian glass, and such is the freemasonry among the trade that an inquiry of any member of it, once you have established your bona fides, will almost certainly be referred to the particular interested expert whether you wish to buy or sell. The Antique Collectors' Club's *Guide to the Antique Shops of Britain*, published annually, gives approximate details of most stocks in shops throughout the country, and membership listings of various North American dealers' associations note special interests, though these listings provide information about only a small percentage of the dealers in the United States (see Appendices 2 and 3).

There are a number of United Kingdom dealers who operate as wholesalers and shippers, generally from warehouses. Their concern is usually with specialized markets abroad, mainly North America, Australia, New Zealand and South Africa. The Arabian and Japanese markets do not justify exclusive specialization, but large stocks in some otherwise general establishments are set aside for them.

Wholesalers and shippers

Some wholesalers have shopfronts and will entertain the public, but most display 'Trade and Export Only' signs. Involvement in the home market introduces tax complications into their otherwise totally export operation, Value Added Tax not being levied on goods sent abroad. One must realize, too, that such businesses are chiefly concerned with assembling large quantities of objects to fill containers, and understandably they do not welcome what amounts to public interference with an automatic and convenient process. Wholesale lots are based on overall, average quality, ranging from good to mediocre, usually at an average price. Selection of the best by the public would upset the balance.

Permanent markets and antique centres

These centres consist of an assembly of small dealers who rent a few square yards of selling space under the same roof at an economical rate. They have mushroomed over the last ten years, the direct outcome of steeply rising overheads coupled with a gradual reduction of the flow of goods into the system at the lowest level, that is direct from the public. In them, it is possible to see a wide range of things, mainly in the smaller categories such as silver, porcelain, glass, jewellery and the like. Such places are convenient for buyers wishing to accumulate quantity, but from the point of view of the smaller private buyer, while there is certainly variety to see, goods appearing among any group of dealers are never cheap. They tend to change hands incestuously until they have reached the maximum economic price, since adjacent dealers all know each other's potential. Nevertheless, there is much for the aspiring enthusiast to learn in any trade gathering. Dealers are garrulous, inclined to discuss their affairs in public, and it would be a mistake to think that the only reason for visiting any one of them is simply to buy and sell. The exchange of information, expertise and gossip is very much a part of the antiques trade's daily routine.

Fringe, fairs and shows

There is a group of amorphous fringe operators who sit on the sidelines, working for their more established colleagues by 'running' for them, for example tracking down an object to meet a particular requirement, finding customers, delivering items to others, arranging repairs and cleaning, etc. Runners often make more profit than their principals, and do so without any outlay. So take care if, having revealed in a saleroom or to a dealer that you require a specific object, you are approached by a would-be supplier. His approach may be perfectly genuine, but the busy antique dealer doesn't usually have time to listen to tittle-tattle, let alone act on it. The runner today usually works with a particular objective. He may bid for a principal at auction, thus earning a commission. He may latch on to a visitor in a bar or at an airport, directing him to sources where a 'rake off' is reserved for him. He may also ask a fee for his services and charge his passenger for transport. Some shippers employ runners on a regular fee basis to assist their customers in putting consignments together.

Fairs, or shows, are of two types. There are those at which a wide variety of operators assemble for a few days (rarely more than a week), in a hotel or rented hall to display their best merchandise and contact new clients. They come from far afield, even abroad. At such shows, remember that the participants have made heavy outlay to prepare and transport their exhibits and will want to recover their overheads. Thus you will tend to be presented with quality that may be costly, but not necessarily overpriced.

The Grosvenor House Fair and the Fine Art and Antiques Fair at Olympia in June and the Burlington House Fair (for which the date is being renegotiated) are the biggest and best-known events in the British art and antiques calendar. There is also the British International Antique Dealers Fair at the National Exhibition Centre in Birmingham in April. These are professionally organized, offering displays of the finest and rarest as well as catering for more mundane tastes. Large, specialist vetting committees of top experts examine all objects on display and try to ensure authenticity, quality, and accuracy of period attribution. There are many smaller, but nevertheless excellent events across the country throughout the year, of which details are announced in specialist periodicals.

Prominent United States fairs – called shows – operate along the lines of British fairs, with vetting committees of dealers and brutal politics about who is to be represented. Major shows include the East Side Settlement House Show (Winter Antique Show) which is held in late January in New York. The Fall Armory Antiques Show and the Fall Antiques Show on the Pier are well-regarded and well-attended, as they usually take place over the same weekend in New York and attract both antique dealers and collectors from across the nation and from Europe. Another North American show that is gaining significant international attention is the Chicago International Art Exposition, which is held in May and which focuses on contemporary and modern fine arts. Both the number and quality of shows are increasing, and, as in the United Kingdom, there are a large number of good, smaller events around the country during different parts of the year. Spring and autumn remain the main show seasons, however.

The second type of antique fair scarcely merits its title at all. It may be held on a circuit, often for the purpose of raising funds for a charity or political party. Obviously, the things to be found in it are small, since they have to be conveniently transportable. There is always a preponderance of unimportant ephemera at such gatherings, and often a great many insignificant decorative reproductions which have no rightful claim to antiquity at all, although there is usually a handful of interesting, if not expensive, items. It is here that knowledge can identify a bargain, for nobody thinks of vetting. Be amused, but don't take such 'fairs' too seriously.

Profit margins

What is the dealer's mark-up? It is a common enough question to which there is no standard answer. Too many people seem to expect an antique dealer to offer his services and make a living on next to nothing. A financial broker who buys shares or property at the right time and 'cleans up', a greengrocer who buys a consignment of cauliflowers cheap, both are regarded as clever. The seller of an antique item to a dealer often resents the latter's profit. What is forgotten is that without the dealer's expertise and without the specific knowledge to direct it to a certain area where the buyer waits, the item would be worthless. Auctioneers achieve the same objective by assembling specialist competing buyers.

On the other hand, there is no excuse for a dealer to 'steal by buying', that is pay next to nothing for an object just because the owner doesn't understand its worth. But however much the dealer enjoys himself one of the main aims of dealing is still to make a profit. Overheads are heavy; mistakes must be paid for.

Not every purchase will yield the same return, nor is it expected to. Where there is competition among dealers of different types to buy certain popular items that are quick sellers, profit margins will be low. A fine period breakfront bookcase, for instance, would be easy to sell to a dealer at a good price if he has several clients waiting to buy one. He will also be fully aware that if he doesn't pay enough for it you will offer it up the road to the next dealer, who will snap it up. In such a situation he will expect to make a small profit, perhaps as little as 10 per cent if he is using his own money. If he works on an overdraft, he will want a little more. He may well take a very short profit if he is selling on to another dealer, since the transaction will probably be settled on the spot — immediate payment, probably in cash, no after-sale service, and collection by the buyer. That is why you will occasionally be asked if you are 'trade'. The private client must pay for the extra service his status requires. The quid pro quo for good service is prompt payment of accounts, especially in these days of high interest rates.

Profit margins can range between, say, 10 per cent for quick-selling stock objects everyone wants, to 100 per cent or more for things liable to hang fire for months. Slow-selling pieces which, admittedly, may increase their worth with time, must nevertheless pay their keep, and a high mark-up on them is to be expected. A dealer is in business to generate turnover and cash flow, not to lock objects away in the hope that they will appreciate in value. In any case, no profit exists in fact until an object has been sold and turned into cash. With the benefit of hindsight, one can see that certain groups of things, such as Victorian glass, silver spoons, some paintings or a host of so-called 'collectibles' held for, say, twenty years, have appreciated to a degree which makes a dealer's profit look silly. Some have gone up in value a hundredfold or more. So, 'if only I'd kept it' is as familiar a lament in the trade as out of it.

Negotiating a deal

Price in the art market is dictated, as in any business, by supply and demand, with the additional elements of fashion, age, quality and rarity to fog the issue. Of course you may try to negotiate, and your success or failure may well depend upon the degree to which your initial efforts to establish a friendly rapport have succeeded.

As to whether the price is 'right', the matter is largely in your hands. Do you argue price with your tailor? You know you can buy a suit for anything from £50 to £500. You don't try to get the most expensive clothes for the bargain figure, you choose what you can afford and what you judge to be best value for money. However, dealers who have no fixed price tags to their goods tend to be more

open to negotiation than dealers whose wares are marked. If you get the feeling that you're being stung, shop around a little and see what others have to offer. In the case of antiques consult a price guide or ring up one of the main auction houses. Both will give an indication of what you might expect to pay, or be paid if you are selling. But remember always that estimates can fluctuate widely. The antiques market, even more than the stock market, changes from day to day and from object to object. Nobody inquires whether one share in IBM is in better condition or of better quality than another, but in the case of an antique both considerations could alter the price by a significant factor.

An interesting comparison can often be made by seeking out the modern equivalent of your prospective purchase. Compare a contemporary chest, for instance, with an old one. The result can surprise you, and whereas the modern piece has an immediate second-hand value of one third of the ticket price as soon as it is paid for, the old piece almost certainly maintains its value for a few years, after which it probably appreciates.

So temper your cupidity with common sense, and remember that the dealer who has become your friend will probably let you in on his bargains. On the whole, too great a preoccupation with price can be counter-productive. If the piece is good and rare, someone else will step in and buy it while you cogitate. If you like a thing, and it suits you, and you can afford it, buy.

Selling

This question is always controversial since the price you obtain for any object depends upon its being offered in the right market. A general trader will make an offer for anything, but he wouldn't perhaps be able to afford a precious diamond. Nevertheless, he might be willing to negotiate the sale of it, although if you do allow him to do so, make sure he explains to you exactly what he is doing. Probably you would be better advised to go straight to a specialist diamond dealer or see what a saleroom expert advises. The latter will obviously want it to go at auction, in which case consider the eventual charges, which may amount to more than a dealer's profit, and the fact that the final buyer may be the specialist dealer

(*Far left*) **Titian: Jacopo Strada** (*detail*) (*Vienna, Kunsthistorisches Museum*). *The portrait was painted in 1567–8. Jacopo Strada was one of the first dealers in the modern sense.*

(*Left*) **Samuel P. Avery.** *Samuel P. Avery (1822–1904) was a highly successful New York dealer who in November 1868 was a moving spirit behind the committee which was formed to found the Metropolitan Museum, New York. He bears a striking resemblance to Jacopo Strada.*

(*Right*) **Daniel-Henri Kahnweiler.** *Kahnweiler was one of the first dealers to champion unknown artists such as Picasso and Braque. Here he is shown in old age, standing in front of Picasso's Cubist portrait of him executed in 1910.*

anyway. Remember also that specialist markets are limited. Specialist dealers make fewer sales than general merchants, and must therefore make higher profits which will be reflected in their price estimates at the outset.

The best general advice is to see a dealer you have come to know and trust. He is in contact with the markets, and if he can't help personally he will direct you to the right quarter.

Becoming a dealer

There remains the curious but understandable urge that comes to so many once they have realized an unexpected windfall for some hitherto unconsidered trifle. Could I become a dealer myself? How should I go about it? Where to start?

A great deal of study and observation is necessary before plunging into very hazardous waters. Establish some favourite interest before you start, then at least you won't find your acquisitions offensive if you have to keep them when they don't sell. Try to locate your potential customer before you buy, but don't be surprised if he suddenly produces some unforeseen snag at the last minute which prevents his going through with the deal; bad condition, wrong period or colour, lack of finance – the permutation of excuses is infinite. Antique shops are full of things bought for specific markets which haven't sold. Three pieces of good advice are: first, always buy quality if you can; second, never buy with only one customer in mind; third, don't try to run before you can walk. Many bankrupt dealers have grasped these rules too late.

If the wish to become a dealer is prompted by a desire to increase income there may well be a corresponding lack of capital. There are two points here. One is the problem of persuading a backer to support you. The other, for those with the necessary finance, is the tempting invitation to join in what is held out to be a lucrative venture. If you are tempted, thoroughly check the bona fides of your prospective partner and have an experienced solicitor (or attorney) draw up any proposed agreement. Partnerships are notoriously short-lived. Don't be seduced, without thorough investigation, into putting money into businesses 'requiring capital', however rosy the financial projections. There are probably reasons for the shortage of capital which the bank has already looked at, and found wanting.

Sometimes you can find an antique dealer who for one reason or another requires help: someone to attend a sale, look up records, visit a museum or mind the shop. If you are a beginner seize the opportunity and listen and learn. The experience may cool your ardour, or stimulate your enthusiasm. Either way it can only be to your benefit.

There remain the markets and fairs. Few survive today of the old-timers who came up the hard way, 'flogging' off a barrow in the Sunday markets the goods they'd culled during a back-breaking week on the 'knocker', going from door to door. In those days there was always something that would make a profit. £10 made you rich enough to fill a barrow, and be sure of 100 per cent profit.

Today, by seeking out with great care what you like, you might furnish a small stall for a Sunday fair with £500. If you find people who like what you've bought more than you did you'll make a few sales and learn. And you'll meet many interesting people.

With very few exceptions you'll find your colleagues helpful. You may be lucky, and you'll go on and buy more until, having weathered the heartbreaks and setbacks, your successes begin to outnumber your failures. You'll start to show a profit and eventually become a member of a carefree brotherhood. They may not, perhaps, be quite as carefree as they once were, but they'll make you welcome nevertheless.

15

SHIPPING AND TRANSPORT, IMPORT AND EXPORT

'It's from Mr. Getty, he says you're to have half each year!' Cartoon by JAK. Titian's Death of Actaeon (formerly owned by Lord Harewood) was sold at Christie's in June 1971 to the dealer Julius Weitzner for £1,680,000. Weitzner immediately sold it to Paul Getty for his museum at Malibu, California. Under UK legislation an export licence was required before the painting could leave the country. The National Gallery through grants and public appeal raised sufficient money to match the price and so prevented the sale to Paul Getty. The cartoon comments on Getty's suggestion that his museum and the National Gallery should share the painting, each displaying it for half the year.

Domestic transport

This chapter deals mainly with international shipping and transport, since it is here that the most acute difficulties and complications arise. However, most of what is said about practical problems, especially in regard to packing, cost and insurance, also applies to domestic transport. The only technical difference between international and domestic transport of antiques and works of art is that in the latter there are no Customs regulations to consider, although in the United States there may be local tax considerations and requirements about the carrier used. For most domestic purposes, door-to-door delivery by car or van will minimize the difficulties and risks, unless the distances are so great as to make this impractical. Small items are best sent by post. Certain removal firms (or shippers) have regular weekly runs between major towns and will arrange to collect and deliver single items to and from addresses within easy reach of their main routes. Inquiries among members of the local antique trade and auctioneers or a few telephone calls to firms listed in the local press or Yellow Pages, will soon reveal what services are available.

International transport

The transport of antiques and works of art across international frontiers is seldom simple. There is a great deal of 'red tape', and the rules and regulations are constantly changing. This chapter sets out the general principles, but keep in mind the saying 'there are exceptions to every rule, and that is a rule'. What may look straightforward could have a hidden snag, and the only way to minimize the difficulties and risks is to use an experienced shipper. He will require a fee, but it may well be worth every penny. When things start to go wrong the time and trouble spent sorting them out yourself can be time-consuming, frustrating and just as expensive as hiring a professional in the first place.

The cost and time involved in sending an object to its destination bear very little relationship to its value or purchase price. Size, weight, tendency to break, and Customs formalities are the chief considerations. Thus there is one rule which allows no exceptions: before buying items abroad which you cannot easily carry yourself, find out how much it will cost to transport them home before sealing the deal. Remember, too, that airlines have cut back the number of flights they operate, and so are often too full to allow large items of hand baggage into the cabin. No one wants to repeat the experience of the collector who was not allowed to take his valuable icon into the cabin of a plane which was fully booked. It travelled in the hold, and when he collected it at his destination it resembled firewood owing the the effect of non-pressurization.

There is considerable choice in forms of transport – air, sea, road, rail – and delivery door to door will probably involve a combination of different forms, with human and mechanical handling between them. The greater the degree of handling and the less specialized the transport, the greater is the risk of damage, loss and delay. In selecting a form of transport, therefore, the main factor to bear in mind is the value of the object and the difficulty in replacing it. A unique object, even though fully insured, is irreplaceable if it is damaged or destroyed.

Choosing a shipper

To find a reliable art shipper or forwarding agent, ask for recommendations from other collectors, auction houses or dealers. You will soon find one who has a good reputation and who specializes in your country or route. Those that run a regular service to your destination will be less expensive. They will also know most of the difficulties that could arise, and it will cut out the need for sub-contracting, which immediately increases the price. Some of the larger shippers advertise in the art trade or antique magazines.

It is advisable to get at least three quotations, as prices can vary considerably. Give each firm exactly the same information: a proper description of the object, with its dimensions; approximate weight; value. The quotation can be a minimum amount, in which case find out what is incorporated in the price, and if you should expect any extras. Better still, ask for a breakdown of the charges, as this will ensure that there are no added extras when the final invoice arrives. It is all too easy to overlook the charges for such items as collection, delivery, insurance, and Customs.

Packing

Unless you are very experienced, or are going to carry the package yourself, get a professional to do the packing for you. They have the proper materials and containers available, they know what dangers to guard against, how to achieve the best results relative to cost and space, and what or how much can be packed together. Some forms of transport have specific regulations about the method and form of packing required. Some insurance claims depend upon proof of adequate and appropriate packing. Since the object of the exercise is to ensure that objects arrive safely, it is false economy to make do with an inadequate and amateurish job.

Air freight

This method is certainly the safest and is advised for all high-value items. The drawbacks are the expense, and the need for the services of a shipper or forwarding agent because of the packing and documentation required. Therefore ask for quotations as previously suggested. The packing should be in wooden

Manet: Bar at the Folies Bergères (*London, Courtauld Institute Galleries*). *The painting is reputedly the first ever to be transported by aeroplane, when it was sent from London to the Manet retrospective exhibition in Paris, in 1932. Painted in 1882, it had been purchased in 1926 by Samuel Courtauld, a noted industrialist and patron of the arts. He presented many of his Post-Impressionist paintings to London University in 1931, and founded the Courtauld Institute, Britain's first university faculty of Art History.*

packing cases. There may be a lot of rough handling, and as a proportion of the total cost, that for wooden packing cases is small. For example: a valuable print which was rolled and sent in a cardboard tube was run over by a forklift truck. The insurance company was not satisfied that it had been adequately packed for air freight and would not settle the claim. The charges you should expect to pay for are: collection; packing; insurance; service charge; airline charges. Customs clearance and delivery to the final destination will usually be charged extra to the above. Find out who the receiving agent is and his scale of charges. Use experienced shippers or agents, because if correct Customs clearance documents are not sent with the consignment, storage charges can rapidly accumulate at the airport while time is wasted obtaining and forwarding the necessary documents. The different documents required for specialized items are discussed later.

Sea freight   This is appropriate only for large and heavy consignments, when it is relatively cheap. The main disadvantage is slowness.

Find a shipper who has a regular container service to your destination. These may not go very frequently, so you must not be in a hurry to receive the objects, and the delays in sea freight are notorious. For example: there was a large estate that had to be sold in the United States for tax reasons. The bulk was sent by sea from England whereas the smaller, more valuable pieces were sent by air. The sea shipment arrived over four months after the air shipment, after a series of disasters including a strike at the New York docks, causing the shipment to be diverted to Montreal where it became icebound, by which time the papers had been mislaid. It finally completed the journey by road. Needless to say the proposed sale date had been missed, and there was a large telephone bill incurred simply trying to keep track of the shipment.

If the final destination is not the actual port, the cost of van or trucking charges for transport between the port and the final destination should be carefully estimated in advance, as they can be a substantial proportion of the whole bill, even though the distance is small compared with the sea journey.

Postal sorting office at Mount Pleasant, London. *Officials are trying to cope with parcels which are damaged or mislaid through inadequate packing.*

This is the most appropriate method for largish items to short-haul destinations, within Europe or North America. It is not suitable for sending small items.

Van and trucking shipments

The main advantage for pictures and furniture is that the amount of packing, an expensive part of shipping, can be cut to a minimum. Where packing cases are necessary, wooden cases can usually be replaced by cardboard and cartons. If cases are not used all corners should have special protection. Insurance rates, especially for china and glass, are higher than for air freight, so that any savings on packing should be weighed against the increased insurance costs.

This is a convenient method for small items, but there are many restrictions, and the appropriate postal authorities should be asked for details.

Postal shipments

Full details of the postal or mail service from the United Kingdom are given in the Post Office Guide. This should be consulted in all instances, as the rules vary considerably from country to country. In the United States similar information will be provided on request by postal workers..

The following points should be noted:

There are size restrictions on all types of packages, such as letters, rolls or parcels, which vary according to the country of destination.

There are weight restrictions on different types of packages.

Parcels cannot be registered if being sent overseas. Only letters, small packets, post cards and printed papers which have to be sent via letter post can be registered.

In the event or loss of damage, compensation on a registered letter is limited to £10.

Insurance may be taken out with the Post Office, but the maximum amount varies depending on which country the package is going to. The top limit is £800 in the United Kingdom and $1,200 in the United States, but for most other countries the amount is much lower. The certificate of posting for a specific parcel must show the amount of insurance paid for, so check that this is correct before leaving the Post Office. Alternatively an insurance broker can be asked to quote for insurance.

The procedures for claims for loss or damage are outlined in the Post Office Guide, but be warned: settlement of a claim can be drawn out over many months.

Everything that is sent abroad by post, except for correspondence, must have a Customs declaration form attached, which states what the contents of the parcel are.

The packing for postal shipments should be robust, as the package has to be able to withstand rough handling. Use plenty of padding and tough, good-quality cardboard and paper. If sent abroad the package must be sealed with wax or lead seals or adhesive tape. Compensation will only be paid for damage if the packing is deemed adequate.

There are some people who do not believe in taking out insurance and maintain that their occasional losses are outweighed by all the insurance premiums they have saved. If you are a gambler and are not dealing in fragile or high-value objects, you may go along with this philosophy, but in this day and age when

Transit insurance

packages can so easily go astray and get damaged it is only sensible to be fully insured. The following are some basic recommendations regarding transit insurance:

1. Always take out insurance coverage from door to door.

2. Airline insurance is not adequate, as it only covers the consignment from airport to airport. The agent who effects Customs clearance and delivery signs for goods as unexamined, and so it is very difficult to pinpoint when the loss or damage occurred.

3. Do not insure for a sum grossly in excess of the value of the object. In the event of damage or loss, the insurance company will conduct an investigation to establish a fair value, and you will have to have concrete evidence to prove the insured value. There is no reason to pay a large premium when you cannot benefit from it.

4. The insured value should include the cost of the packing and shipping which you would want refunded in the event of loss.

Importing into the United Kingdom

All antiques and works of art can be imported as long as the correct paperwork is completed. A private individual can import objects purchased abroad, but is subject to the normal Customs restrictions. This means that if you have purchases over the duty-free limit they should be declared. Everything is deemed subject to duty and Value Added Tax unless you can prove exemption from it. When sending items to the United Kingdom for sale from overseas, everything without exception must be declared at Customs at the port of entry. Generally speaking, if there is an exemption from VAT, duty is not payable either, but there are various exceptions depending on particular circumstances, which is why it is best to seek professional advice. You obviously do not want to pay unnecessary duty. Exemption from VAT is dealt with below. A list of addresses of Government Departments to whom inquiries can be addressed is also given below. The procedures involved in importing are basically the same for private individuals bringing in items for their own collections, for dealers importing goods, and for people sending objects to be sold by auction in the United Kingdom. Expatriates returning to the United Kingdom with their personal effects are subject to different rules which can vary greatly according to circumstances and are not dealt with here.

Import documents: when importing items by air, sea or van, it is essential to have the following documents for all shipments:

An invoice for Customs purposes, which sets out a brief description of the item or items, giving an exact or approximate age.

In the objects are over 100 years of age this must be stated on an antique declaration. There must be an original signature stating that to the best of your knowledge and belief this is a correct statement.

If the items are packed in more than one case, there must be a packing list indicating the contents of each case.

The importer must sign a VAT 905 Customs form to claim exemption from VAT. The following categories are not liable to VAT: 1 antiques over 100 years of age other than pearls and loose gem stones; 2 original works of art disposed of by the creator or as part of his estate before 1 April 1973; 3 a collection or collector's piece of zoological, botanical, mineralogical, anatomical, historical, archaeological, palaeontological or ethnographic interest. Category 1 must be accompanied by an antique declaration from an authorized expert if it does not qualify under either 2 or 3. Category 2 covers original paintings, drawings, prints and sculptures.

The following documents are required for special shipments:

If importing objects incorporating the tusks (ivory), feathers, skins, furskins (except where the fur is only a trimming) etc. from endangered animals, birds or reptiles, it is necessary to have an Endangered Species Import Licence. This will only be granted if there is a corresponding Export Licence from the sending country. Endangered Species licences are obtainable from the Department of the Environment in Bristol.

A jade declaration must be signed for the importer by a jade expert who has actually examined all pieces of jade to confirm that they are over 100 years of age. If the objects have not been seen abroad, the expert will have to request a site to examine the items before signing the declaration.

If a shipment is sent from Hong Kong the British Customs require a certificate from the Hong Kong Chamber of Commerce granting permission for the shipment.

Penalties: there are severe penalties for making inaccurate declarations on Customs documents, and for not declaring objects at Customs. Do not give misinformation. Customs officers may call upon experts to give a ruling on age as well as on price. There is a stiff fine to be paid on top of the duty and VAT for making inaccurate declarations.

Payment of VAT and duty: when an item is liable to duty, VAT is payable on the declared value of the item, the duty and the shipping charges. Once duty is paid, there is no refund if the item is re-exported.

If items that do not qualify for exemption from VAT are being imported for resale, the VAT can be deferred at the time of importation against the importer's VAT registration number. VAT at the current rate has to be collected from the purchaser at the time of sale. If the item is unsold and is returned to the original owner, no VAT is payable. No duty is payable if the item is consigned from another EEC country and is accompanied by a T2L form which shows that all necessary taxes have already been paid. Any duty paid is on the declared value. If the item does sell, the Customs require an accounting of how much it sold for and will readjust the duty payable. If too much duty was paid they will refund the difference, but if not enough duty was paid the balance has to be remitted immediately.

If you are planning to hand-carry objects which are to be sold, whether arriving by air or sea, it is best to send all the necessary invoices and antique declarations well ahead of time to the importer. This will ensure that the C10 Customs import documents can be completed by the importer's agent, who can then meet you and hopefully grant you a swift and smooth passage through Customs.

Exporting from the United Kingdom

With certain specified exceptions, it is necessary for all overseas purchasers to apply to the Department of Trade to export any goods produced or manufactured more than 50 years before the date of exportation and valued at £8,000 or more. If it can be shown conclusively that the article had been imported into the United Kingdom within 50 years of the date of application to export, then a licence will be granted, although this does not dispense with the need to apply for a licence. Articles, or matching sets of articles, less than 50 years old or valued at less than £8,000 can be exported under Open General Export Licence with no further documentation (but if you are selling abroad and wish to claim back Value Added Tax you will need documentation even here).

Export licences may be obtained from the Export Licensing Branch of the Department of Trade. The form must be filled out with two extra copies of the description of the object, and must be accompanied by a photograph of the object (an illustration from a catalogue is not acceptable), and, if available, the import documents if imported within the last 50 years. If the import documents are available the licence should be granted within a week; if not, it may be three weeks. If the item is of national importance it has to go before the Export Review Committee, who can refuse to grant a licence (see below).

Individual licences: under the Export of Goods (Control) Order, an individual licence is needed to export from the United Kingdom and the Isle of Man to any destination the following: photographic positives and negatives produced more than 60 years before the date of exportation and valued at £200 or more per item (excluding items personally belonging to the producer or spouse); any other goods manufactured or produced *more than 50 years* before the date of exportation (excluding postage stamps or other items of philatelic interest, and other personal documents) and valued at over £8,000 per article or matching set of articles.

Where the item consists of a portrait or sculpture of a British historical personage who appears in the *Dictionary of National Biography* and has a value in excess of £2,000, then H.M. Customs, at the port of exit, require a certificate from the National Portrait Gallery (or Scottish National Portrait Gallery) stating that the item is not a work of national importance.

Bulk licences are available to regular exporters of documents, manuscripts or archives, but specific licences are required for manuscript Books of Hours, Missals, Psalters, Antiphoners and Graduals; illuminated or illustrated manuscripts in Arabic, Persian, Turkish, Urdu, and other oriental languages, and miniature paintings by Persian, Chinese and other Eastern artists, whether in or extracted from albums, where the value is in excess of £2,000; any papers and memoranda of those who have held public office; any document, manuscript or archive valued at more than £200 per article (or group of documents, etc.).

Marine Chronometer no. 176 by John Arnold (*sold by Christie's 25 November 1981*). *Chronometers were issued by the Admiralty in London to ships of the Royal Navy on voyages of exploration. This was first issued in 1791 to Captain George Vancouver RN, after whom the Canadian city is named. It was reissued to Captain Bligh in 1806, who failed to return it, and since then it had remained in private hands in England. The Vancouver Maritime Museum bid £39,600 ($76,032) at auction in 1981, and were immediately granted an export licence in view of the important historical connection with Vancouver.*

If diamonds are unmounted, a specific licence is required whatever age or value. Mounted diamonds can be exported without a licence provided they are exported through the special channels provided by the Post Office relating to registered letter post and/or insured parcel post. A licence is not required for gemstones, including synthetic or reconstructed diamonds.

A specific licence is required for archaeological items recovered at any time from the soil of the United Kingdom (including the bed of the sea within territorial waters), with the exception of coins or articles recovered after burial or concealment less than 50 years before the date of exportation.

An export licence is required for items made wholly or partly from endangered species, for example, ivory, horn, bone. Pre-authenticated licences are available from the Shipping Department for African elephant ivory only. A separate application must be made to the Department of the Environment, Bristol, for articles made of other endangered species, for example, rhinoceros horn.

Export Reviewing Committee: the Department of Trade refers all applications to export to the appropriate 'expert adviser', who in certain instances will recommend that the licence be withheld. Such cases are then referred to the Reviewing Committee, who arrange for the object to be produced at their meeting (at the applicant's expense) in order to consider whether the object satisfies the 'Waverley Criteria', that is: is the object so closely connected with our history and national life that its departure would be a misfortune? Is it of outstanding aesthetic importance? Is it of outstanding significance for the study of some particular branch of art learning or history? Where the Committee consider an object does meet one or more of these criteria, they will recommend that an export licence be withheld, and notify the applicant without giving reasons.

A decision not to allow export is normally subject to an offer by a public institution being made within a specified time for the purchase of the object (which the exporter is not obliged to accept); failing such an offer, the export licence is granted. The price recommended by the Reviewing Committee as the basis of an offer by a public collection is that which the Committee considers reasonable. If the exporter makes it publicly clear that he will not sell to a public collection, an indefinite stop is placed on the export, and a further application will be considered after an interval of 10 years only if there has been a significant change in status. Neither the Department of Trade nor an 'expert adviser' can give an advance ruling on the question of whether or not an export licence will be refused for a particular object on grounds of national importance.

The United States

In nearly all cases, export licences are not required to take art and antiques out of the United States. The only exceptions are works of art made partly or wholly from parts of animals covered by the various lists of endangered species. Regrettably the laws regarding the export of such works cannot be summed up neatly, but copies of the legislation, which is the Endangered Species Act of 1973 and the Marine Mammal Protection Act of 1972, are available through the United States Fish and Wildlife Service whose address is listed overleaf.

Foreign dealers who buy property from New York dealers or auction houses must pay New York State and City taxes unless they have an Out of State Resale License. These licences may be received through the New York State Technical Services Bureau, whose address is listed overleaf.

Import regulations are similar in principle to those for the United Kingdom. Listed overleaf are some major differences that should be noted when importing into the United States of America.

1. All objects made in the United States may return to the United States duty free. This does not apply to items created by American nationals when abroad.

2. The frames on pictures, drawings and prints are subject to duty unless they are over 100 years old. Since the documentation and charges involved in proving this are usually more than the duty, it is better to pay the duty or leave the frames behind.

3. Sculptures that are not over 100 years old must be within the first ten casts to be free of duty. This must be readily provable.

4. The duty rate for functional items such as vases is much higher than for purely decorative objects. If an item that is over 100 years old has been converted, say, into a lamp, the date of the conversion is taken as the age of the object. If this has happened in the last 100 years the item becomes dutiable as an electrical appliance.

   Similarly, precious gemstones (diamonds, rubies, sapphires, emeralds) may be brought into the United States without incurring a duty unless the gemstones are in a setting, in which case they are considered jewellery and are subject to duty. Semi-precious stones are subject to a duty in either case.

5. Rizzas on icons are very rarely over 100 years of age and are therefore dutiable. If the rizza is sealed on to the icon then the whole icon becomes dutiable. If it is possible to remove the rizza and pack it separately, then duty is payable on the rizza only.

6. The importation of Fabergé is complicated. Only certain workmasters are accepted as producing works of art. Work by the others is dutiable if less than 100 years old. All items made in Russia attract a very high rate of duty.

7. Pre-Columbian art may be imported into the United States only if accompanied by an export licence that shows the work was legally brought out of the country of origin.

8. As a rule, objects made partly or wholly of parts of endangered species may not be brought into the United States unless the object is over 100 years old. Even then, however, there are difficulties since age must be proven by the importer, unless the Customs agent recognizes the work as an antique. There are over 700 species considered endangered, so when purchasing objects (from scrimshaw to tortoiseshell spectacle frames) buy carefully.

9. If you do pay duty and then re-export within 24 months, you are entitled to a 99 per cent rebate. This entails filling out numerous forms, and if you ask a broker to do it for you he will charge approximately $250.

France   Antiques and works of art usually require a licence for export from France, and advice on the subject should be sought from a reliable shipper or agent. Items

Brancusi: Bird in Space (*Philadelphia Museum of Art, Louise and Walter Arensberg Collection*). *The artist sought to import a similar work into the United States in 1927 for an exhibition of his work. It was seized by custom officials who sought to impose a 40 per cent* ad valorem *duty on the grounds that it was 'a metal utensil' and 'an object of manufacture' (duty was not payable on works of art). Brancusi took the case to court, which ruled in his favour, saying 'by its harmonious proportions, elegant lines and the beauty of its execution it is a work of art.'*

exported for resale need a Temporary Export Licence. This is issued by the Commission des Beaux Arts in Paris, which meets every Wednesday. There is a Curator for each specific field who has to sign the release for each item to leave the country. The Commission can authorize the purchase of the item at the declared value for a museum in France. The licence is valid for twelve months and then can be renewed for a further twelve months. The item may not be sold for less than the declared value, and the proceeds for the sale have to be returned to France. In the event of the items failing to sell within a specific time, proof of the object returning to France must be produced.

There is a range of VAT rates for items that have been purchased abroad entering France, depending upon the type of object.

Italy, Spain and Portugal

The export of antiques and works of art is not allowed, and household effects may be exported only if the country of residence is being changed to the importing country.

Australia and South Africa

All antiques being imported into these countries have to have special Customs invoices which are obtainable from the local Embassy. These have to be accompanied by a BADA or LAPADA certificate obtained from the British Antique Dealers' Association in London or through agents at the airport.

Canada

The Canadians also have a special Customs invoice for imports but do not require the BADA certificate.

Addresses

Below are some of the most important addresses in the United Kingdom and the United States for those wishing to make inquiries about importing and exporting. Addresses and advice for other countries can be obtained from shippers, or from the trade associations or embassies of the individual countries.

United Kingdom: general export inquiries: Export Licensing Branch, Department of Trade, Sanctuary Buildings, 16/20 Great Smith Street, London SW1P 3DG, Tel. 01 215 7877.

Relief from Value Added Tax on goods bought for export: H.M. Customs & Excise, VAT Machinery Division E, Knollys House, 11 Byward Street, London EC3R 5AY, Tel. 01 623 3010.

Customs duty payable abroad, preferential tariffs, restrictions on imports by overseas countries: Export Services & Promotions Division, Department of Trade, Export House, 50 Ludgate Hill, London EC4M 7HU, Tel. 01 248 5757.

Endangered Species Import and Export Licences: Department of the Environment, Tollgate House, Houlton Street, Bristol BS2 9DJ.

United States: export licences for objects made from parts of endangered species: United States Fish and Wildlife Service, Public Affairs Office, 1375 K Street N.W., Washington, D.C. 20005.

Customs information: United States Customs Service, Public Affairs Office, 1301 Constitution Avenue N.W., Washington, D.C. 20229.

Out of State Resale Licenses: Technical Services Bureau, Sales Tax Instruction and Interpretation Unit, Room 104, Building 9, State Campus, Albany, New York 12227.

16
LEGAL RIGHTS
AND OBLIGATIONS

'Perkins, you call my lawyers and I'll call Christie's.'
Cartoon by Charles Addams.

While most people go through life without being involved with 'the law', in the sense of being involved in a court case, everyone unwittingly meets the law many times each day: each time one buys a cabbage or travels on a bus one makes a contract which has legal implications.

The law is a framework of rules for conduct in society; some of these rules are concerned with criminal behaviour, but others govern relations between citizens as they go about their ordinary business, including buying and selling. The latter rules ('the Civil Law') are framed in such a way as to be applicable to the most varied circumstances. How they will be applied to any particular circumstances is ultimately a matter for the courts, but the same basic principles apply equally to the sale of a packet of pins as they do to the sale of a baronial mansion. Indeed, if a collector were to make a claim against an auctioneer who had sold a worthless painting as 'by Rubens', relevant legal principles would be found in a case involving a heifer which the auctioneer said was 'unserved' and which promptly died bearing a calf!

This chapter is only intended to serve as a general introduction to some of the main rules that are most likely to apply to collecting, and is principally concerned with the rights of the buyer. It should not therefore be taken as a complete statement; furthermore, the law is changing or developing each day as Parliament makes new laws and judges make new decisions.

Where knowledge of technical terms is desirable or their use unavoidable, the appropriate expression appears in inverted commas, for example, 'negligence'. The law stated is English law; the laws of other countries – including Scotland – may differ.

The basic principle applicable to buying and selling is usually expressed in Latin as 'caveat emptor' – meaning 'let the buyer beware'. In other words, the buyer takes the risk and will bear any loss unless there is a specific rule giving him some protection; where there is no such rule, even though the buyer may feel he has a moral right to have his money back, he may have no legal claim. Sellers, often dealers, may be well aware of the relevant legal principles, and, except as a matter of goodwill, may be entitled to refuse any redress where no such specific legal protection exists.

Largely for the benefit of buyers of new 'consumer' goods there are laws which give legal protection to the buyer, or consumer, who is usually in a weaker economic position than the seller. These rules do not, however, offer the same degree of protection to the buyer of secondhand goods and antiques or to people who buy from private sellers as opposed to dealers. Accordingly collectors should heed the 'caveat emptor' rule and, before buying, thoroughly satisfy themselves that they are buying what they think they are buying.

There is one other important practical respect in which a buyer should also beware: that is the identity and substance of the seller; it is of no use to a buyer that he has a watertight legal claim only to find that the seller has wheeled his barrow away, shut up shop or gone bust.

Buying and selling – basic legal considerations

When you buy or sell, whether a Rembrandt or a cabbage, you make a contract. The contract sets out the rights and obligations of the buyer and seller which are enforceable by law. There are three main elements, each of which must be present in order for a contract to come into existence:

Contracts of sale

Offer: an offer may be oral, written or even by conduct; if a buyer picks up an item in a shop and silently takes it to the cashier, he is making an offer to buy it.

Acceptance: an offer is not binding until accepted; until then, it can be withdrawn. Again, acceptance may be written, oral or by conduct.

Consideration: this is the benefit that each party confers or promises to confer on the other; in a sale of goods, the consideration given by the seller will be delivery of the goods and that given by the buyer will be the price. A gift, when the recipient gives no consideration, does not amount to a contract.

Neither party is bound by a contract until an offer has been made and accepted. If a dealer puts the wrong price tag on an item on display, the buyer cannot force the dealer to sell at that price; by displaying goods, a dealer is not making an offer, he is making what is called 'an invitation to treat' – an invitation to the buyer to make an offer. Similarly, a buyer is not bound to proceed with the purchase until an offer made by him has been accepted. (It should be noted that a buyer who damages an item in a dealer's shop will nevertheless be liable for that damage on grounds arising other than in contract.)

The rights of a buyer and seller under a contract depend upon its terms. Some terms may be expressly agreed and some implied by an Act of Parliament. Other terms may be implied in other ways, such as by the custom of a particular trade.

Expressly agreed terms: such matters as arrangements for repair or restoration, disclaimers of liability and whether the cost of removal of a bulky item is included in the price may be discussed and agreed between buyer and seller in the case of more expensive items. In other cases, there may be no express terms other than the price which may be 'agreed' by the buyer handing a priced item to the dealer. Other matters may become express terms of the contract (for example, a sign

'It isn't every day, Sir, you can get a chair straight from a Continental Palace.' 'Why, you told me the same thing last week about a vase.' 'Quite right, Sir; at the moment crowned 'eads are taking no risks.' Cartoon by E. H. Shepard, Punch, *15 November 1911. The fundamental legal principle is 'caveat emptor' – let the buyer beware.*

hanging in the shop to the effect that 'All watercolours are original unless otherwise stated'; in this case the buyer of a work which turns out to be a print will generally be entitled to return it and have his money back). Similarly an auctioneer's printed conditions will be terms of the contract. But for a statement or notice to be a term of the contract it must have been expressly or implicitly agreed by the parties before the contract is made, in other words, before acceptance. If a dealer sells an item, is paid and hands over the item but then gives the buyer a receipt on the back of which are set out the conditions of the transaction (for example, 'No refund unless goods returned within ten days'), the buyer, who will not have seen them before, will not be bound by them and they will not be terms of the contract (unless perhaps the buyer is a regular customer and therefore familiar with the shop's procedures).

Express terms are equally binding whether in writing or not. Written terms are, however, more effective since they are easier to prove at a later date. No one can deny the existence of a written term, but an unscrupulous dealer may more easily deny that he said something.

Implied terms: in any contract of sale of goods, the seller guarantees that he has a right to sell. If goods are sold solely by description or by reference to a sample, where the buyer does not inspect the goods (as in a mail order purchase), the seller guarantees that the goods will accord with the description or sample.

There are two terms concerning quality which are also implied when a dealer sells. The first is that the goods are of the kind of quality a reasonable man would expect having regard to all the circumstances; if, however, the buyer inspects the goods and that inspection reveals or ought reasonably to have revealed the defect complained of, this implied term will be of no avail to a buyer, nor will it apply to any defect to which the dealer draws attention. The second is that the goods must be reasonably fit for any purpose made known expressly or impliedly by the buyer to the seller. These terms are designed largely to protect the buyer of everyday items. It is virtually impossible for a dealer to exclude the application of these terms by means of a disclaimer.

In the context of antiques and collectors' items, the implied terms regarding quality are likely to be of less significance, one of the relevant circumstances being the very fact that reasonable people would expect to find defects in secondhand goods.

Ownership and risk: under a contract of sale, ownership of the goods ('property in the goods') passes from seller to buyer when the two agree that it should. Normally, few buyers and sellers discuss or make any such express agreement (although most auctioneers' conditions will contain such a term), so the Sale of Goods Act 1979 lays down certain complex rules which apply in the absence of an express agreement.

Where, as will usually be the case, the goods are identified at the time of sale and available for immediate delivery, ownership passes at the time the contract is made. This will be so even if, for example, payment is deferred (on credit for example) or actual delivery delayed for some days. It will be otherwise, however, if the goods have to be manufactured, adapted or repaired before, under the terms of the contract, the buyer is bound to take them. In that case, ownership will not pass to the buyer until he has notice that the goods are ready. The question may be important for two main reasons, namely the amount which can be claimed by the seller if the buyer wrongly defaults on the contract and the effect of damage or destruction of the goods after the contract of sale has been made. The passing of ownership does not necessarily give a buyer who has not paid for an item the right to take possession of it; that right is dependent upon payment of the price or the seller agreeing credit terms.

If ownership has passed to the buyer, the seller can sue for the agreed price. But if a buyer defaults before ownership has passed, the seller can only sue for the amount of his loss, which may not necessarily be the full price of the goods, and must take steps to minimize ('mitigate') his loss. For example, suppose a seller agrees to have a painting cleaned before delivery to the buyer; before the cleaning is completed, the buyer makes known to the seller that he has changed his mind and does not wish to take the painting; the seller can only claim from the buyer his loss – perhaps storage charges and work on cleaning – and not the agreed price.

Unless otherwise agreed, the risk of accidental damage or destruction passes to the buyer at the same time as ownership. If, therefore, the ownership has passed to the buyer but the goods are left with the seller whose shop and contents are totally destroyed by fire through no fault of his own, the buyer will bear the loss; the buyer will still be bound to pay for the goods if he has not done so and will have no right to recover from the seller if he has paid. The seller is legally bound to take reasonable care of the goods, and may still be liable to the buyer if he has not done so. The conditions of sale of most auctioneers provide that risk will pass on the fall of the hammer even though property may not pass until later (usually when payment in full has been made).

Buyers who do not collect their purchases immediately should, for these reasons, take care that the goods are covered by their own insurance.

Breach of contract: if one party to a contract fails to do what he has promised to do, in other words is 'in breach of a term of the contract', the other will have a legal right to redress. First, the latter must prove that the former is in breach; although in many cases that may be obvious, in others it may be difficult to prove.

When a breach of contract has been established, the object of the law is to put the injured party in the same financial position as he would have been if there had been no breach. This may involve a complete refund against return of the goods; payment of compensation ('damages') equivalent to the loss which has been suffered or of an amount necessary to put the defect right; or a court order instructing the party in default to perform his promise. The most usual judgement awarded by the courts will be damages, even though that may not, in the mind of the buyer, be a sufficient compensation for the time, trouble and disappointment which he has suffered. Which judgement is given will depend upon the seriousness of the breach and may depend upon the speed with which the buyer makes his claim once he has discovered the breach.

For example, assume that a collector of working models buys from a shop a model steam engine described as a 'working model'. If it turns out that the boiler is solid steel and the model would never have been capable of being a working model, the seller will be in breach of a term of the contract; the breach is probably sufficiently serious to make compensation an inadequate remedy for the buyer. If so, the court would allow the collector to return the model and have his money back. If, on the other hand, the steam engine had a normal boiler but the whistle was badly fitted and allowed steam to escape, reducing the efficiency of the engine, the shopkeeper may be in breach of the implied term relating to quality (see 'Implied terms'), but the breach may not be sufficiently serious to entitle the buyer to return the engine; instead, he should be entitled to claim damages equal to the cost of having the whistle correctly fitted. If a collector of furniture buys an 'original' Chippendale chair and finds that one leg is a modern replacement, he may similarly not be entitled to return the chair, but may only be entitled to a partial refund equivalent to the difference in value between the chair as it is and as it would have been had the leg not been a replacement.

Seller's rights: a seller has a right to have the promises of the buyer under the contract enforced or to receive compensation if the buyer is in breach of contract. The main concern of a seller is obviously to ensure that he receives effective payment. Payment in cash is clearly effective payment, but payment by cheque is not, in law, the same as payment in cash since a buyer can stop payment on a cheque before it is cleared or his bank account may be overdrawn.

Until payment the seller has a right to retain goods (a 'lien'), and will usually be entitled to re-sell them to a third party if he is not paid. If ownership of the goods has passed to the buyer the unpaid seller may sue for the price, but when paid he must be prepared to deliver the goods to the buyer.

Sellers should take care when selling to persons under 18; contracts with minors may not be enforceable unless the subject-matter is what the law considers to be 'necessary' for the minor. The law takes a somewhat broad and unforeseeable view of what is 'necessary': it depends partly on the station in life of the minor and his existing possessions. Antiques or collections are rarely likely to be 'necessary' in the legal sense.

Legal protection for buyers

The main requirement of the buyer is to obtain what he bargained for and be satisfied with his purchase. Simply because the buyer has paid more for an item than he need have paid had he bought it elsewhere will not of itself give rise to any grounds for complaint; buyers should therefore be aware of current market prices and prepared to look around or bargain to get a satisfactory price.

If the seller is in breach of a term of the contract, the buyer has a legal right to have the seller's promises enforced or to claim compensation. It most commonly happens that a collector is unsatisfied with his purchase in one of the following cases:

  if the seller refuses to hand over the goods;
  if the seller hands over the goods but they turn out to be faulty or defective;
  if a description attached to the goods turns out to be wrong;
  if the goods turn out to be stolen.

Refusal to hand over the goods: if a contract has been made, the buyer will be entitled to obtain the goods or to receive compensation. For example, a bric-a-brac dealer sells to a buyer, B, an old chest of drawers for £50 for which B pays and which he agrees to collect next week. Before collection, the dealer realizes that the item is a valuable commode worth £5,000; B may or may not have spotted that the item is valuable and either be pleased with his secret bargain or as yet unaware of its value. B has a legal right to have the commode delivered to him when he calls to collect. If B fails to persuade the dealer to hand over the item, he may get an order from the Court requiring the dealer to do so ('specific performance'), or alternatively he could claim compensation of £5,000. If, before B calls to collect, the dealer has sold to a third party who has bought in good faith, B can claim £5,000 from the dealer; he cannot claim the commode from the third party unless the third party was in collusion with the dealer.

While an order to hand over the goods may be refused by the Court if it considers that damages would be adequate satisfaction for the buyer, such an order will normally be made if the item is unique or if there are other circumstances, such as the bankruptcy of the dealer, which would make damages ineffective. If the dealer has sold on to a third party, *and* gone bankrupt, the unfortunate buyer probably has no redress in practice, and the best advice for any collector who spots a bargain is to pay for it and take it away as quickly as possible.

Defective or faulty goods: unlike new goods where the implied term as to quality may be of assistance (see 'Implied terms'), defective or faulty secondhand goods are less likely to be the subject of compensation or subject to return if they are substantially in order and the seller has made no express statements describing the condition of the goods. A buyer would have no right to claim against a seller of a secondhand table which turns out to have some woodworm – unless perhaps the rot is so bad that the table collapses and could not even be used as a table. On the other hand, if the new frame of a painting collapses when first hung so that the painting is destroyed, the buyer should be entitled to compensation.

It is best for collectors to ensure that no such claim is likely to arise by taking precautions before contracting to buy. In practice, collectors should:

inspect their purchases very carefully before agreeing to buy;

if buying without such an inspection (for example, as a result of an advertisement), inspect carefully as soon as the goods are received and immediately return any goods which turn out to be unsatisfactory;

make any complaints known to the seller as soon as possible and if practical return the goods to him;

ask the advice of the seller on any points of particular importance; for instance, ask the dealer whether the table is free of woodworm. In this way, the dealer may make statements with a view to achieving a sale which become express terms of the contract or representations giving a right to return. It is easier to get satisfaction for such terms or representations than to rely simply on implied terms. (As to such statements, the same principles apply as mentioned below under 'Wrong descriptions and attributions'.)

Wrong descriptions and attributions: a dealer or auctioneer may make a descriptive statement about the goods in many ways; there may be a label attached to them, he may express a view on the provenance, make or condition of the goods in reply to a question from a buyer or there may be statements of description in an auctioneer's catalogue. Not all such statements, if they turn out to be wrong, give a right to the buyer to return the goods and have his money back; the legal rules are complex. In general, however, a buyer who feels aggrieved by a false description or false attribution should immediately complain to the person who sold the item and if he fails to get satisfaction, take legal advice upon whether he has any rights. What follows is a very rough guide.

Some statements and descriptions give rise to no legal liability; extravagant praise by salesmen of their goods is one example and is called a 'mere puff' ('the most beautiful example of its kind', 'a once-in-a-lifetime bargain' – describing a Far Eastern mass-produced ashtray). If a dealer or seller expresses a genuinely held opinion about, say, the identity of a painter, this being an opinion which he has reached after careful research, he will not be liable simply because he turns out to be wrong. It is otherwise if, for instance, a dealer describes a painting as by Rubens when no reasonable person would have done so, provided the buyer can show that he relied upon that description in deciding to buy.

If goods are sold by description alone, so that the buyer has no opportunity to inspect, and the goods do not conform with the description, the buyer can get his money back. For example, if a buyer answers an advertisement for a 'gold-plated carriage clock' which arrives but turns out to be made of bronze, he can return it and have his money back.

If a dealer or auctioneer orally or in writing makes a statement of fact about an item which the buyer can prove that he relied upon and can show to be false or misleading, the buyer can claim his money back together with legal expenses. It makes no difference whether the statement was made deliberately, innocently or carelessly. If, however, the deception was deliberate (for example, if the maker of a fake or forgery, his accomplice or a seller who knows it to be a fake seeks to pass the goods off as the genuine article), the buyer may have an additional or alternative right to claim for deceit and the person who made the statement may be guilty of a crime. Dealers are also under an obligation not to give misleading descriptions which constitute an offence under the Trades Description Acts.

For the seller to be liable, the description must be one of fact, not opinion, and the buyer must have relied upon the statement in deciding to buy. If therefore a buyer has relied upon his own judgement and his own inspection, the dealer may not be liable. It is also sometimes difficult to tell whether a statement is one of fact or opinion: a statement that a painting is oil on canvas is clearly a statement of fact. A statement that a painting is by a particular artist, when it cannot be scientifically proven one way or the other, is probably a statement of opinion. In practice, nearly all descriptions, attributions and opinions about authenticity given by dealers and auctioneers will be statements of opinion, not fact.

The basic rule, despite the protection afforded to buyers, is still 'caveat emptor' – let the buyer beware. This rule is more than likely to be applicable in the context of antiques and collectors' items. Unless some deliberate false description or fraud has been perpetrated by the seller, a collector who buys a piece which turns out to be a forgery or fake will not automatically have any right of redress. In practice, collectors should:

- ask specific questions of dealers and auctioneers ('Does the table have woodworm?' or 'Is the chair by Chippendale?');
- if dissatisfied, make complaints known to the seller as soon as possible;
- if possible, only pay when satisfied with a purchase;
- make written notes of statements made by the seller which seem important to the collector;
- ask the dealer to give a written description of the item to be bought. If the dealer says a painting is by Rembrandt, insist that he writes 'painting by Rembrandt', not just 'painting'.

Exclusion clauses: because of the liability which may attach to attributions and descriptions, most auctioneers and some dealers will seek in their conditions to exclude liability for misleading or false representations. They are only legally entitled to do so insofar as the courts consider it reasonable that they should be allowed to rely upon their exclusion clauses. It is unlikely that a seller who carelessly or deliberately describes a glass necklace as made of diamonds would be able to escape liability by means of a printed disclaimer in his conditions of sale that he is not liable for false descriptions.

Even if there are clauses purporting to exclude liability, they may be overridden by subsequent statements; for instance, specific statements by an auctioneer about the condition of a lot may override a printed condition that goods are 'sold with all faults and imperfections'.

Stolen goods: it is an offence knowingly to buy stolen goods, punishable by a fine or imprisonment. No crime, however, is committed by someone who buys goods which have been stolen unless he knew or believed them to have been stolen.

A person who purports to sell stolen goods (whether or not he knows them to have been stolen) has no legal right to sell them, and the true owner of stolen goods will generally have a right to recover the goods even from an innocent buyer. The buyer can claim his money back from the person who sold them to him – if that person can still be traced and has sufficient means.

In the United Kingdom there are some exceptions to the rule that a person who purports to sell stolen goods has no right to sell them, the main one arising from what is known as 'sale in market overt' – open market. Any sale which takes place in market overt will give good title to the goods to the buyer with the result that the true owner cannot reclaim them. However, not all markets are 'market overt': all shops in the City of London are market overt provided the goods in question are the shop's usual type of merchandise; any legally constituted public open market is market overt, but few street markets fall into this category.

Auction sales   A sale by auction is a sale at which goods are sold to the highest bidder, and, apart from some special rules, is governed by the same basic legal principles as set out above. At the sale, the auctioneer's request for bids is not an offer but merely an invitation to the bidders to make offers. A bid is an offer and the auctioneer is free to accept or reject a bid until the fall of the hammer which constitutes acceptance. Similarly, until the fall of the hammer, any bid may be withdrawn. Any lot may be withdrawn before it has been sold, even if included in the catalogue; a disappointed buyer who has incurred expense in travelling to attend an auction has no right to compensation if a lot is withdrawn or indeed if the auction is cancelled.

Most auctioneers have extensive conditions of sale which constitute the terms of the contract for sale which is a contract between the seller (not the auctioneer) and the buyer. The auctioneer is an agent of the seller and so the conditions of sale will be weighted in favour of the auctioneer and the seller.

Some descriptions in auction catalogues will be statements of fact and some will be statements of opinion. If they are statements of fact, and they prove to be misleading or false, a disappointed buyer should be entitled to have his money back in exchange for return of the lot on the basis of the general principles mentioned above.

Most auctioneers seek to exclude liability for the condition of lots, and for misattributions and misdescription in their catalogues (see above, 'Exclusion clauses'). Such exclusions are likely to be effective as a matter of law, although in practice, for commercial reasons, reputable auctioneers may not seek to rely on them. It is therefore not a good course, except perhaps with reliable and well-established auctioneers, to buy at an auction without a thorough prior personal inspection of the lot.

If a buyer bids a high price for goods in the mistaken belief that he is getting a bargain and the goods are knocked down to him, he cannot back out unless he can show that there was a genuine fundamental mistake about the contents of a lot or that he was persuaded to bid in reliance for instance upon a false statement of fact ('misrepresentation') made about the goods by the auctioneer or by the seller. A buyer at auction is obviously in a stronger position if he has not paid for goods, since it will then be up to the auctioneer or seller to sue for the price; they will often be unwilling to do so, particularly if the buyer is counterclaiming for misdescription. However, auctioneers generally reserve the right to refuse to admit people to auctions or to refuse bids, and may exercise these rights at future auctions against a buyer who has refused to pay.

Despite many myths, it is unlikely for a bidder to find himself accidentally the buyer of a lot by scratching an itch on his nose. It is also unlikely that, if a dispute arises, a bidder who thinks he has made the final bid could force the auctioneer to acknowledge that the contract of sale was made with him; most auctioneers reserve a right in their conditions of sale to put up a lot again for sale if, in their view, a dispute has arisen (see also Chapter 12).

Where a sale is expressed to be 'subject to reserve' this will be a price below which the goods will not be sold. The auctioneer is not bound to disclose what reserve has been fixed by the seller. If the reserve is not reached in the bidding, the auctioneer will withdraw the goods from the sale on behalf of the seller. It is not lawful for the seller to bid for his own goods unless an appropriate announcement has been made either from the auctioneer's rostrum or in the catalogue; it is usually one of an auctioneer's standard notices or conditions of sale that the auctioneer may bid on behalf of the seller.

Compensation for poor service

A collector may have a right to compensation if he seeks and receives advice on a prospective purchase, on restoration or conservation or on other matters from an expert, whether an auctioneer or a dealer or some third party, and suffers financial loss because that advice turns out to be bad having been carelessly given. The right to compensation is based on 'negligence' if it can be shown that the person giving the advice was under a duty to take care in giving the advice and failed to take care, resulting in financial loss to the claimant (this concept of negligence is part of the 'fiduciary trust' relationship in the United States). Again the effectiveness of disclaimers of liability is restricted.

Examples: (1) Before bidding for an item at auction, a collector seeks a valuation from some expert valuer; the valuer gives a valuation without inspecting the lot, and on the strength of that advice, the bidder bids a high price for what turns out to be an obvious copy without any significant value; he may be entitled to compensation from the valuer. (2) An expert restorer advises a particular treatment to clean a painting when it is well known that the treatment would cause damage to the particular painting; the owner would be entitled to compensation for the loss in value of the painting if it is damaged.

Similar provisions apply to contracts for repairs and other services as apply to contracts for sales of goods. The person undertaking the service is legally obliged to use proper materials and good workmanship and, in the absence of any agreement, to charge a reasonable charge. He is also under an obligation to carry out the service within a reasonable time.

Some repairers or restorers may seek to exclude liability for damage or negligence, for example a sign in the shop saying 'All repairs carried out at customer's risk'. As with other exclusion clauses, the law will only allow the repairer to rely upon such an exclusion clause to the extent that it is reasonable to allow him to do so. As with any other rights, the legal remedies may be no more than theoretical unless the repairer or restorer is a man of sufficient substance to honour his obligations.

Sorting out problems

If a legal problem arises and it is intended to consult a solicitor, it is advisable to consult him without delay. In other cases the first step is obviously to make the complaint known to the other party, and it will usually be advisable to refuse to pay any amounts outstanding; that may be sufficient in itself to bring about

"LA BELLE FERRONNIÈRE": A PICTURE IN THE LOUVRE, PARIS, GENERALLY REGARDED AS AN AUTHENTIC WORK BY LEONARDO DA VINCI (FOR COMPARISON WITH THE ADJOINING ILLUSTRATION).

THE SUBJECT OF A "SLANDER OF TITLE" ACTION BROUGHT BY ITS OWNER AGAINST SIR JOSEPH DUVEEN, FOR CALLING IT "A COPY": MRS. HAHN'S PICTURE (FOR COMPARISON WITH THE ADJOINING ILLUSTRATION).

SIR JOSEPH DUVEEN, BT.: THE FAMOUS ART DEALER, FROM WHOM MRS. HAHN CLAIMED £100,000 DAMAGES FOR "SLANDER OF TITLE."

In the Supreme Court at New York, on February 5, a suit for 500,000 dollars (£100,000) damages for slander of title was begun by Mrs. Andrée Ledoux Hahn against Sir Joseph Duveen. The action arose out of his alleged statement, nine years ago, that Mrs. Hahn's picture, "La Belle Ferronnière," purporting to be by Leonardo da Vinci, was only a copy of that master's work. Mrs. Hahn contended that Sir Joseph's declaration had "killed" a proposed sale of the painting to the Kansas City Art Institute. This long-standing art dispute was discussed by a committee of experts in Paris in 1923, and we reproduce above two photographs taken on that occasion and published in our issues of Sept. 22 and 29 in that year. It was reported at the time that the experts were understood to have pronounced the Louvre picture to be an original Leonardo and Mrs. Hahn's picture a copy, opinions being based partly on artistic quality and partly on the nature of the pigment. Mrs. Hahn's pending action against Sir Joseph Duveen was also mentioned at that time. It was stated in a message from New York on February 16 last that the suit recently begun there had lasted for ten days, and that Sir Joseph Duveen had been in the witness-box for five days. He was reported to have maintained his ground that an art expert is entitled to give his opinion. In the interests of art and his profession, he had refused an opportunity given him to retract. He submitted that if, as he believed, the Louvre portrait was Da Vinci's original, he had no alternative but to deny the claims of Mrs. Hahn's picture.

THE 1923 DISCUSSION OF THE CLAIM OF MRS. HAHN'S PICTURE TO BE AN ORIGINAL LEONARDO: ART EXPERTS IN CONCLAVE IN PARIS SHOWING PROFESSOR VENTURI (CENTRE BACKGROUND).

EXPERTS WHO PRONOUNCED ON THE 1923 DISPUTE: (L. TO R.) SIR MARTIN CONWAY, SIR CHARLES HOLMES, M. NICOLLE, PROFESSOR VENTURI, MR. ROGER FRY, MR. L. S. LEVY, M. LURFROSE, AND CAPTAIN L. DOUGLAS.

The Leonardo da Vinci dispute. One of the most extraordinary legal actions ever fought, as reported by the Illustrated London News, *2 March 1929. The jury failed to agree, and a new trial was ordered, but Duveen settled out of court for $60,000. Duveen had, in fact, never seen the Hahn picture when he stated it to be a copy.*

redress. In addition pressure may be brought upon dealers who belong to trade organizations and associations. Citizens' Advice Bureaux (Better Business Bureaux in the United States) may also be able to refer a complainant to sources of reference or advice. Where a false trade description has been applied, a complaint may be made to the local trading standards officer, but he cannot pursue individual claims.

Court actions: if no satisfaction is obtained, an action may be started in the courts. Most claims, unless very substantial, will be started in the local County Court, and it is possible for a claimant to handle his own case without a lawyer. Care should be taken, however, that the claim is well-founded, because if the claimant fails or withdraws he may be ordered to pay the legal costs incurred by the other side. (By contrast, in the United States, defendants are responsible for their legal fees, though plaintiffs may ask for the legal expenses in their suit.) The County Courts do have a procedure which is designed to be simple and quick whereby small disputes can be referred to arbitration in the Court; both parties must agree to submit the dispute to arbitration. Guidance on the Court procedure can be obtained from Court officials.

In England, legal actions cannot generally be brought in the courts more than six years after the wrong complained of – which will usually be the date the item was bought.

Solicitors: everyone wants to avoid being involved in a court case, perhaps for fear of the expense, delay and worry. Nevertheless, the legal profession does have its uses. Advice can be obtained from a solicitor on the various rights and types of action and the merits of a claim. His trained eye may see aspects of a case which had not occurred to the client. Often, one reasoned letter from a solicitor will produce a speedy and satisfactory conclusion if the other party, perhaps a dealer, thereby realizes that the buyer 'means business'. A great majority of claims, even where a writ has been issued or a summons served, are settled without ever reaching the Court.

If a collector does not already have a solicitor, the best way to find one is on the personal recommendation of a friend or business colleague. In the absence of a recommendation, lists of solicitors are usually available in classified telephone directories or in specialized publications in most local libraries. Solicitors are not allowed to advertise, but the problems discussed in this chapter would be within the normal practice of most solicitors.

The charges of a solicitor vary by reference to certain factors, particularly the amount of time required, but the charge must be what is fair and reasonable. Few solicitors will be able to give a binding estimate of costs, but some may be prepared to give an indication and will certainly say whether the claim is worth pursuing from a financial point of view.

If a claim succeeds, it may be possible for the successful party to have some (but rarely all) of his own solicitor's costs paid by the other side. Likewise the party who fails may be ordered to pay the other side's costs. Clients who object to the amount of a solicitor's fee have a right to have the costs reviewed by the Law Society (which is the body governing the profession of solicitors) or by Court officials.

Some towns have community or voluntary legal advice centres where free advice and legal assistance may be obtained. In addition, the Legal Aid Schemes funded by the government provide assistance to persons with limited means. Not all solicitors undertake work under these schemes, and the financial limits for eligibility are fairly low. If a client thinks he qualifies, he should ask the solicitor for advice on this point at the outset. Many solicitors offer a fixed fee interview service where the client may have up to half an hour's advice and assistance for a fairly nominal fee.

It is scarcely necessary to say that prevention is the best cure. Sometimes, however, the most careful person meets an unforeseen problem and may even have no redress either in law or in practice, however 'morally' justified he may feel his claim to be. Perhaps, therefore, it is as well for a collector to assume that he has no rights; he will then be pleasantly surprised to find that he is protected by the law. It follows from this that if you are buying you should:

inspect thoroughly and carefully;

if seeking advice, make clear to the dealer or expert that you are relying on that advice;

keep written notes and records of dealings and statements;

obtain written confirmation from the seller of descriptions and other important matters;

submit any complaints as soon as possible and confirm in writing;

withhold any outstanding payment if you feel the claim is justified.

Reference books   The Law of England is contained in Acts of Parliament, local laws and the cases which have been decided in the courts, and as such fills many volumes; there are no simple reference books in which the layman could hope to find the whole answer to any problem. Legal text books are expensive and it is inadvisable for the layman to rely upon his own reading of a specialist publication. For this reason, it is not appropriate to set out a selective bibliography of legal text books.

Acts of Parliament and other Government publications are available from Her Majesty's Stationery Office and larger bookshops. Local reference libraries may contain some useful publications. Collectors of certain items, such as firearms, will also have to consider the relevant laws. Note also that there are laws controlling the export of certain antiques and collectors' pieces.

Taxation   Taxation is as much a part of everyday life in the twentieth century as infant mortality, illiteracy, disease and slums were part of the nineteenth. In fact the two are connected since the progress made in this century in social welfare, education and public health have mostly been paid for by the State, and direct and indirect taxation are the Government's method of raising revenue to pay the bills.

There is no point in becoming obsessed about tax liabilities. The small private collector has nothing to be anxious about or fear, and if collecting is going to give you sleepless nights worrying about real or imaginary tax problems and ruin your pleasure, you should find something else to do. If you think you have, or may have, a tax problem then it is only sensible to take proper advice. If you are trading in works of art rather than genuinely collecting, or if you are in the fortunate position of inheriting, acquiring, possessing, or disposing of works with a substantial value or of national importance, then advice must be sought about both tax liability and possible exemptions from tax. Government policy and tax legislation tend, nowadays, to change quite frequently, so that up-to-date advice is essential. You should find a lawyer or accountant with specialized knowledge of taxation relating to collectors. Major organizations such as Christie's have resident experts offering a tax advisory service. The leading or local experts with a good name are well known to the fine art profession, and a few inquiries of reputable firms will enable you to discover who they are.

Joos van Cleve: The Virgin and Child Enthroned with Angels (*Liverpool, Walker Art Gallery*). *United Kingdom legislation allows for works of art to be surrendered in lieu of tax in certain circumstances, and since the Finance Act of 1956 Christie's have negotiated many such transactions on behalf of clients. Joos van Cleve's painting, acquired by Charles Blundell between 1835 and 1841, was bought by the Walker Art Gallery, Liverpool, through a negotiated sale in 1981.*

CLASSIC BOOKS
FOR THE COLLECTOR

The books given below are recommended by the specialist departments in Christie's to collectors who wish to develop (rather than perfect) an interest in the subjects listed. The list makes no claim to be comprehensive but all books listed are well recognized, reliable and authoritative. Many of them are long established classics, and most contain bibliographies for further reading. Monographs on individual artists and craftsmen have in general not been included in the list, and with a few exceptions it is confined to works published in the English language. There are extensive and most useful bibliographies in the *Oxford Companion to Art*, and the *Oxford Companion to the Decorative Arts* (both edited by Harold Osborne and published by the Oxford University Press, 1970 and 1975 respectively), and in the *Penguin Dictionary of the Decorative Arts* (edited by John Fleming and Hugh Honour, published by Allen Lane in 1977). All three are essential reference works for the collector's bookshelf.

Museum and exhibition catalogues are invaluable, since they often contain the detailed information about specific works and objects that is most useful to collectors, but because of their relative unavailability (especially in libraries) they have not in general been included in this bibliography.

Aircraft

A. J. Jackson, *De Havilland Aircraft since 1915*, London, 1962

F. T. Jane (ed.) & others, *Jane's All the World's Aircraft*, London, annually since 1911

American Indian Art

F. J. Dockstader, *Indian Art in America: The Arts and Crafts of the North American Indian*, Greenwich, 1961

Antiquities

Classical

J. Boardman, *Athenian Black Figure Vases*, London, 1974
J. Boardman, *Athenian Red Figure Vases*, London, 1975
M. Henig (ed.), *A Handbook of Roman Art*, Oxford, 1983
R. A. Higgins, *Greek and Roman Jewellery*, London, 1961
G. Richter, *A Handbook of Greek Art*, London, 1959

Egyptian

W. C. Hayes, *The Scepter of Egypt*, parts I–II, New York, 1953

Near East

H. Frankfort, *The Art and Architecture of the Ancient Orient*, 3rd (revised) impression, London, 1963

Arms and Armour

C. Blair, *European and American Arms*, London, 1962
C. Blair, *European Armour*, London, 1958
J. Hayward, *The Art of the Gunmaker*, vols. I and II, London, 1962, 1963; 2nd edn., 1965
H. L. Peterson, *Arms and Armor in Colonial America, 1526–1783*, 2 vols., Harrisburg, Pa., 1956
G. Stone, *A Glossary of the Construction, Decoration and use of Arms and Armor*, New York, 1934, 1961

Arts and Crafts, Art Nouveau and Art Deco

I. Anscombe and C. Gere, *Arts and Crafts in Britain and America*, New York, 1978
V. Arwas, *Art Deco*, London, 1980
B. Catley, *Art Deco and other Figures*, London, 1978
R. J. Clark, *The Arts and Crafts Movement in America 1876–1916*, Princeton, N.J., 1972
P. Evans, *Art Pottery of the United States: An Encyclopedia of Producers and Their Marks*, New York, 1974
R. & T. Kovel, *The Kovels' Collectors' Guide to American Art Pottery*, New York, 1974
G. Naylor, *The Arts and Crafts Movement*, London, 1971
C. V. Percy, *The Glass of Lalique: A Collectors' Guide*, London, 1977
T. Préaud & S. Gauthier, *Ceramics of the Twentieth Century*, Oxford, 1982
M. D. Schwartz & R. Wolfe, *A History of American Art Porcelain*, New York, 1967

Barometers

E. Banfield, *Antique Barometers*, Hereford, 1976
N. Goodison, *English Barometers 1680–1860*, London, 1968; 2nd edn., Woodbridge, Suffolk, 1977

Books

J. Carter, *ABC for Book Collectors*, 6th edn., London, 1982
J. Carter, *Taste and Technique in Book Collecting*, London, 1970
P Gaskell, *A New Introduction to Bibliography*, Oxford, 1972
J. Peters (ed.), *Book Collecting: A Modern Guide*, New York & London, 1977
A. Thomas, *Great Books and Book Collectors*, London, 1975
P. H. Muir, *Book Collecting as a Hobby: a Series of Letters to Everyman*, London, 1945
P. H. Muir, *Book Collecting: More Letters to Everyman*, London, 1949

Chinese Works of Art

C. Deydier, *Chinese Bronzes*, Munich, 1981
A. du Boulay, *Chinese Porcelain*, London, 1963

G. Ecke, *Chinese Domestic Furniture*, Hong Kong, 1942; reprinted, Vermont, 1962

H. Garner, *Chinese Lacquer*, London, 1979

H. Garner, *Oriental Blue and White*, London, 1954

D. Howard & J. Ayers, *China for the West*, London, 1978

D. Howard, *Chinese Armorial Porcelain*, London, 1974

S. Jenyns, *Later Chinese Ceramics*, London, no date

S. Jenyns, *Ming Pottery and Porcelain*, London, 1954

D. F. Lunsingh-Scheurleer, *Chinese Export Porcelain*, London, 1974

R. C. Stevens, *The Collector's Book of Snuff Bottles*, New York, 1976

Clocks and Watches

G. H. Baillie, *Watchmakers and Clockmakers of the World*, vol. I, London, 1929, and subsequent editions; vol. II by B. Loomes, London, 1976

F. J. Britten, *Old Clocks and Watches and their Makers*, London, 1899. 6th edn., 1932, is best of the original format, but also revised edns. by G. H . Baillie, C. Clutton and C. R. Ilbert, London, 1956; and by C. Clutton and G. Daniels, London, 1983.

T. P. Camerer Cuss, *The Camerer Cuss Book of Antique Watches*, Woodbridge, Suffolk, 1976

C. Clutton & G. Daniels, *Watches*, London, 1965; 3rd (revised) edn., London, 1979

P. G. Dawson, C. B. Drover & D. W. Parkes, *Early English Clocks*, Woodbridge, Suffolk, 1982

W. Edey, *French Clocks*, New York & London, 1967

R. Gould, *The Marine Chronometer*, London, 1923 and subsequent reprintings

E. Jaquet & A. Chapuis, *Technique and History of the Swiss Watch*, London, New York, Sydney, Toronto, 1970

Cigarette Cards

The Catalogue of International Cigarette Cards, London, 1982

London Cigarette Card Company, *The Complete Catalogue of British Cigarette Cards*, London, 1982

Coins and Medals

C. L. Krause & C. Mishler, *Standard Catalog of World Coins*, Iola, Wis., 1983

J. Porteous, *Coins in History*, London, 1969

P. Seaby & F. Parvey, *Coins of England*, London, 1983

D. Sear, *Greek Coins*, London, 1978

D. Sear, *Roman Coins*, London, 1983

Drawings

P. Rawson, *Drawing*, London, 1969

F. Ames-Lewis, *Drawing in Early Renaissance Italy*, New Haven and London, 1981

Furniture

American

E. H. & J. A. Bjerkoe, *The Cabinetmakers of America*, New York, 1967

H. Comstock, *American Furniture: Seventeenth-, Eighteenth- and Nineteenth-Century Styles*, New York, 1962

W. M. Hornor, Jr., *Blue Book: Philadelphia Furniture*, Philadelphia, 1935

R. & T. Kovel, *American Country Furniture, 1780–1875*, New York, 1965

English

Antique Collectors' Club, *Pictorial Dictionary of British Nineteenth-Century Furniture Design*, Woodbridge, Suffolk, 1977

W. A. Coleridge, *Chippendale Furniture*, London, 1968

R. Edwards, *Shorter Dictionary of English Furniture*, London, 1977

R. Edwards & M. Jourdain, *Georgian Cabinet Makers*, London, 1955

C. Gilbert, *Chippendale*, London, 1978

E. Harris, *Adam Furniture*, London, 1963

M. Jourdain, *Regency Furniture*, revised edn., London, 1965

D. Watkin, *Thomas Hope and the Neoclassical Idea*, London, 1968

French and Continental

G. de Bellaigue, *The James A. de Rothschild Collection at Waddesdon Manor: Furniture, Clocks and Gilt Bronzes*, London, 1974

G. Himmelheber, *Biedermeier, Furniture*, London, 1974

H. Honour, *Cabinet Makers and Furniture Designers*, London, 1969

P. Verlet, *French Royal Furniture*, London, 1963

F. J. B. Watson, *Louis XVI Furniture*, London, 1960

F. J. B. Watson, *Wallace Collection Catalogue: Furniture*, London, 1955

F. J. B. Watson, *The Wrightsman Collection: Furniture*, New York, 1966

Glass

V. Arwas, *Glass: Art Nouveau to Art Deco*, London, 1977

E. Barrington Haynes, *Glass Through the Ages*, London, 1948; revised 1959; reprinted 1966

L. M. Bickerton, *Illustrated Guide to Eighteenth-Century Drinking Glasses*, London, 1971

H. Tait, *The Golden Age of Venetian Glass*, London, 1979

W. A. Thorpe, *A History of English and Irish Glass*, 1924; reprinted, London, 1969

Japanese Works of Art

The Netsuke Handbook of Ueda Reikichi, adapted from the Japanese by R. Bushell, Tokyo, 1961

W. H. Edmunds, *Pointers and Clues to the Subjects of Chinese and Japanese Art*, London, 1934; reprint, Geneva, 1974

M. Feddersen, *Japanese Decorative Art*, London, 1962

S. Jenyns, *Japanese Porcelain*, London, 1965

S. Jenyns, *Japanese Pottery*, London, 1971

A. Koop & H. Inada, *Japanese Names and How to Read Them*, London, 1972

Jewellery

J. Anderson Black, *The Story of Jewelry*, New York, 1974

J. Evans, *A History of Jewellery, 1100–1870*, 1st edn., London, 1951; 2nd edn., Boston, 1970

Y. Hackenbroch, *Renaissance Jewellery*, London, 1979

I. Kuntzsch, *A History of Jewels and Jewelry*, New York, 1981

G. F. Kunz & C. H. Stevenson, *The Book of the Pearl*, New York, 1908

H. Newman, *An Illustrated Dictionary of Jewellery*, London, 1981

Lord Twining, *A History of the Crown Jewels of Europe*, London, 1960

Miniatures

E. Auerbach, *Nicholas Hilliard*, London, 1961

D. Foskett, *Collecting Miniatures*, London, 1979

D. Foskett, *A Dictionary of British Miniature Painters*, London, 1972

B. Long, *British Miniaturists*, London, 1929

Murdoch, Murrell, Strong and Noon, *The English Miniature*, New Haven, 1982

R. Strong, *The English Renaissance Miniature*, London, 1983

Motor Cars

G. N. Georgano (ed.), *The Complete Encyclopaedia of Motor Cars*, London, 1968, 1973, 1983

C. Mortimer, *The Constant Search*, London, 1982

M. C. Sedgwick, *Cars of the 1930s*, London, 1970

M. C. Sedgwick, *The Motor Car 1946–1956*, London, 1979

W. C. Williams, *Motoring Mascots of the World*, London, 1980

Musical Instruments

A. Baines, *European and American Musical Instruments*, New York, 1966

A. Baines, *Woodwind Instruments and their History*, London, 1967

D. M. Boalch, *Makers of the Harpsichord and Clavichord 1440–1840*, Oxford, 1974

W. Hammer, *Master Italian Violinmakers*, Munich, 1976

R. E. M. Harding, *The Piano-Forte: its History Traced to the Great Exhibition of 1851*, London, 1933; reprint, Woking Surrey, 1978

W. Henley, *Universal Dictionary of Violin and Bow Makers*, Brighton, 1979

L. G. Langwill, *An Index of Musical Wind Instrument Makers*, Edinburgh, 1980

Objects of Vertu

H. Ricketts, *Objects of Vertu*, London, 1971

Paintings

Italian Renaissance

M. Baxandall, *Painting and Experience in Fifteenth-Century Italy*, Oxford, 1974

S. Freedberg, *Painting in Italy 1500–1600*, London, 1976

F. Hart, *Italian Renaissance Art*, London, 1980

M. Levey, *The Early Renaissance*, London, 1967

M. Levey, *High Renaissance*, London, 1975

J. Shearman, *Mannerism*, London, 1967

A. Smart, *The Dawn of Italian Painting 1250–1400*, Oxford, 1978

J. White, *Art and Architecture in Italy 1250–1400*, London, 1966

Seventeenth- and Eighteenth-Century

A. Blunt, *Art and Architecture in France 1500–1700*, London, 1953; 2nd edn., 1973

A. Crookshank & the Knight of Glin, *The Painters of Ireland c.1660–1920*, London, 1978

J. Egerton, *British Sporting and Animal Pictures 1655–1827*, London, 1978

M. J. Friedlander, *Van Eyck to Bruegel*, 2 vols., London, 1969

H. Honour, *Neo-Classicism*, London, 1968

W. G. Kalnein & M. Levey, *Art and Architecture of the Eighteenth Century in France*, Harmondsworth, 1972

M. Levey, *Rococo to Revolution*, London, 1978

G. H. Marius (ed. G. Norman), *Dutch Painters of the Nineteenth Century*, Woodbridge, Suffolk, 1973

J. R. Martin, *Baroque*, London, 1977

J. Rosenberg & S. Slive, *Dutch Art and Architecture 1600–1800*, London, 1977

E. Waterhouse, *Painting in Britain 1530–1790*, London, 1978

R. Wittkower, *Art and Architecture in Italy 1600–1750*, London, 1973

Nineteenth-Century

H. Honour, *Romanticism*, London, 1979; new edn. 1981

L. Nochlin, *Realism*, Baltimore & Harmondsworth, 1971

J. Rewald, *The History of Impressionism*, London & New York, 1961

J. Rewald, *The History of Post-Impressionism*, London & New York, 1978

R. Rosenblum & H. Janson, *Art of the Nineteenth Century*, London, 1984

C. Wood, *Dictionary of Victorian Painters*, Woodbridge, Suffolk, 1972

The Second Empire 1852–1870: Art in France under Napoleon III, Philadelphia, 1978

Modern Movement

Arts Council Exhibition Catalogue, *Dada and Surrealism Reviewed*, London, 1978

J. Golding, *Cubism, A History and Analysis*, London, 1971

C. Gray, *The Russian Experiment in Art 1863–1922*, London, 1971

G. H. Hamilton, *Painting and Sculpture in Europe 1880–1940*, London, 1972

N. Lynton, *The Story of Modern Art*, Oxford, 1980

R. Rosenblum, *Cubism and Twentieth-Century Art*, New York, 1961; revised edn., 1976

I. Sandler, *The Triumph of American Painting: A History of Abstract Expressionism*, New York, 1970

Modern British

W. Baron, *The Camden Town Group*, London, 1977

R. Cork, *Vorticism and Abstract Art in the First Machine Age*, vols. I & II, London, 1976

J. Rothenstein, *Modern British Painters*, vols. 1–3, London, 1952, 1956, 1974

R. Shone, *The Century of Change: British Painting since 1900*, Oxford, 1977

G. M. Waters, *Dictionary of British Artists 1900–1950*, vols. I & II, Eastbourne, 1975

American

M. Fielding, *Dictionary of American Painters, Sculptors and Engravers*, New York, 1965

G. C. Groce & D. H. Wallace, *The New York Historical Society's Dictionary of Arts in America, 1564–1860*, New Haven, 1964

J. H. Lipmann & H. M. Franc, *Bright Stars: American Painting and Sculpture since 1776*, New York, 1976

J. Wilmerding, *American Art*, London, 1976

Pewter

P. R. G. Hornsby, *Pewter of the Western World 1600–1850*, Exton, Pa., 1983

L. I. Laughlin, *Pewter in America: Its Makers and their Marks*, 3 vols., Barre, Mass., 1969

R. F. Michaelis, *Antique Pewter of the British Isles*, London, 1955

C. F. Montgomery, *A History of American Pewter*, New York, 1978

A. J. G. Vester, *Old European Pewter*, London, 1958

Photography

M. Auer, *The Illustrated History of the Camera from 1839 to the Present*, Boston, 1975

C. Beaton & G. Buckland, *The Magic Image: The Genius of Photography from 1839 to the Present Day*, Boston, 1975

B. Coe, *Cameras from Daguerreotypes to Instant Pictures*, New York, 1978

H. and A. Gernsheim, *The History of Photography*, New York, 1969

E. S. Lothrop, *A Century of Cameras*, New York, 1973

B. Newhall, *The History of Photography from 1839 to the Present*, New York, 1982

L. D. Witkin & B. London, *The Photograph Collector's Guide*, London, 1979

Postcards

A. Byatt, *Picture Postcards and their Publishers*, Malvern, Worcs., 1978

Pottery and Porcelain

(See also *Arts and Crafts, Art Nouveau and Art Deco*)

English
Blue and White Porcelain

B. Watney, *English Blue and White Porcelain of the 18th Century*, London, 1963; 2nd edn., 1973

Bow

E. Adams & D. Redstone, *Bow Porcelain*, London, 1981

A. Gabszewicz & G. Freeman, *Bow Porcelain, the Collection Formed by Geoffrey Freeman*, London, 1982

Chelsea

G. E. Bryant, *The Chelsea Porcelain Toys*, London, 1925

F. S. Mackenna, *The Gold Anchor Wares*, Leigh on Sea, Essex, 1952

F. S. Mackenna, *The Red Anchor Wares*, Leigh on Sea, Essex, 1952

F. S. Mackenna, *The Triangle, and Raised Anchor Wares*, Leigh on Sea, Essex, 1948

Derby

H. G. Bradley (ed.), *The Ceramics of Derbyshire 1750–1975: an Illustrated Guide*, privately published, Tiverton, Devon, 1978

J. Twitchett, *Derby Porcelain*, London, 1980

Figures

P. Bradshaw, *Eighteenth-Century English Porcelain Figures 1745–1795*, London, 1981

A. Lane, *English Porcelain Figures in the Eighteenth Century*, London, 1961

Liverpool

K. Boney, *Liverpool Porcelain of the 18th Century and its Makers*, London, 1957

Longton Hall

B. Watney, *Longton Hall Porcelain*, London, 1957

Lowestoft

G. A. Godden, *Illustrated Guide to Lowestoft Porcelain*, London, 1969

C. Spencer, *Early Lowestoft: a Study of the Early History and Products of the Lowestoft Porcelain Manufactory*, Redhill, 1981

Nineteenth-Century and General

G. A. Godden, *British Porcelain, an Illustrated Guide*, London, 1974

G. A. Godden, *Chamberlain-Worcester Porcelain 1788–1852*, London, 1982

G. A. Godden, *Encyclopaedia of British Pottery and Porcelain Marks*, London, 1970 (reprinted)

G. A. Godden (ed.), *Staffordshire Porcelain*, London, 1983

G. Savage, *Eighteenth-Century English Porcelain*, London, 1952

Pottery

F. Britton, *English Delftware in the Bristol Collection*, London, 1982

F. H. Garner & M. Archer, *English Delftware*, London, 1972

D. Towner, *Creamware*, London, 1988

Wedgwood

R. Reilly & G. Savage, *The Dictionary of Wedgwood*, London, 1980

Worcester

Branyon, N. French & J. Sandon, *Worcester Blue and White Porcelain 1751–1790*, London, 1981

F. S. Mackenna, *Worcester Porcelain*, Leigh on Sea, Essex, 1950

H. R. Marshall, *Coloured Worcester Porcelain of the First Period*, Newport, Gwent, 1954; reprinted 1976

European

C. H. de Jonge, *Delft Ceramics*, London, 1970

R. de Plinval de Guillebon, *Paris Porcelain 1770–1880*, London, 1972

S. Ducret, *German Porcelain and Faience*, New York, 1962

A. W. Frottingham, *Lustreware of Spain*, New York, 1951

E. Hannover, *Pottery and Porcelain*, London, 1924

J. Hayward, *Viennese Porcelain of the du Paquier Period*, London, 1952

W. B. Honey, *Dresden China*, London, 1954

W. B. Honey, *European Ceramic Art*, London, 1952

W. B. Honey, *French Porcelain of the Eighteenth Century*, London, 1950

W. B. Honey, *German Porcelain*, London, 1947

A. Lane, *French Faience*, London, 1948

A. Lane, *Italian Porcelain*, London, 1954

G. Liverani, *Five Centuries of Italian Maiolica*, London, 1960

B. Rackham, *Italian Maiolica*, London, 1963

P. Verlet, *Sèvres*, Paris, 1954

Prints

E. Garvey, *The Artist and the Book*, Boston, 1972

A. M. Hind, *A History of Etching and Engraving*, New York, 1923; reprinted, 1984

A. M. Hind, *An Introduction to a History of Woodcuts* (2 vols), New York, 1963

W. M. Ivins, *Prints and Visual Communication*, Cambridge, Mass., 1953

F. H. Man, *150 Years of Artists' Lithographs 1803–1953*, London, 1953

H. Mayor, *Prints and People*, New York, 1971

F. Weitenkampf, *American Graphic Art*, New York, 1970

Rugs and Carpets

I. Bennett, *Country Life Book of Rugs and Carpets of the World*, London, 1977

C. Edwards, *The Persian Carpet*, London, 1975

M. L. Eiland, *Chinese and Exotic Rugs*, Boston, 1979

K. Erdmann, *The History of the Early Turkish Carpet*, London, 1977

K. Erdmann, *Oriental Carpets*, London, 1962

Y. Petsopoulos, *Kilims*, London, 1979

Russian Works of Art

V. Lossky & L. Ouspensky, *The Meaning of Icons*, Boston, 1969

M. C. Ross, *Russian Porcelains*, Oklahoma, 1968

A. K. Snowman, *The Art of Carl Fabergé*, London, 1962

G. von Habsburg-Lothringen & A. von Solodkoff, *Fabergé, Court Jeweller to the Tsars*, London & New York, 1979

A. von Solodkoff, *Russian Gold and Silver*, London & New York, 1981

Scientific Instruments

M. Daumas, *Scientific Instruments of the Seventeenth and Eighteenth Centuries, and their Makers*, London, 1972

S. Guye & H. Michel, *Time and Space, Measuring Instruments from the Fifteenth to Nineteenth Century*, London, 1971

H. Wynter & A. Turner, *Scientific Instruments*, London, 1975

Sculpture

M. Baxandall, *The Limewood Sculptors of Renaissance Germany*, London & New Haven, 1980

S. Beattie, *The New Sculpture*, London & New Haven, 1983

W. Bode (ed. & rev. by J. D. Draper), *The Italian Bronze Statuettes of the Renaissance*, New York, 1980

R. Gunnis, *Dictionary of British Sculptors 1660–1851*, London, 1953

G. F. Hill, *A Corpus of Italian Medals of the Renaissance before Cellini*, London, 1930

J. Mackay, *The Dictionary of Western Sculptors in Bronze*, Woodbridge, Suffolk, 1977

J. Pope-Hennessy, *Catalogue of Italian Sculpture in the Victoria and Albert Museum*, London, 1964

E. J. Pyke, *A Biographical Dictionary of Wax Modellers*, Oxford, 1973; supplement printed privately, 1981

F. Souchal, *French Sculptors of the Seventeenth and Eighteenth Centuries: The Reign of Louis XIV*, illustrated catalogue A–F, Oxford, 1977 and idem., G–L, Oxford, 1981 (M–Z in preparation)

P. Verdier, *The Walters Art Gallery: Catalogue of the Painted Enamels of the Renaissance*, Baltimore, 1967

Silver

American

S. G. C. Ensko, *American Silversmiths and their Marks*, 3 vols., New York, printed privately, 1927–48

M. G. Fales, *Early American Silver*, New York, 1973

D. T. Rainwater, *Encyclopedia of American Silver Manufacturers*, New York, 1975

D. T. Rainwater & H. Ivan, *American Silverplate*, Nashville, 1968

Continental

J. F. Hayward, *Virtuoso Goldsmiths*, London, 1976

C. Hernmarck, *The Art of the European Silversmith 1430–1830*, London, 1977

H. Honour, *Goldsmiths and Silversmiths*, London, 1971

English

M. Clayton, *The Collector's Dictionary of the Silver and Gold of Great Britain and North America*, London, 1971

J. Culme, *Nineteenth-Century Silver*, London, 1977

A. G. Grimwade, *Rococo Silver*, London, 1974

J. F. Hayward, *Huguenot Silver in England 1688–1727*, London, 1959

C. Oman, *English Domestic Silver*, London, 1934 (many editions)

R. Rowe, *Adam Silver*, London, 1965

G. Taylor, *Silver through the Ages*, Harmondsworth, Middx., 1958

Textiles

E. S. Bolton & E. J. Coe, *American Samplers*, Boston, 1921

H. Clouzot, *Painted and Printed Fabrics*, New York, 1927

M. T. Landon & S. B. Swan, *American Crewelwork*, New York, 1970

R. W. Moncrieff, *Man-made Fibres*, London, 1963

F. W. Montgomery, *Printed Textiles, English and American Cottons and Linens 1700–1850*, London, 1970

B. Morris, *Victorian Embroidery*, London, 1962

B. Palliser, *History of Lace*, London, 1902

C. L. Safford & R. Bishop, *America's Quilts and Coverlets*, New York, 1972

W. G. Thomson, *A History of Tapestry*, London, 1972

L. W. van der Meulen-Nulle, *Lace*, London, 1963; New York, 1964

Toys

Model Engineer Magazine, M.A.P. Publications, Hemel Hempstead, published fortnightly since 1900

J. G. Garrattt, *Model Soldiers: A Collectors' Guide*, London, 1958

G. Kichenside, *A Source Book of Miniature and Narrow Gauge Railways*, London, 1981

C. E. King, *The Collector's History of Dolls*, London, 1977

C. E. King, *The Encyclopaedia of Toys*, London, 1978

A. Levy, *A Century of Model Trains*, London, 1974

D. Pressland, *The Art of the Tin Toy*, London, 1976

G. White, *Toys, Dolls, Automata: Marks and Labels*, London, 1975

Tribal Art

T. Barrow, *Art and Life in Polynesia*, London, 1971

E. Elisofon & W. Fagg, *The Sculpture of Africa*, London, 1958 (also French & German translations)

W. Fagg, *Tribes and Forms in African Art*, London, 1965

W. Gillon, *Collecting African Art*, London, 1979

S. Hooper, *Art and Artefacts of the Pacific, Africa and the Americas: The James Hooper Collection*, London, 1976

F. Willett, *African Art*, London, 1971

Watercolours

D. Clifford, *Collecting English Watercolours*, London, 1970

E. Croft-Murray & P. Hulton, *Catalogue of British Drawings in the British Museum (16th and 17th Centuries)*, London, 1960

M. Hardie, *Watercolour Painting in Britain*, 3 vols., London, 1966

S. Houfe, *The Dictionary of British Book Illustrators and Caricaturists 1800–1914*, Woodbridge, Suffolk, 1978

L. Lambourne & J. Hamilton, *Catalogue of British Watercolours in the Victoria and Albert Museum*, London, 1980

H. L. Mallalieu, *The Dictionary of British Watercolour Artists up to 1920*, Woodbridge, Suffolk, 1976

I. A. Williams, *Early English Watercolours*, Bath, 1970

A. Wilton, *British Watercolours 1750–1850*, Oxford, 1977

Wine

S. Bradford, *The Story of Port*, London, 1983

M. Broadbent, *The Great Vintage Wine Book*, London, 1980

M. Broadbent, *Wine Tasting, Enjoying, Understanding*, London, 1979

Christie's Price Index of Vintage Wine, London, 1983

A. Lichine (ed.), *Encyclopedia of Wines and Spirits*, London, 1975; 5th edn., 1982

H. Johnson, *World Atlas of Wine*, London, 1977

E. Penning-Rowsell, *Wines of Bordeaux*, London, 1979

PROFESSIONAL ASSOCIATIONS

Introduction

There are few, if any, official or government bodies that accredit professionals in the art community (dealers, appraisers, restorers), and a number of self-policing associations have been established. Some of these associations admit members by invitation only, others take applications, some test applicants and others do not. Nearly all have codes of ethics. However, many highly qualified people in arts-related professions are not members of any association at all. References from friends, fellow collectors, museums, curators, or art historians are just as important to the collector seeking such services, if not more so, than referrals from one of the associations' staff members. There are any number of qualified dealers, appraisers, and restorers providing good service each day, but one must look for them. An impressive logo and name do not necessarily mean that there is effective authority behind them. As in all things, check first.

Listed below are the chief professional organizations worldwide that are of importance for collectors and dealers. Much fuller listings, including many regional and specialized groups, are listed in the *International Directory of Arts* (see Appendix 3).

Trade and Professional Bodies in the United Kingdom

The main organizations in the United Kingdom are:

The British Antique Dealers' Association Ltd (BADA)

The BADA was established in 1918 and was born out of action taken by a group of members of the trade who opposed a government proposal concerning a tax on luxury goods. The action was successful.

Since that time the membership has almost always numbered 500. The members are primarily elected for their integrity and knowledge. Their membership is reviewed annually and thus the reputation of the Association is jealously guarded. The purpose of the Association is to protect its members, but in doing so also to protect the public from unscrupulous behaviour, and thus it devotes much time to its public relations.

The Association regularly stages exhibitions, as it has done since it was founded. It is closely involved in much government departmental work and regards itself as a watchdog for any unpalatable proposals likely to affect the trade and the general public where the buying, selling and restoration of antiques and works of art are concerned.

BADA runs one- and two-year courses in the restoration of clocks, furniture and porcelain at West Dean College. It also recently agreed to promote and maintain the annual Grosvenor House Fair in order to support its members and commerce in general.

Address: 20 Rutland Gate, London, SW7 1BD

The London and Provincial Antique Dealers' Association Ltd (LAPADA)

LAPADA provides active representation for those in the antiques and fine art trade who meet the Association's requirements in terms of knowledge, experience, probity and commercial soundness. It gives members a wide range of services and tangible benefits, including discounts on insurance premiums; assistance with tax and legal problems; reduced rates for certain hotels, publications, car and van hire, security equipment, etc.; informative quarterly newsletters; corporate publicity. The Association welcomes inquiries from the trade and the public and will take appropriate action in cases involving breach of the Association's code of practice or disputes with members. LAPADA is active on behalf of its members endeavouring to ease the weight of fiscal bureaucracy and arbitrating in cases of dispute. In 1983 membership of LAPADA numbered 600 in the United Kingdom and 85 overseas.

Address: 112 Brompton Road, London, SW3 1JJ

The Cotswold Antique Dealers Association (CADA)

CADA represents a group of antique dealers situated in the heart of England. The aims are to promote and encourage trade in the Cotswold area, and to assist all visiting dealers and collectors in locating antiques and works of art. The members will give advice on where to stay in the area, and assistance with packing and shipping, insurance, and exchange of foreign currencies.

Address: High Street, Blockley, near Moreton-in-Marsh, Gloucestershire

The Society of London Art Dealers

The Society brings together companies, firms and individuals engaged in the sale or exhibitions of pictures, drawings, prints and sculpture in London. Its purpose is to advance and promote the interests of the trade, both home and export.

Address: c/o The Fine Art Society, 148 New Bond Street, London, W1Y 0JT

Society of Fine Art Auctioneers (SOFAA)

The Society is a professional body representing approximately two dozen fine art auctioneers in Great Britain who offer a comprehensive service. The aim of the Society is to insist on high standards among its members so that vendors received the best possible service.

Address: 7 Blenheim Street, New Bond Street, London W1Y 0AS

Antiquarian Booksellers' Association

The Antiquarian Booksellers' Association is the recognized trade body for dealers in rare books and manuscripts in the United Kingdom. Its members are pledged to uphold the status of the antiquarian book trade and to promote just and honourable methods in the conduct of business. It was founded in 1906 and was the first organization of its kind in the world. A list of members with their fields of specialization where appropriate is available free of charge from the Associations's Secretary.

The Association does not itself buy or sell books or provide a valuation service, but all its members are either prepared to do so or to refer inquiries to other firms better able to meet the needs of a collector or owner. Membership of the Association is restricted to booksellers who have a minimum of five years' trading experience.

One of the ABA's more important functions is to sponsor the annual Antiquarian Book Fair (normally held each June in the Europa Hotel in London). There is an International Directory of Antiquarian Booksellers (see Appendix 3).
Address: 154 Buckingham Palace Road, London, SW1

Trade and Professional Bodies in the United States

International Foundation for Art Research (IFAR)

IFAR was incorporated in 1968 to provide authentications to collectors on paintings. Over the years, IFAR's function has changed, and although its staff still work on authentications a large part of their efforts go towards gathering and disseminating information on stolen art and forgeries. They also recently undertook a project to document and catalogue Pre-Columbian art in the Cuzco region of Peru so that should the art hanging in churches there be smuggled out some record of Peru's national treasures will survive and the loot may be reclaimed more easily.

Because IFAR is not a professional organization but one given to research, its membership has more in common with the museum world than with that of dealers or appraisers. Members receive bulletins and invitations to lectures generated by the foundation.

The IFAR lecture series, held during each winter, covers legal and art-historical issues. IFAR also publishes two periodicals, *Art Research News* and *Stolen Art Alert*.
Address: 46 East 70 Street, New York, NY 10021
Telephone: (212) 879–1780

American Society of Appraisers (ASA)

In 1952, the American Society of Technical Appraisers and the Technical Valuation Society, groups of appraisers centred on the East and West coasts of the United States, merged to form the American Society of Appraisers.

Only 800 or so of the 4,500 members of the ASA specialize in appraising personal property (art, antiques, collectables). The rest handle real estate, machinery (farm tractors), and other non-arts related properties. Members fall into three categories: Associate, Member, and Senior Member. Applicants for Associate must provide several references and Associates need not be practising appraisers. If the applicant has been a full-time appraiser (either as an appraiser solely or as a dealer as well) for two years and can pass the ASA's eight-hour exam that covers the ASA's code of ethics, the principles of appraising, and specific technical questions about a particular field of art or antiques then the applicant can become a Member. Senior

Members must have been a full-time appraiser for five years and have the same qualifications as Members. The ASA's members are listed by speciality and geographic location in a booklet published by the ASA and available for $5.00. The ASA also publishes a bimonthly newsletter, *Newsline*, and an annual or semi-annual, depending on the year, technical journal, *Valuation*, as well as a code of ethics. Seminars are conducted for members on both national and regional levels.
Address: P.O. Box 17265; Washington, DC 20041
Telephone: (703) 620–3838

Appraisers Association of America (AAA)

Founded in 1949, the AAA exists to further the art of appraising and to match collectors in need of appraisals with appraisers qualified to undertake them.

Membership in the AAA numbers roughly 1,200 and membership is reviewed if complaints are received about individual members. Applicants to the AAA must provide references and three appraisals performed recently. The AAA publishes a monthly newsletter, *The Appraiser*, which contains information about legal, ethical, and educational aspects of appraising.
Address: 60 East 42 Street, New York, NY 10165
Telephone: (212) 867–9775

Art and Antique Dealers League of America (AADLA)

AADLA, founded in 1926 and thus the oldest dealers' association or league in the United States, is a member of CINOA (see below). There are nearly 110 members of AADLA in the United States and Canada, all of whom ascribe to the League's code of ethics. As with other such associations, the purpose of the League is to distinguish its members by virtue of their membership, and membership is by application and is reviewed annually. Members handle primarily antiques and largely those that pre-date 1830.
Address: 353 East 53 Street, New York, NY 10022
Telephone: (212) 838–7520 or (212) 355–0175

Art Dealers Association of America (ADAA)

The ADAA, a group of well-established dealers, was formed in 1962 partly in response to governmental dissatisfaction with inflated valuations being prepared as the basis for excessive taxation deductions following gifts to non-profit educational or cultural institutions. Six years later, the ADAA worked in conjunction with the Internal Revenue Service to establish the IRS's Commissioners Art Advisory Panel which is a group of curators, academics, historians, and dealers who review values listed for tax deductible donations.

The ADAA devised what it feels is an answer to the question of conflict of interest in appraising fine arts that have been donated to institutions for tax considerations (the ADAA does not perform estate or insurance appraisals save in rare circumstances). Rather than referring requests for names of appraisers to their members the ADAA administrative offices require that collectors provide information about and photographs of the item to be appraised. This information, without the collector's name, is sent out to three ADAA members who prepare appraisals and valuations independently of each other and return the materials to the ADAA offices. If there is a significant disagreement regarding value or identity of the work of art the three members meet and discuss the bases of their opinions and arrive at a consensus. The ideas here are that three heads are better than one and that because the appraisers are acting on behalf of the ADAA rather than the collector, there is no pressure to weight the valuation in the collector's favour. ADAA members appraise only fine arts – paintings, prints, drawings, etchings, and sculpture.

The problem of excessive valuations still exists, and so does the ADAA. The Association has roughly 120 members who sell for the most part fine arts – that is, paintings, drawings, etchings, prints, and sculpture. Membership is by invitation rather than application. The Association gives out two annual awards, one a $5,000 award for outstanding contribution to art historical study, and the other a $20,000 fellowship to a doctoral student at a United States university whose studies focus on American or European fine arts. The ADAA also sponsors a series of panel discussions on the art world each November. Their publication, the *Art Theft Archives*, is a free service that lists art recently stolen. ADAA is a member of CINOA.
Address: 575 Madison Avenue, New York, NY 10022
Telephone: (212) 940–8590

The National Antique & Art Dealers Association of America (NAADA)

In 1954 a group of dealers split off from AADLA to form NAADA. Membership of NAADA is by invitation only and the membership is both small (only 39) and select. As the Association's name suggests, its members deal more heavily in antiques than in fine art. Its members must ascribe to the Association's code of ethics, which is pledged to safeguard the interests of collectors.

Although NAADA does not give grants or awards it does sponsor periodic lectures and symposia, in 1983 topic being 'In Quest of Quality'. NAADA is a member of CINOA.
Address: 15 East 57 Street, New York, NY 10022
Telephone: (212) 355–0636

National Institute for the Conservation of Cultural Property (NIC)

The NIC grew out of the National Conservation Advisory Council (NCAC), a United States group formed in 1973 to identify national needs and problems in the field of conservation and to recommend solutions. The NCAC disbanded in 1982 after publishing eight reports on the state of conservation in the United States and sanctioning the creation of the NIC to continue efforts in promoting and coordinating national programs whose end is to safeguard publicly and privately owned cultural property, assist efforts of conservators, and enhance public understanding of conservation principles and problems. Essentially, the NIC acts as a clearing house for information on techniques and problems in restoration and as a study centre for administrative and operational problems within institutions.

The NIC's members are institutions and associations. It is not a professional association. Quite aside from its work with institutions and various governmental agencies the NIC aids collectors in finding reputable conservators. Although collectors can simply call museums near where they live to get a referral, some museums are reluctant to provide this information because referrals are tantamount to endorsements, and many museums do not like to endorse anything save the works in their collections and some museums regret having gone that far. Upon a request from a collector, a member of the NIC staff will call a museum to get the information a collector needs, but because of the NIC's position in the art community they may obtain information a collector could not get.
Address: A & I – 2225, Smithsonian Institution, Washington, DC 20560
Telephone: (202) 357–2295

American Institute for Conservation of Historic and Artistic Works (AIC)

The AIC started off in 1959 as the American group of the International Institute for Conservation of Historic and Artistic Works (IIC), whose headquarters are in London. In 1973 the AIC was incorporated as an independent organization. Unlike the NIC, the AIC is a professional association whose members are conservators or people interested in the field of conservation.

The AIC's 2,100 members are conservators, restorers, and people interested in conservation. Associate Members include conservation students, conservators, art historians, museum curators, museum professionals, librarians and archivists, though anyone interested in conservation may become an Associate Member. Professional Associates are practising conservators with two years in the field who agree to uphold the AIC's code of ethics and must submit two treatment reports on works they have restored, as well as information about their education or training and references from two Professional Associates. The rank of Fellow in the AIC indicates a minimum of five years' full-time practice as a conservator and candidates must be recommended by five other Fellows. Applications for both the Professional Associate and Fellow categories are reviewed very carefully by a five-person membership committee. There is also an Institutional Membership.

Members receive the AIC's journal and newsletter. The Institute publishes a pamphlet that lists names and addresses of all AIC members and includes the Bylaws and Code of Ethics of AIC.
Address: 3545 Williamsburg Lane NW, Washington, DC 20008
Telephone: (202) 364–1036

Trade and Professional Bodies in Europe and Worldwide

CINOA (Confédération Internationale des Négociants en Oeuvres d'Art)

The International Art Dealers' Association is a non-profit-making organization founded in Amsterdam in 1936. Its purpose is to promote good feeling and goodwill between dealers in all member countries and to consult on any international matter relating to antiques and works of art. The headquarters were later transferred to Brussels and have remained there ever since. There are thirteen member countries at present: Belgium, Holland, New Zealand, Eire, France, Western Germany, Austria, Italy, South Africa, Great Britain, the United States of America, Sweden and Switzerland.
Head Office: 27 rue Ernest Allard, Brussels, Belgium.

Australia

Antique Dealers' Association of New South Wales, 354 Dowling Street, Paddington, Sydney 2021
Antique Dealers' Association of Victoria, Malvern, P.O.B. 24, Melbourne 3144

Austria

Bundesberufsgruppe des Kunst- und Antiquitätenhandels, Bauernmarkt 13, 1011 Vienna

Bundeskammer der Gewerblichen Wirtschaft, Sektion Handel, Gremium Antiquitätenhandel, Schwarzenbergplatz 14, 1041 Vienna

Sales are held by the state-run Dorotheum, Dorotheegasse 11, Vienna.

Belgium

Chambre des Antiquaires de Belgique, 27 rue Ernest Allard, 1000 Brussels

Chambre Syndicale des Salles à Ventes de Belgique, 3 sq. de Biarritz, 1050 Brussels

Union Professionelle des Marchands d'Antiquités, Objets d'Art, Curiosités et Brocante, Chaussée de Wavre 1422 à 1162, Brussels

Canada

Canadian Antique Dealers' Association, Box 517, Station K, Toronto M4P 2EO

Denmark

Dansk Kunst- und Antikvitetshandler-Union, Larsbjornstraede 6, 1454 Copenhagen

France

Association des Antiquaires et Brocanteurs de France, 31 rue de Peletier, 75009 Paris

Chambre des Commissaires-Priseurs de Paris, Hôtel Drouot, 9 rue Drouot, 75009 Paris

Chambre Nationale des Commissaires-Priseurs, 13 rue de la Grange-Batellière, 75009 Paris

Société des Antiquaires de France, Palais du Louvre, Pavillon Mollieu, 75001 Paris

Syndicat Français des Experts Professionels en Oeuvres d'Art, 15 rue Vaneau, 75007 Paris

Syndicat National des Antiquaires, Négociants en Objets d'Art, Tableaux anciens et modernes, 11 rue Jean Memoz, 75008 Paris

Syndicat National du Commerce de l'Antiquité et de l'Occasion (SNCAO), 18 rue de Provence, 75009 Paris

Ireland

Irish Antique Dealers' Association, 27 South Anne Street, Dublin 2

Italy

Associazione Antiquari d'Italia, Lungarno Soderini 5, Firenze, Italy

Federazione Italiana Mercanti d'Arte, Corso Venezia 47–9, 20121 Milan

Sindicato Nazionale Mercanti d'Arte Moderna, Corso Venezia 47–9, 20121 Milan

Japan

There are closely connected Dealers' Associations in Tokyo, Osaka, Kyoto, Nagoya and Kanayawa.

Netherlands

Nederlands Antiquairs Genootschap, Van Broeckhuijsenstraat 1–3, 6511 PE Nijmegen

Stichting Oude Kunst- en Antiekbeurs, Keizersgracht 207, 1016 DS Amsterdam

Vereeniging Nederlands Antiquairs Genootschap, Postbus 246, 2980 AE Ridderkerk

Vereeniging van Handelaren in Oude Kunst in Nederland, Keizersgracht 207, 1016 DS Amsterdam

New Zealand

General Auctioneers' Association of New Zealand, P.O.B. 11–253, Wellington

New Zealand Antique Dealers' Association, 99 Shortland Street, Auckland

Norway

Norges Kunst & Antikvitethandleres Forening, Universitetsgaten 12, Oslo

Sweden

Sveriges Konst- och Antikhandlare Forening, Västerlanggatan 43, 1129 Stockholm

Switzerland

Schweizerische Gesellschaft der Freunde von Kunst Auktionen, Werdmühlestrasse 11, 8001 Zürich

Verband Antiquare und Restauratoren, Kirchgasse 33, Postfach 1139, 8001 Zürich

Verband Schweizerischer Antiquare und Kunsthändler, Sachsenstrasse 23, 4562 Biberist

Verband Schweizerischer Auktionatoren von Kunst und Kulturgut, Laupenstrasse 41, 3008 Bern

West Germany

Bundesverband des Deutschen Kunst- und Antiquitätenhandels e.V., Stadtwaldgürtel 32A, 5000 Cologne 41

Deutscher Fachverband für den Antiquitäten- und Kunsthandel e.V., Lindenallee 6–8, 4300 Essen

Landesverband Deutscher Auktionatoren für Rheinland und Westfalen e.V., Klusenhof 12, 4010 Hilden

Verband Deutscher Kunst- und Antiquitätenhändler e.V., Schloss Sickendorf, 6420 Lauterbach 7

There is also a Berlin auctioneers' society (but apparently no national one) and several regional antique dealers' associations.

APPENDIX 3

DIRECTORIES OF AUCTION HOUSES AND DEALERS

Introduction

The most comprehensive international directory is the *International Directory of Arts*, published annually in English by the Art Address Verlag, Munich, and by Bowker and Company in the United States. The 1983/84 edition, in two volumes, comprises the following sections:

Volume I: Museums and Art Galleries; Universities, Academies, Colleges; Associations; Artists; Collectors.

Volume II: Art and Antique Dealers; Numismatic Dealers; Galleries; Auctioneers; Restorers; Art Publishers; Art Periodicals; Antiquarian and Art Booksellers.

Listings are alphabetical by country, filling a total of 1,378 closely printed pages. Under 'Art Periodicals' it lists antique trade periodicals published in several countries; where national directories are not published, many of these periodicals will contain regular advertisements from dealers and auctions houses.

The trade Associations listed in Appendix 2 will also supply lists of their members.

United Kingdom

The Antique Collecting Directory (ed. Lorraine Johnson), London, 1983

Antiques Trade Gazette, a weekly newspaper with copious trade advertisements, detailed listings of forthcoming sales, and reports on the current art market.

The Auction Companion (ed. D. and K. Leab), London, 1981

British Art and Antiques Yearbook, National Magazine Company, London, 1984

The Guide to the Antique Shops in Great Britain, Antique Collectors Club, Woodbridge, 1984

United States

American Art Directory (ed. J. Cattell Press), published annually by Bowker, New York and London.

The Antique World Travel Guide to America (ed. P. Bayer and M. Goldrum), New York, 1982

The Auction Companion (ed. D. and K. Leab), London, 1981

Collectors' Guide to US Auctions and Flea Markets (ed. Susan Wasserstein), New York, 1981

Collectors' Market Place Directory, published annually by Artepreneur Inc, New York. Lists New York only

Fine Arts Market Place (ed. P. Cummings), New York, 1978. Also includes details of art material suppliers; services such as restorers, insurers, packers, custom brokers; and art associations, print clubs, arts councils, and Foundations

Flea Market America (ed. McCree), Santa Fe, 1983

The Kovels' Collectors Source Book (ed. Ralph and Terry Kovel), New York, 1983

Europe and Worldwide

Art Diary: The World's Art Directory (ed. G. Politi), published annually in Milan

The Auction Companion (ed. D. and K. Leab), London, 1981

Catalogo dell' Antiquariato e del Collezionisimo, published by Mondadori, Milan

Guida OPI dell' antiquariato Italiano, published by the Organizzazione Publicazioni Italiane, Genoa

Guide Emer, published biennially by Guide Emer, Paris. Comprehensive listing of auction houses, dealers and associated services in Paris, the French provinces and Europe

International Art and Antiques Yearbook, a worldwide dealers' and collectors' guide to the antiques trade published by Art and Antiques Yearbook Publishers, London. Lists dealers, dealers' associations, art and antique periodicals, antique fairs.

International Directory of Antiquarian Booksellers, 1976/77. Members of the 16 national associations affiliated to the League of Antiquarian Booksellers are listed alphabetically or geographically and by specialization.

International Directory of Arts (see above).

APPENDIX 4

DIRECTORIES OF MUSEUMS, GALLERIES AND PRIVATE COLLECTIONS

General

There are many general guide books which contain information about museums, galleries and private collections. The most detailed listing of museums worldwide is to be found in *The Directory of Museums* edited by Kenneth Hudson and Ann Nicholls, published in London by MacMillan in 1975 (published in the United States by Columbia University Press in 1974 as the *Directory of World Museums*). It contains a brief description of each museum, with addresses. It also has a classified subject index of specialized and outstanding collections, and a bibliography of national museum directories. *The International Directory of Arts* (see Appendix 3) also gives a comprehensive list, as does *Museums of the World* (2nd edition 1975) published by Verlag Dokumentation, Munich.

English-speaking travellers to Europe and North America are very well catered for with the famous series of Green Guides, published by Michelin, and by the Blue Guides, published by Benn, which are very readily available and inexpensive, and they are informative, reliable, and indispensable. Tourist offices, both national and local, will also give advice and information.

A selection of specialized publications for the United Kingdom and the United States is given below, and it is worth re-emphasizing the richness and importance of the British country houses and their contents, which are unique and of the greatest importance and interest to collectors (see chapter 2).

United Kingdom

Arts Review Year Book, published annually by *Arts Review* Magazine. Lists museums and public galleries; London galleries; regional museums and galleries; art in country houses; friends' associations; art societies and organizations; arts councils; book publishers; print publishers; art and design colleges; craft shops and workshops.

Country House Treasures (by Arthur Foss), London, 1980

The Good Museums Guide (by Kenneth Hudson), London, 1980

Historic Houses, Castles and Gardens in Great Britain and Ireland, published annually by ABC Historical Publications

The Historic Houses Handbook (by Neil Burton), London, 1981/2

The Libraries, Museums and Art Galleries Yearbook, published annually by James Clark & Co., Ltd., Cambridge

Museums and Galleries in Great Britain and Ireland, published annually by ABC Historical Publications

Museums Yearbook, published annually by the Museums Association.

United States

American Art Museums (by E. Spaeth), New York, 1969

Art in America. The August issue of the magazine *Art in America* is an annual guide to galleries, museums and artists of contemporary art.

The Art Museums of New England (by S. L. Faison), Boston, 1982

Looking at Art: a Visitor's Guide to Museum Collections (by A. M. Gealt), New York, 1983

Manual for Museums (by R. H. Lewis), Washington, 1976

Museums USA: A History and Guide (by H. and M. Katz), New York, 1965

The Official Museum Directory, published annually for the American Association of Museums by the National Register Publishing Company.

On Understanding Art Museums (ed. S. E. Lee), Englewood Cliffs, 1975

APPENDIX 5

CHRISTIE'S SALEROOMS AND REPRESENTATIVES

1. Salerooms

United Kingdom
Head Office
Christie, Manson & Woods Ltd,
8 King Street, St. James's, London SW1Y 6QT
Telephone: (01) 839 9060 Telex: 916429
Chairman: J. A. Floyd

South Kensington
Christie's South Kensington Ltd,
85 Old Brompton Road, London SW7 3JS
Telephone: (01) 581 2231 Telex: 922061
Chairman: W. F. Brooks

Scotland
Christie's & Edmiston's Ltd,
164–166 Bath Street, Glasgow
Telephone: (041) 332 8134/7 Telex: 779901
Chairman: Sir Ilay Campbell

Robson Lowe at Christie's (stamp auctions)
47 Duke Street, St. James's, London SW1Y 6QX
Telephone: (01) 839 4034

Europe
Italy
Christie's (International) SA,
Palazzo Massimo Lancellotti, Piazza Navona 114, Rome
00186
Telephone: (396) 654 1217 Telex: Rome 611 524
Directors: Tom Milnes Gaskell; Maurizio Lodi-Fé
Consultant: d. ssa. Luisa Vertova Nicolson

The Netherlands
Christie's Amsterdam B.V.,
Cornelis Schuytstraat 57, 1071 JG Amsterdam
Telephone: (3120) 64 20 11 Telex: 15758
Cables: Christiart, Amsterdam
Director: Harts Nystad

Switzerland
Christie's (International) S.A.,
8 place de la Taconnerie, 1204 Geneva
Telephone: (4122) 28 25 44 Telex: Geneva 423 634
Cables: Chrisauction, Geneva
Directors: Richard Stern; Georges de Bartha; Hans
Nadelhoffer

United States
Christie, Manson & Woods International, Inc.

502 Park Avenue, New York, N.Y. 10022
Telephone: (212) 546 1000 Telex: International, New York
620721 Domestic, 710 581 2325
Cables: Chriswoods, New York
President: David Bathurst

Christie's East
219 East 67th Street, New York, N.Y. 10021
Telephone: (212) 570 4141 Telex: Domestic 710 581 4211
President: J. Brian Cole

2. Representatives
United Kingdom and Ireland
Christie's in the City
Simon Birch,
10/12 Copthall Avenue, London EC2R 7DJ
Telephone: (01) 588 4424

Inverness
Jack Buchanan,
111 Church Street, Inverness
Telephone: (0463) 234603

Perthshire
Sebastian Thewes,
Strathgarry House, Killiecrankie by Pitlochry, Perthshire
Telephone: (079681) 216

Argyll
Sir Ilay Campbell, Bt.,
Cumlodden Estate Office, Crarae, Inveraray, Argyll
Telephone: (05466) 633

Edinburgh
Michael Clayton,
5 Wemyss Place, Edinburgh
Telephone: (031) 225 4756/7

Ayrshire
James Hunter Blair,
Blairquhan, Maybole, Ayrshire
Telephone: (06557) 239

Northumbria
Aidan Cuthbert,
Eastfield House, Main Street, Corbridge, Northumberland
Telephone: (043471) 3181

North-West
Victor Gubbins,

Eden Lacy, Lazonby, Penrith, Cumbria
Telephone: (076883) 8800

Yorkshire
Sir Nicholas Brooksbank, Bt.,
46 Bootham, York
Telephone: (0904) 30911

West Midlands
Michael Thompson,
Stanley Hall, Bridgnorth, Shropshire
Telephone: (07462) 61891

East Anglia
Ian Henderson-Russel,
Davey House, Castle Meadow, Norwich
Telephone: (0603) 614546

Mid-Wales
Sir Andrew Duff Gordon, Bt.,
Downton House, New Radnor, Presteigne, Powys
Telephone: (0242) 518999

Cotswolds
111 The Promenade, Cheltenham, Glos.
Telephone: (0242) 518999
Consultant: Rupert de Zoete

West Country
Richard de Pelet,
Monmouth Lodge, Yenston, Templecombe, Somerset
Telephone: (0963) 70518

South Dorset & Solent
Nigel Thimbleby,
Wolfeton House, Dorchester, Dorset
Telephone: (0305) 68748
    and at
Bournemouth
39 Poole Hill, Bournemouth, Dorset
Telephone: (0202) 292740

Devon and Cornwall
Christopher Petherick,
Tredeague, Porthpean, St. Austell, Cornwall
Telephone: (0726) 64672

South East
Robin Loder,
Leonardslee Gardens, Lower Beeding, Sussex
Telephone: (040386) 850

Ireland
Desmond Fitz-Gerald,
Knight of Glin, Glin Castle, Glin, Co. Limerick
Private Residence: 52 Waterloo Road, Dublin 4
Telephone (0001) 68 05 85

Northern Ireland
John Lewis-Crosby,
Marybrook House, Raleagh Road, Crossgar, Downpatrick,
    Co. Down
Telephone: (0396) 830574

Channel Islands
Richard de la Hey,
8 David Place, St. Helier, Jersey
Telephone: (0534) 77582

United States
California
Russell Fogarty,
Christie, Manson & Woods International, Inc.,
342 North Rodeo Drive, Beverly Hills, California 90210
Telephone: (213) 275 5534

San Francisco
Ellanor Notides,
3667 Sacramento St., San Francisco, Ca. 94118
Telephone: (415) 346 6644

Florida
Helen Cluett,
225 Fern Street, West Palm Beach, Fla. 33401
Telephone: (305) 833 6952

Massachusetts
Edgar Bingham, Jr.,
32 Fayette Street, Boston, Mass. 02116
Telephone: (617) 338 6679

Mid-West
Frances Blair
46 East Elm Street, Chicago, Illinois 60611
Telephone: (312) 787 2765

Mid-Atlantic
Paul Ingersoll,
P.O. Box 1112, Bryn Mawr, Pa. 19010
Telephone: (215) 525 5493

David Ober,
2935 Garfield Street, N.W., Washington D.C. 20008
Telephone: (202) 387 8722
Consultants: Nuala Pell; Joan Gardner

Texas
Linda N. Letzerich,
Suite 702, 2001 Kirby Drive, Houston, Texas 77019
Telephone: (713) 529 7777

Carolyn Foxworth,
7047 Elmridge Road, Dallas, Texas 75240
Telephone: (214) 239 2093

Europe
Monsieur Gérald Van der Kemp, President d'Honneur of
Christie's, Europe, is based in Christie's Paris office.

Austria
Vincent Windisch-Graetz,
Ziehrerplatz 4/22, 1030 Vienna
Telephone: (43222) 73 26 44

Belgium
Richard Stern; Janine Duesberg,
Christie, Manson & Woods (Belgium) Ltd.,
33 Boulevard de Waterloo, 1000 Brussels
Telephone: (322) 512 8765 or 8830 Telex: Brussels 62042

Denmark
Birgitta Hillingso,
20 Parkvaenget, 2920 Charlottenlund
Telephone: (451) 62 23 77

France
Princesse Jeanne-Marie de Broglie,
Caroline de Roussy de Sales
Christie's France SARL,
17 rue de Lille, 75007 Paris
Telephone: (331) 261 1247 Telex: 213468

Italy
Giorgina Venosta,
Christie's (Italy) S.r.l.,
9 via Borgogna, 20122 Milan
Telephone: (392) 794 712 Telex: 316464

Sandro Perrone di San Martino,
Corso Vittorio, 86, 10121 Turin
Telephone: (3911) 548 819

Norway
Ulla Solitair Hjort,
Riddervoldsgt. 10b, Oslo 2.
Telephone: (472) 44 12 42

Portugal
Antonio Santos-Mendonça,
Rua Conde de Alnoster –44–1° ESQ, 1500 Lisbon
Telephone: 786383

Spain
Casilda Fz-Villaverde y Silva,
Valenzuela 7, Madrid 14
Telephone: (341) 223 66 27 Telex: 46681E
Cables: Christiart, Madrid

Sweden
Lillemor Malmström,
Hildingavägen 19, 182 62 Djursholm, Stockholm
Telephone: (468) 755 10 92 Telex: Stockholm 12916

Baroness Irma Silfverschiold,
Klagerups Gard, 230 40 Bara
Telephone: (040) 44 03 60

Switzerland
Maria Reinshagen,
Christie's (International) A.G.,
Steinwiesplatz, 8032, Zürich
Tel: (411) 69 05 05 Telex: Zürich 56093

West Germany
Jörg-Michael Bertz,
Alt Pempelfort 11a, 4000 Düsseldorf
Telephone: (49211) 35 05 77 Telex: 8587599
Cables: Chriskunst Düsseldorf

Isabella von Bethmann Hollweg
Wentzelstrasse 21, D-2000 Hamburg 60
Telephone: (4940) 279 0866

Charlotte Fürstin zu Hohenlohe-Langenburg
Reitmorstrasse 30, 8000 Munich 22
Telephone: (4989) 22 95 39

Worldwide
Argentina
Consultant: Cesar Feldman,
Libertad 1269, 1012 Buenos Aires
Telephone: (541) 41 1616 or (541) 42 2046
Cables: Tweba, Buenos Aires

Australia
Sue Hewitt,
298 New South Head Road, Double Bay, Sydney, 2028
Telephone: (612) 326 1422 Telex: AA26343
Cables: Christiart Sydney

Brazil
Consultant: Vera Duvernoy,
Caixa Postal 1769, 20100 Rio de Janeiro
Cables: Christiart, Rio de Janeiro

Canada
Murray Mackay
Christie, Manson & Woods International, Inc.,
94 Cumberland Street, Suite 803, Toronto, Ontario, M5R 1A3
Telephone: (416) 960 2063 Telex:065 23907

Japan
Sachiko Hibiya,
c/o Dodwell Marketing Consultants,
Kowa Building No. 35, 14–14, Akasaka 1-chome, Minato-ku, Tokyo 107
Telephone: (03) 584 2351 Telex: J 23790

Mexico
Consultant: Ana Maria de Xirau,
Callejon de San Antonio 64—San Angel, Delegacion Villa Alvaro Obregon 01000, Mexico D.F.
Telephone: (905) 548 5946

INDEX

Numbers in italic refer to illustrations and their captions

ACKNOWLEDGEMENTS

The publishers would like to thank the following owners and copyright holders for permission to reproduce photographs. Illustrations not listed below come from Christie's archives. Numbers refer to pages.

© ADAGP, Paris, 1984, 188; By courtesy of Thos Agnew & Sons, London, 171; Griffith Institute, Ashmolean Museum, Oxford, 17; BBC Copyright Photograph, 45; Bibliothèque Nationale, Paris, 13; Bodleian Library, Oxford, 41, 200; The Bridgeman Art Library, 122; Reproduced by Courtesy of the Trustees of the British Museum, 31; Caisse Nationale des Monuments Historiques et des Sites, Paris, 14; Country Life, London, 55, 125; Courtauld Institute Galleries, London (Courtauld Collection), 181; By kind permission of the Society of Dilettanti: photograph Courtauld Institute, 49; John Donat, London, 121; Textile Conservation Centre, Apartment 22, Hampton Court, 102, 103, 105; Japan Information Centre, 119; A. F. Kersting, London, 18; Keystone Press Agency, 130; Liebermann, 172; Lloyds of London, 133; All rights reserved. The Metropolitan Museum of Art, 60; Patrick Roach, 53; Royal Commission on Historic Monuments (England) London, 117; Sotheby's, 138; Towneley Hall Art Gallery and Museums, Burnley Borough Council, 50; Crown Copyright, Victoria and Albert Museum, 68, 88, 89, 95, 99; Reproduced by permission of the Trustees of the Wallace Collection, 65, 79.